ordinary theologies

BLACK STUDIES & critical thinking
BLACK LEADERSHIP

Judy Alston, *Series Editor*

Rochelle Brock and Richard Greggory Johnson III
Executive Editors

Vol. 39

The Black Studies and Critical Thinking series
is part of the Peter Lang Education list.
Every volume is peer reviewed and meets
the highest quality standards for content and production.

PETER LANG
New York • Washington, D.C./Baltimore • Bern
Frankfurt • Berlin • Brussels • Vienna • Oxford

Noelle Witherspoon Arnold

ordinary theologies

Religio-spirituality and the Leadership of Black Female Principals

PETER LANG
New York • Washington, D.C./Baltimore • Bern
Frankfurt • Berlin • Brussels • Vienna • Oxford

Library of Congress Cataloging-in-Publication Data

Arnold, Noelle Witherspoon.
Ordinary theologies: religio-spirituality and the leadership
of black female principals / Noelle Witherspoon Arnold.
pages cm. — (Black studies and critical thinking; v. 39)
Includes bibliographical references and index.
1. Women school principals—United States. 2. African American school principals.
3. Educational leadership—United States. 4. School principals—
United States—Religious life. 5. African American women—Religious life.
6. Black theology. 7. Womanist theology. I. Title.
LB2831.93.A76   371.2′012—dc23   2013038197
ISBN 978-1-4331-1636-0 (hardcover)
ISBN 978-1-4331-1635-3 (paperback)
ISBN 978-1-4539-1243-0 (e-book)
ISSN 1947-5985

Bibliographic information published by **Die Deutsche Nationalbibliothek**.
Die Deutsche Nationalbibliothek lists this publication in the "Deutsche
Nationalbibliografie"; detailed bibliographic data is available
on the Internet at http://dnb.d-nb.de/.

Cover image credits:
Model: Ursula Thomas
Headshot: James Paul, JPaul Photography
Styling and Photo: Bruce Makoto Arnold

© 2014 Peter Lang Publishing, Inc., New York
29 Broadway, 18th floor, New York, NY 10006
www.peterlang.com

All rights reserved.
Reprint or reproduction, even partially, in all forms such as microfilm,
xerography, microfiche, microcard, and offset strictly prohibited.

Dedication

To my wonderful husband, Bruce,

and

To the One at Whose feet lie my own ordinary theologies

(John 6:68)

Contents

ix	Acknowledgments	
1	Introduction	
15	Chapter 1	Contextual Constructs
41	Chapter 2	Womanist Theology as Methodology and Method
79	Chapter 3	Testimony: Presentation of Narratives
		Bobbie
		Avery
		Toni
		Pattie
155	Chapter 4	Exegesis
211	Chapter 5	Spirit-led: The Dialogic of Womanist Theology and Educational Leadership
233	Conclusion	Meditations and Musings
237	References	
259	Index	
267	The Author	

Acknowledgments

At issue for many educators is the intersection of the public and the professional self. This is not a useful distinction to make in many ways. Actually, it is a distinction that I myself find difficult. So much of what individuals value and believe impacts life and work and sometimes it is difficult to separate the two. We carry these beliefs and experiences with us, and our actions in varying situations and contexts are impacted by our private and public selves. These spaces often overlap, transcend, frame, and are used to negotiate the other, different selves.

Theories of "the everyday" can be described in "terms of the categories and social relations of the operative in everyday life" (Essed, 1991, p. 186). We are located physically and socially in the structure of life. For some, these structures are demarcated in all sorts of categories that serve as binaries. For others, these structures of being and doing traverse each other as complex practices. Structures such as personal and professional beliefs and practices are articulated as multiple meanings. In this same way, the idea of the "ordinary" (Mitchem, 2002) encompasses the expression of daily practice and issues of daily life.

Ordinary Theologies explores the religious and spiritual in the leadership practices of Black female principals. Due to the paucity of research concerning Black female principals, this book aspires to add to the small body of that literature by adding the voices of African American women leaders who live, work, and lead through religion or spirituality. Religion and spirituality provide a space for agency and highlight the multiple ways Black women leaders navigate their intersecting public and private lives as they engage in social justice. Both the "product and the process" (Romo & Roseman, 2005) of justice are articulated in "ordinary," day-to-day realities of life and work that are influenced by religion and spirituality.

The writing of this book has much to do with my own journey as a Black female educator who identifies as a person of faith and what this faith means for my own work and life. I sometimes feel under/mis/re/presented in theories and theologies concerning women and their work. As a university professor, I deal often with conceptual and theoretical perspectives.

This book would not have come about were it not for Toni, Pattie, Bobbie, and Avery, who allowed me tell their stories and gave me permission to be creative with them. I was a captive to making this good because they and the stories meant so much to me. I owe them tremendous thanks for making the process of writing a book something I could love.

Thank you to the editor of the series, Judy Alston. Your life shows that God has a place in the academy and scholarship is made that much richer because of it. Thank you for helping to bring this book to life.

My dissertation committee at the University of Alabama gave me the perfect mix of expertise, guidance, and contribution while working on the study that informed this book. Utz McKnight, Joyce Stallworth, Angela Benson, and Heather Pleasants made me work hard and dig deep. Thanks to the chair of that committee, Natalie Adams, who has always had my admiration. I thank her for the constant encouragement, compassion, and "swift kicks." She makes life and the academy seem easy. I am especially thankful for the late Dr. Harold Bishop, who passed away before my study was completed. He always told me I was a star and he made me believe it. I truly miss him.

My professional colleagues offer me a rich circle in which to be creative and scholarly, particularly those whom I have written with: Bruce Arnold, Jeff and Melanie Brooks, Sarah Diem, Emily Crawford, Ty-Ron Douglas, Cosette Grant, Muhummad Khalifa, Dianne Taylor, Roland Mitchell, Azadeh Osanloo, Dymaneke Mitchell, Ursula Thomas, Samantha Briggs, Mark Gooden, Autumn Tooms, Mark Giles, Michelle Young, Cindy Reed, and the *University Council of Educational Administration*. I also extend many, many thanks to my best Graduate Assistant ever, Iman Poostdoozan, for his assistance on this project. I could not have completed the final manuscript changes without you.

Finally, I am indebted to the many womanist researchers, authors, theologians, and ethicists in whose works I seem to have found myself. I want to be you when I grow up.

Introduction

"Despite the constitutional separation of church and state, a concept understood differently by different Supreme Courts, there has been keen...interest in the matters associated with religion" (Pinar, Reynolds, Slattery, & Taubman, 1996, p. 9). That battle extends beyond the places of worship and a certain economy finds itself in public schools. Educational issues and religion and spirituality have engaged parents, students, educators, the media, and politicians on a grand scale. One characteristic in these issues is the notion that students, teachers, and administrators leave their personal beliefs at the schoolhouse door. This is an improbability at best. Moreover, dialogue concerning religion, spirituality, and education has largely been linked to "hot-button" issues such as the separation of church and state, evolution versus creationism, and instruction of religion in schools. By focusing on these few issues of faith and education, discussions are one-dimensional, corrosive, and unconstructive. Although there is a legal but ill-perceived notion of church and state, educational practice still presents itself through religious or spiritual activity and the personal faith of individuals posits itself in the everyday actions of school.

Engagement concerning religion, spirituality, and education only allows for partial exploration and ignores certain epistemological and ontological histories such as faith. When and if faith is discussed in schools, the dialogue is neutered and diminished to more acceptable concepts such as spirituality, ethics, or character development. Moreover, a binary between the spiritual and the secular is false at best (Lorde, 1984). In reality, the religious and the spiritual often co-exist and complement in the totality of experience for those to whom they matter (Moody, 1997).

Nash argues that religion and spirituality give meaning to lives and can be found in narrative (Nash, 1998). Postman (1996) asserts that religion and spirituality provide a sense of identity, community, a basis for conduct, and explanations for life (p. 7). Because of this, telling spiritual stories provides vital ways to view professional work. For many, there is an overlap of public and private spaces. Too often, the conflicts among these public and private personas and contexts leave one with more questions than answers. In my interactions with other Black female principals, I found questions similar to my own, "What happens to one's religious or spiritual belief in the different contexts in which we find ourselves, particularly in the principalship?"

Principals' values and beliefs influence their vision of the school as well as their behaviors (Glasman, 1984; Greenfield, 1991; Hallinger, Bickman, & Davis, 1990; Krug, Scott, & Ahadi, 1990). Greenfield (1991) states that the principal's belief system is important to understand because it colors practically everything the principal does on a daily basis (p. 6). Krug et al. (1990) concluded that the principal's interpretation of that belief or leadership activity is of primary importance. In spite of these facts, traditional educational leadership research has completed only a partial exploration and has ignored certain epistemological and ontological frames such as culture, gender, and faith. Owing to a "steady stream of educational litigation and jurisprudence" (Long, 2005, p. 28), school practice has become mired in what educators can or cannot do by the law. Religion is seen as an entity separate from spirituality, with the latter as a satisfactory replacement for the former (Long, 2005). When and if faith is discussed in schools, the dialogue is neutered and diminished to more acceptable concepts such as spirituality, ethics, or character development (Dantley, 2003; Noddings, 1984; Shields, 2005; Starratt, 2005a, 2005c).

Black, Female, Spiritual: Leadership in the Margins

The masculine enterprise of leadership (Blackmore, 1993) has often embodied women in prescribed roles of femininity, leadership, and professionalism. Blackmore (1999) underscores the fact that "leadership is treated...as a set of generic competencies rather than holistically; the social, ethical...dimensions of leadership are leached out" (p. 5). It is my hope this research foregrounded these concerns and deconstructed normed epistemologies, descriptors, articulations, and enactments of the principalship. The research on females leading in education is slim, yet our knowledge of women of color is even thinner. There is a silence of the voices of administrators of color, and it is in this silence that my research and the narratives of the participants are situated. Emerging literature on leaders of color teaches us that "their ways of leading may be as diverse as their cultural heritages but all rise from their own complex social and cultural histories" (Ah Nee-Benham & Cooper, 1998, p. 40).

Religion and spirituality manifest themselves in very real ways and are present whether we discuss them or not. Research has shown that educators do not just bring these beliefs with them to school. These beliefs actually inform and frame pedagogy, decision making, activism, and social justice (Capper & Keyes, 1999). There has been much research on the significance of teachers' experiences and the import of religio-spirituality, but few individual accounts of principals. In addition, Black leadership narratives and those of women persist as underrepresented viewpoints in educational leadership (Murtadha & Watts, 2005) or are explored as a peculiar phenomenon associated with urban communities and schooling (Lomotey, 1989). The little research that has been conducted has been limited to those Black female principals leading urban schools, and even then that research is limited (Bloom & Erlandson, 2003; Loder, 2005).

Narrating Leadership and Spirituality

Starratt (2005a) noted that in the field of educational leadership, one should not examine merely theories or what others say about a phenomenon, but close attention should be paid to actual practice in schools. Where simply examining practice ends, meaning-making can be explored in the words, lives, and stories of those who make the meaning. Historical narratives are one example of ways in which meaning-making is fostered. In the case of this book, historical spiritual narratives of Black women, from early nineteenth- and twentieth-century writing, provide context for current inquiry into contemporary spiritual narratives. Hine (1994) writes:

> It is not enough simply to uncover the hidden facts, the obscure names of black foremothers. [What we need is] the development of an array of analytical frameworks that allow us to understand why black women of all classes behave in certain ways, and how they acquired agency. (p. 12)

This book examines historical spiritual narratives to focus not only upon the accumulation of data, but also upon how certain knowledges and truths for the individual lead to certain choices (Floyd-Thomas, 2006b). These historical spiritual narratives become a means to examine the "testimony and witness" often inherent in them as a framework for understanding how Black women narrate leadership. This book takes the ideas of testimony and witness and rearticulates these concepts into a workable process whereby Black women recounted stories of their personal religious experiences and daily practice and highlighted how these beliefs affected all aspects of their lives, including their work.

Religious belief and practice are not merely idiomatic Black religious experiences. The narratives are meant not to generalize the religious experiences of Black women principals, but to shed a broader light upon the intersection of the religion and spirituality in the narrating and performing of leadership. Examining the spiritual narratives of Black female principals allows exploration of "the interweaving of Black women's religious, biblical, theological, and sociopolitical thought and reflection as it often emerges in autobiography, biography, and other narrative forms" (Bellah et al., 1985, p. 27). This book allows the story of religio-spirituality and leadership to develop and become more legitimated in the broader field of educational leadership. The multiple stories of spirituality and leadership then become a part of the larger understandings that shape our work as researchers and educational leaders. In other words, the religious context of spiritual narratives "is not viewed as separate from the social and [the] professional is not divorced from the personal...[They] are active...with life decisions" (Mitchem, 2002, p. 59). In like manner, the contemporary spiritual narratives and autobiographical accounts in this book serve as windows into the workings and outcomes of spirituality in the lives of individuals. "There is a power and persuasive nature of faithful lives, and...biographies, autobiographies and memoirs of spiritual people" (Gilmour, n.d.). Not only how spirituality is defined for a group of Black female leaders, but also how spirituality is "used" takes particular importance. For example, these principals discuss how their spirituality supports them in performing the duties of the principalship, and how their interpreted religious faith impacts their decision making.

Womanism/Womanist Theology

Womanist theology serves as the major frame for this work. The six tenets of womanist theology served as methods for this narrative research and guided analysis. The six tenets are 1) radical subjectivity, 2) critical engagement, 3) traditional communalism, 4) redemptive self-love, 5) appropriation/reciprocity, and 6) Spirit-love. The result was the creation of four alternative research texts written as spiritual narratives, written in the vein of historical and contemporary narratives to highlight religio-spirituality in the writers' lives and principalships. The study contributes to the understanding of the principalship by adding the voices of Black women to the understanding of educational leadership experiences and expressions.

Philomena Essed (1991) coined the term "everyday racisms" to describe the intersecting oppressions that Black women face in society. These intersections can traverse race, gender, class, religion, and sexual orientation, among other things. The standpoint of womanist theology names "ordinary theologies" (Mitchem, 2002) to describe the intersection of public and private religious acts and beliefs and how these deeply held beliefs respond to life situations and occupy daily practice. Using a womanist theological framework, the religion and spirituality of four Black female principals are explored. Each of the four women on which this book is based exemplifies the idea of the African inseparability of spirit and soul and a long tradition and history of spirituality and religion in the African American community, particularly among Black women (Bennett, 1975). What results is a creation of spiritual narratives to explore how religious and spiritual values and beliefs influence practice in the principalship.

Some scholars use the terms *womanism* and *Black feminism* as synonyms, yet others view them as separate. Early Black feminists have been deemed separatist (McDowell, as cited in Williams, 2000). However, one could hardly make the claim today. Many leading Black feminists (Collins, 2000; hooks, 1999) see Black feminism as a struggle for injustice anywhere for anyone. Black feminism may tend to see itself as "a distinct Black female culture...and as a separate cultural form" (Williams, 2000, p. 219), birthed of its experience of white female counterparts, that has little to do with the actual "truth" of what it means to be Black. Yet womanism is depicted in literature as a more inclusive epistemological and ontological theory "that is committed to the wholeness and survival of entire people" (Williams, 2000, p. 219). It is important to note that this does not mean that all "Black women are womanists and (all womanists are not Black women" (Beauboeuf-Lafontant, 2002, p. 437). This book does not purport this notion either. This book portrays Black feminism and womanism as intersecting realities and standpoints for Black women and integrates both as a more fruitful inspection of Black womanhood.

Womanist theory, originally coined by Alice Walker (1983), was named to make visible the most salient values of Black people, particularly Black women. Walker's four-part definition is as follows:

> WOMANIST 1. From womanish. (Opp. Of "girlish" i.e., frivolous, irresponsible, not serious.) A Black feminist or feminist of color. From the Black folk expression of mother to female children, "you acting womanish," i.e., like a woman. Usually referring to outrageous, audacious, courageous or willful behavior. Wanting to know more and in greater depth than is considered "good" for one. Interested in grown up doings. Acting grown up. Being grown up. Interchangeable with another black folk expression: "You trying to be grown." Responsible. In charge. Serious.
> 2. Also: A woman who loves other women, sexually and/or nonsexually. Appreciates and prefers women's culture, women's emotional flexibility (values tears as natural counterbalance of laughter) and women's strength. Sometimes loves individual men, sexually and/or nonsexually. Committed to survival and wholeness of entire people, male and female. Not a sepa-

ratist, except periodically, for health. Traditionally universalist, as in: "Mama why are we brown, pink, and yellow, and our cousins are white, beige, and black?" Ans: "Well, you know the colored race is just like a flower garden, with every color flower represented." Traditionally capable, as in: "Mama, I'm walking to Canada and I'm taking you and a bunch of other slaves with me." Reply: "It wouldn't be the first time."

3. Loves music. Loves dance. Loves the moon. Loves the Spirit. Loves love and food and roundness. Loves struggle. Loves the Folk. Loves herself. Regardless.

4. Womanist is to feminist as purple is to lavender. (pp. xi–xii)

In its application to schooling, the womanist educational framework includes concepts such as othermothering, communalism (Beauboeuf-Lafontant, 2002; Collins, 1991); spirituality (Townes, 1995, p. 13); and risk, acting with care with risk to oneself while recognizing there is no security of success (Beauboeuf-Lafontant, 2002). Womanism values women's ways of knowing, particularly those of African American women, in every sphere of life.

Womanism entered the theological arena as a gender-based movement in the 1980s (Williams, 2000). Walker's four-part definition forms a critical and methodological framework for various disciplines exploring the lives of Black women, including theology. Womanist theology offers a way to record and examine women's religious meanings and epistemology, but is also a way to contest and eradicate oppression and inform social justice (Mitchem, 2002). Delores Williams (1993) states some defining features of womanist theology:

> Womanist theology attempts to help Black women see, affirm, and have confidence in the importance of their experience and faith for determining the character of the Christian religion in the African-American community. Womanist theology challenges all oppressive forces impeding Black women's struggle for survival and for the development of a positive, productive quality of life conducive to women's and the family's freedom and well-being. Womanist theology opposes all oppression based on race, sex, class, sexual preference, physical disability and caste...Womanist theology...also branches off in its own direction, introducing new issues and constructing new analytical categories. (p. xiv)

Womanist theology offers a way to "consider how the Divine becomes manifested in the everyday experience of women,...women who are left out of its discourses" (Floyd-Thomas, 2006b, p. 8). The use of Black women's spiritual narratives presents an opportunity to give voice and to "put at the center Black women's sacred worlds" (Chireau, 1995, p. 67) and their intersection and oneness with everyday life.

Womanist theologians appropriate Walker's four-part definition to examine biblical scholarship, Christology, ecumenics, and Christian practice (Mitchem, 2002). In addition, womanist theologians apply womanist hermeneutics to challenge oppressive religious traditions, patriarchy, notions of sexuality, and other theological and societal constructions (Gilkes, 1993; Mitchem, 2002). Floyd-Thomas (2006b) gathers Walker's four-part definition into five principles that are used in my research: To these, I add what I call 6) Spirit-love to highlight the religious spirituality that binds these creeds together. Expanding these tenets and the ways in which womanist theologians frame them creates a model framework in this research for exploring religion and spirituality for African American women in everyday life and work.

Studies that examine religion still do so from largely white, Eurocentric notions of religion that are a departure from the Black feminist notion of spirituality (Mitchem, 2002). An examination of spiritual narratives through a womanist lens offers an opportunity to engage Black women's life stories and how what one believes is salient in one's life history (Floyd-Thomas, 2006b). Black women's lived experiences allow me to explore to which end women are empowered toward activism and social justice in everyday practice. Using a womanist theology frame particularly allows me the epistemological and ontological use of a theory to bridge the unique experiences of the Black female. While womanism is sufficient in exploring matters of spirituality, culture, gender, and work, womanist theology allowed me to explore the unique experiences from the standpoints of Black women who position themselves theologically. Womanist theology is located in a particular belief system, yet it stands in opposition to traditional Western religious belief and challenges all the status quos, oppressions, and privileges that come with it (Mitchem, 2002). Womanist theology provides a framework from which to view ways that educators integrate spirituality in the form of personal faith and how they use that faith to interrogate marginality, promote social justice, and initiate social activism in schools.

Particularly important in womanist theology is the concept of intersection. Intersectionality denotes the connections among oppressions, race, class, gender (Crenshaw, 1991). Intersections can also include sexual orientation, religion, and dis/ability. Alone, each of these can be a rather sterile category. Neither construct is sufficient to examine Black women's participation with religion or spirituality, life, schools, or the principalship. However, by examining religio-spirituality and these other constructs as intersectionalities, I desterilize these categories and provide a more fruitful examination of religion and spirituality and the impact they have upon the principalship. I am able to regard each of the four women's narrative experience in Chapter Three as Christian Black females and in larger historical, sociocultural, religious, and institutional contexts. Race-only or gender-only frameworks limit the unpacking of power relations in social groups (Collins, 1998). However, intersectionality is used to "think though all social institutions, organizational structures, patterns of social interaction and other social practices on all levels" (Collins, 1998, p. 205). Intersectionality is a way to view the collective experiences of women while not essentializing one way to be a Christian Black female principal. Intersectionality allows the book to focus on a unit of analysis from the standpoint of the individual and the group without losing the uniqueness of either.

Religio-spirituality

Spirituality and religion are not always the same, but for many they are interrelated (Mitchem, 2002; Tisdell, 2003). Religion, in many instances, serves to inform and connect to our spirituality (Tisdell, 2003). Yet, this vagueness or lack of concreteness led some researchers to consider that there is not a definitive description of either. Mott-Thornton (1998) identifies the dangers of a common usage of spirituality. Many of the definitions are mismatched and irreconcilable. Because of this many researchers agree that spirituality is personally defined (Dantley, 2005; Tisdell, 2003).

Conversations with the principals in this book make some things clear and align with recent research: Spirituality is personally defined

(Dantley, 2005; Tisdell, 2003), is culturally located (Tisdell, 2003; West & Glaude, 2003; Wiggins, 2004; Williams, 2000), and exists as a form of meaning-making and guides life and work (Capper & Keyes, 1999; Webb, 2000). Some literature maintains that it is not possible to separate religion and spirituality completely (Slife & Richards, 2001) or to explore concepts of justice without it. In fact, in Slife and Richards' (2001) idea of holism, it is suggested that the components of a theoretical or theological position are vitally related and find meaning in its relation to other positions. I recognize the interrelatedness of religion and spirituality as operationalized by examining what I call religio-spirituality. Doing so allows me to acknowledge the participants' relationship between spirituality and religion without the problems associated with using spirituality and religion synonymously or separately. The four women in this book self-identified as spiritual rather than religious, although they identified spirituality through the lens of religion. They often use the terms *faith, belief,* and *values* synonymously with *religio-spirituality*, and these are discussed in their individual narratives. I must note that this book is grounded in the women's individual conceptions of spirituality as it is rooted in a Judeo-Christian, Baptist inclination of religious values and ideals.

Social Justice

While there is research on the silencing of Black women, educational research does not fully examine how religion and spirituality have impacted Black women in actively resisting the status quo in schools, despite the fact that historically Black spirituality has been located in resistance (West & Glaude, 2003). This research highlights the role of religio-spirituality in performing the duties of the principalship; interpreting policy individually and collectively, resisting the status quo in schools, and challenging traditional roles of the principalship. Religio-spirituality becomes a way to interrogate marginality and initiate social justice in schools. Rather than focusing on a specific framework for social justice, discussions are framed around the meanings of social justice, the frames of reference (in this instance, religious spirituality) for these meanings, and the leadership behaviors that arise.

Often located in spiritual narratives are notions of "witnessing" and "testifying" (Ross, 2002). Within the Black community, these terms mean more than just telling the stories; they highlight personal and social praxis through religious spirituality. Ross concludes:

> Testifying occurs both as an interpersonal narration of divine interaction with everyday life and as a formal portion of worship wherein believers share in community what God has done in their lives… Testimonies require the presence of witnesses, persons who also have seen or experienced God's work and who are able to certify or attest to the truth of it in the testimonies they hear. By identifying oneself as a witness, a believer asserts that she has personally experienced God's provision or other intervention. Moreover…the term witnessing has arisen as a complementary way of naming the believer's ordinary moral practice—way of living—as religious practice. (p. 14)

Methodology

When I decided to explore and privilege the spiritual, personal, and professional life narratives of Black female principals, I initially began to consider life history narratives. However, as I continued a review of the literature, I wanted to focus particularly upon the role of religion in Black women principals' lives and professions. During this time, I "fell in love with" historical and contemporary spiritual narratives of African American women. The writings often apply and explicate the facets of religion and spirituality against the backdrop of the larger whole of the life (Moody, 2003).

As a researcher, I wanted to privilege real, everyday-lived experiences of the principals. The women I talked to often spoke of the disconnect between what they saw as the spiritual—"who we really are"—and the secular—"what we are supposed to do and be"—in schools. For these principals, the "story" or narrative of their religious spirituality defined their experiences as principals. They acknowledged that their spirituality is "always present," yet there is a conflict between maintaining full fidelity to religious or spiritual enactments and to those of the principalship. Through the use of personal narratives, the relationship of religion and spirituality to the private and public life were explored. Because of the particular emphasis upon spirituality, their stories followed the tradition of *spiritual narratives* and are named as such throughout this book. The women are also referred to as *spiritual historians*.[1] Historical and contemporary spiritual narratives come in various nonfiction and fiction forms, including, but not limited to, poems, novels, sermons, songs, diaries, letters, and speeches (Brown, 2000). The four spiritual narratives in this book are presented as a jeremiad, a poem, a psalm, and a public address. Mining spiritual narratives, much like life history narratives, is useful because "public and private cannot…be separated…. Life historians do not ask for such separation" (Bullough, 1998, p. 20). Spiritual auto/biography validates the personal, professional, and social activities of these Black women and how religious "beliefs and values reveal themselves within our words, thoughts, and deeds" (Floyd-Thomas, 2006b, p. 154). It has been said that "historically the African American bears the impulse of biography" (Gates, 1991, p. 3).

Overview of Chapters

Spirituality has been characterized as the real, lived "historic force of African American women's spirituality with the demand of the Spirit to contextualize and live one's faith" (Townes, 1995, p. 13). Warnick (2004) suggests that education must engage religious thought or it risks becoming extraneous to the field and alienating those to whom religious thought matters. A large number of people look to their religion for meaning and guidance and education is not exempt (Warnick, 2004). In an effort to provide space in education for work that centers on religion, I "interpret religion and its influences on contemporary life" (Warnick, 2004, p. 346) and "what a religious tradition means, or what its import is" (Warnick, 2004, p. 347). This book does not attempt to answer whether the religious tradition is true.

Using the research questions as a guide, in Chapter One I give a review of womanism and womanist theology and its tenets, which serve as conceptual and contextual frames of this work, and a review of historic and contemporary spiritual narratives. I also provided a brief overview of the Black Church and the National Baptist Conven-

---

[1] The term *life historian* is suggested by Marjorie Mbilinyi (1989) as an alternative to the objectifying labels of *informant* and *subject*. Some other researchers have also considered the use of *collaborator* and/or *participant* to promote research collaboration. In the case of this research, I use the term *spiritual historian*.

tion, USA (NBC-USA), which serves as the denomination of choice for each spiritual historian. Additional history and tenets of the Black Church movement and the NBC-USA are more fully explored in Chapters Four and Five. Within my literature review, I linked spiritual narratives to an exploration of pertinent literature of educational leadership and spirituality as it pertains to Black female principals. In Chapter Two, I explore womanist theology as methodology and method and present each tenet as it relates to the product and process of narrative research. In Chapter Three, I offer a presentation and analysis of the data of each spiritual historian as "testimonies" or religious stories/narratives from which we can learn with an analysis of each. Chapter Four presents an "exegesis" or a discussion and cross-testimonial analysis of major themes and concepts explicated in the narrative process. Chapter Five stands as a synthesis of the findings in the research and offers future instruction on implications for practice, preparation, research, and emergent theory. This research is related particularly to religio-spirituality and its impact by asking, "What can these spiritual narratives tell us about performing the principalship in schools?"

Chapter 1

Contextual Constructs

Inquiry, discovery, and theoretical interpretations exist simultaneously in the entire process of the research project.

(Mitchell & Cody, 1993, p. 170)

Ain't I a Womanist?

In the summer of 2006, I was enrolled in a class that dealt with church and state issues and schooling. During this class, the professor had us locate ourselves in one religious narrative according to certain characteristics of those narratives. Almost all of us in the class could not pick just one and concluded that we were some funky hybrid of two or more. I mention this because it was a pivotal time in which I was forced to confront what my religious spirituality, gender, class, and race meant for me as an educator and as a human being in general. I realized that I had been treating certain aspects of myself in certain contexts as things to be protected from, when in actuality they served as lenses through which I viewed the whole of my life. My personal and professional life had seemed to make demands of these identities (or vice versa), yet up to this point, the academy had not seemed to do so. Others seemed to locate themselves somewhere (Marxist, feminist poststructuralist, pragmatist, etc.), and I couldn't find theoretical space that made total sense to me. Sure, the Marxists and feminists and poststructuralists around me would agree that they too were "funky hybrids," yet they still seemed to have a "home" and I did not. Once again, certain parts of me that I held most precious in private seemed ancillary to those lived in public. As a principal, I dealt with many issues and tensions among what I considered the unifying and sense-making system of the whole of my life and school issues. I believed my gender, race, culture, and religious spirituality demanded certain responses from me that were often at odds with district policy and the traditional performance of the principalship. But also these same identities colored what I believed. I was also undergoing some tensions among my theological and hermeneutical interpretations of the Bible and "being Christian" in comparison to some of those held by individuals in my church.

So am I getting closer to a theoretical framework for my work and for my life? I am not sure (I am evolving), but remain amazed by the Black women whose works take up most of my bookshelf, the historical foremothers who serve as their inspiration, and the "everyday" womanists who live the womanist life whether they name themselves as such or not. A womanist theological stance becomes an "opportunity to state the meanings of God in the real time of Black women's lives…Historical and cultural realities, from Black women's perspectives, also need expression in theological terms" (Mitchem, 2002, p. 60).

Womanist Theology

The defined area of womanist theology is relatively new. However, it provides a way to explore the many facets of African American women's religious and spiritual beliefs. "It is used to shape personal and communal meaning in faith, to analyze church doctrines, and challenge ecclesiastical operations" (Mitchem, 2002, p. ix.). Womanist theology also contributes to the understanding of Black religious life, activism, and newfound ways to explore oppression and justice (Floyd-Thomas, 2006a). While these are functions that are beneficial to the religious enterprise, I believe that womanist theology can serve as a framework for other disciplines to understand "Black women's faith experiences and gain a clearer understanding of the link between faith and life" (Mitchem, 2002, p. xi).

Womanist theologians have appropriated Walker's (1983) four-part definition to examine biblical scholarship, Christology, ecumenics, and Christian practice (Mitchem, 2002). Though the word *womanist* was coined by Walker, *womanism* was created by Black women scholars of religion to define the newfound movement in the academy. In 1985, womanism debuted at the American Academy of Religion and Society of Biblical Literature and introduced theoretical examinations of religion and society to explore "Black women's concerns from their own intellectual, physical and spiritual perspective" (Floyd-Thomas, 2006a, p. 3). Womanism utilized, employed, and theorized faith formation at the intersections of race, class, and gender.

Prior to womanist theology, theological study and development had existed largely in the perspectives of Black men and white women. During this time, several seminal works began the formation and progression of womanist theology. Delores Williams (1986) first highlighted the necessity of a theological analysis that was not based in white feminist theology. Williams stressed Cheryl Townsend Gilkes (1987), who completed religious sociology studies in the 1980s that investigated Black denominations. She highlighted that Black churchwomen were subsumed in frameworks created by Black men. These frameworks did not examine the unique needs, knowledges, and ways of doing theology from a woman's perspective. Katie Cannon's (1988) *Black Womanist Ethics* brought to the forefront Black women's ethical agency as found in theology. Cannon followed this work with *Katie's Canon* (1995), which highlighted her own personal narrative and the importance of womanism to the Black community. Renita Weems (1993) interpreted nine biblical stories featuring women, starting with the story of Hagar, the slave. Weems linked the oppression and subsequent redemption of Hagar to the plight of Black women. Her Hagar metaphor has been used in womanist theological works since that time. In *White Women's Christ, Black Women's Jesus*, Jacquelyn Grant (1989) explored the unique relationship of Black women to Jesus and His care for them. By the 1990s these signal texts led the way for other distinctive approaches to theology and ethics. Emilie Townes' (1993b) *Womanist Justice, Womanist Hope* "took ethics further on a path that was grounded in history" (Mitchem, 2002, p. 74). Townes (1993a) edited *Troubling in My Soul: Womanist Perspectives on Evil and Suffering*, which linked biblical suffering to Black women and spirituality. Marcia Riggs (1994) looked at the Black women's club movement in the nineteenth century to examine justice.

In addition, womanist theologians have applied womanist hermeneutics to challenge oppressive religious traditions, patriarchy, notions of sexuality, and other theological and societal constructions (Gilkes, 1993; Mitchem, 2002). Womanist theologian Stacy Floyd-Thomas (2006b) gathered Walker's four-part definition into five principles: 1) radical subjectivity, 2) traditional communalism, 3) redemptive self-love, 4) critical engagement, and 5) appropriation and reciprocity. To these, I add what I call 6) Spirit-love to highlight the religious spirituality that binds these principles together. By expanding these tenets, womanism, as theologians have framed it, becomes a model framework in this research for exploring religion in everyday life and becomes a vital epistemology for exploring religious spirituality.

Radical Subjectivity

Radical subjectivity denotes the formation of Black women's subjectivity in light of intersecting oppressions that they face. This tenet also denotes how women have contested forced identities and hegemonic truth claims. For instance, the first part of Alice Walker's definition comes from an African American idea that meant you were acting "grown" or too old for your age. Many Black women grew up hearing the term that carried the admonition to "keep out of grown folks' business." Yet what was so powerful in Walker's definition is that it seemed to encourage Black women to mind their own business and others' as well. Simply put, we are to step outside of silencing identities and behaviors of any kind. This may include challenging stereotypes and prescribed gendered notions. One such womanist describes this "as the right of Black women to have the freedom and space to define themselves as beings and Black women in their own right rather than how others define them" (Floyd-Thomas, 2006a, p. 9). Diana Hayes (2006) defines it this way:

> Womanist theologians use the stuff of women's lives to spin a narrative of their persistent effort to rise above and beyond those persons and situations, which attempt to hold them down...Each of us who claims womanist as a critical aspect of our self-understanding does so from with this context of own lives. (pp. 57, 63)

Black women do not have to live by any prescriptive code that the world has to offer. We make a demand to challenge our "exoticized, eroticized, anomalized, masculinized, and demonized" (duCille, 1996, p. 72) existence and present positive narratives of ourselves as having all the validity and veracity inherent in us as with the dominant culture. Womanism becomes an "audacious act of naming and claiming voice, space, and knowledge" (Floyd-Thomas, 2006a, p. 16). A womanist is "in charge, a gatherer of knowledge,...and serious about her task. Who she is makes her dangerous to hegemony (Townes, 1995, p. 9).

Traditional Communalism

Traditional communalism is taken from the ways that Black women have nurtured and supported other Black women (and men) in the individual and collective struggle for freedom from oppression. This definition takes womanism past an oversimplified version of taking care of the community as cited in some literature. It goes beyond community as just taking care of a physical space and those in it, to one of spiritual and philosophical significance. "The womanist cares about her people—contemporary and historical" (Townes, 1995, p. 9). Stated in Walker's definition is the "commitment to the survival and wholeness of entire people, male *and* female" recognizing that to promote and uplift oneself is to do the same for others. The needs of Black women and the Black community are considered, and activism is enacted on behalf of all. Traditional communalism includes other womanist concepts such as othermothering, having interpersonal and political commitment to the development of all children in a community (Beauboeuf-Lafontant, 2002); and an ethic of risk, acting with risk on behalf of oneself and others while recognizing there is no security of success (Beauboeuf-Lafontant, 2002) on behalf of the "beloved community."

Redemptive Self-Love

Although Walker addresses the communal aspects of womanism that focus on community, she also clearly makes space for the individual. *Redemptive self-love* makes space for the Black woman to love herself *and* others. Regardless, she behaves as if she is no longer a victim of oppression. Womanist sociologist Cheryl Townsend Gilkes (1989) says this about Alice Walker and self-love:

> If we are to explore the work of Alice Walker for ethical content or for direction in constructing ethics and in thinking theologically, I think that the most fruitful course is her artful advocacy of unconditional love that starts with our acceptance of ourselves as divinely and humanly lovable...[T]his love is the greatest issue in human existence. (p. 109)

In the face of an intersecting barrage of oppressions, self-love allows the Black woman to "demystify the perceptions of Black women's bodies, ways, and loves" (Floyd-Thomas, 2006b, p. 10). The Black woman becomes a lover of her body, her race, and her gender even in the face of the social norm that says she shouldn't. bell hooks (1995) speaks of this self-love in *Sisters of the Yam: Black Women and Self-Recovery*. Even in Black women's quest to be communal, serving, nurturing, and caring (which are hallmarks of the Black community), we must not be (self) sacrificial lambs and forget to nurture and serve ourselves. So while self-love serves communally and is reconciled with the dominant culture, it is also in protest to a culture that systematically and institutionally assaults the worth of Black women (Gilkes, 1993, p. 239). Black women are called to love themselves in spite of circumstances and intersecting oppressions. Self-love is a reaffirmation of Black womanhood and to know "that it is all right to be Black and female" (Douglas, 2006, p. 142).

Critical Engagement

Critical engagement calls for Black women to remove themselves from the margins by constant critique of the hegemonic conditions in society. This also involves Black women negotiating and managing these same hegemonic conditions. Floyd-Thomas (2006a) says that womanists

> critically engage their world at the intersection of their oppressions since they have borne the brunt of social injustice throughout the history of the modern world...Most obviously as a counterbalance to feminism, womanism is always cognizant that the life chances and potential of Black women are circumscribed by more than sexism alone. (p. 11)

Womanists are "serious" in recognizing interlocking oppressions and working to dismantle them. It acknowledges Black women's intensity toward praxis for those situated in the margins and disrupts the status quo. It has also been said that critical engagement is a "hermeneutical suspicion" (Floyd-Thomas, 2006a, p. 208) and a "nitty-gritty hermeneutic" (Harris, 2006, p. 54). This includes taking Black women's stories and everyday experiences, without "sugarcoating" oppressive realities, and naming them as valid epistemologies. Black women can "outwit, outmaneuver, and outscheme" (Copeland, 2006, p. 228) dominant social systems and structures, which involves "debunking, unmasking, and disentangling" (Cannon, 1996, p. 138) dominant ideologies.

Appropriation and Reciprocity

"Womanist approaches to religion and society have not only been invested in knowledge production and reconstruction only for themselves and their mainstreaming disciplines but also for other scholars...and those who remain on the margins" (Floyd-Thomas, 2006b, p. 11). Womanist theologians are also committed to appropriating and being reciprocal to other scholarship and maintaining a constant reflection and interpretation of historical figures and events to continue to advance their cause. Even in the dialogic process, there is also a commitment to the everyday "vernacular" (Phillips, 2006, p. xxiv) of ordinary life and the ways in which individuals describe it.

Appropriation and reciprocity seek to identify and coordinate others' standpoints, issues, and identities in eradicating oppression. "It affirms that Black women are connected to—and generally live their lives as part of—the primary site of today's most entrenched social problems: the masses" (Phillips, 2006, p. xxxix). Despite the interrogation and activism in achieving justice for Black women, appropriation and reciprocity recognize and demand justice for all oppressed and marginalized peoples (Floyd-Thomas, 2006b). "Human equality is categorical, absolute, and unconditional, and universally applicable" (Townes, 1993b, p. 138).

Love of Spirit

In Walker's definition, love of Spirit seems to be ambiguous. One does not know if she means religion, spirituality, or even the notion of a Christian God. "Loves the Spirit" by Walker's standard is not intrinsically religious or Christian. And there is some discussion as to whether womanism can truly inform womanist theology. Cheryl Sanders (1989) writes:

> The fact [is] that womanist is essentially a secular cultural category whose theological and ecclesial significations are rather tenuous...Walker's definition comprises an implicit ethics of moral autonomy, liberation, sexuality and love that is not contingent upon the idea of God or revelation...The use of Black women's experience as a basis for theology is futile if that experience is interpreted apart from a fully theistic context. (p. 87)

Still, many womanist theologians offer that since we are called to love everyone, regardless of religion, Walker's definition still serves to be inclusive of the religious spirituality and have secular moral appeal (Harris, 2006). However, this tenet was added due to the role that Walker's definition has offered womanist theology. The definition *has* affirmed for Christian Black women their right in society and the religious community. "Womanist theology is informed and inspired by traditions of Black women working with religious thought in new ways" (Mitchem, 2002, p. 55).

Why womanist theology? Womanist theology "affirms Black women's connection with both feminism and with the history, culture, and religion of the African American community" (Martin, 1998, p. 56). Womanist theology begs a response to questions surrounding religious spirituality and its impartation to the lives and work of leaders, educational and otherwise. More than just denoting the journey of one Black woman literary genius or a scholarly trend or fad, womanism has become an answer for many Black women scholars in studying religious spirituality (Floyd-Thomas, 2006b, p. 7).

Up to this point, I have discussed womanist theologians as firmly rooted in the canons of religion. However, womanist theology also interrogates the religions to which these theologians firmly attach themselves. Identity, intersectionality, and oppression within religion are also explored to radically reinterpret all elements of society (Floyd-Thomas, 2006b). Daphne Wiggins (2004) posits:

> Womanists are not wed to biblical authority that is predicated on the Bible's being inerrant or infallible...Most have not rejected the Bible or Christianity in total as some radical feminist theologians have. They value and advocate for the physical and spiritual salvation of the family, redistribution of wealth, goods, and services in American society, and the end of race, sex, and class supremacy. In addition, they are devoted to articulating a theological liberative position for women even when it might be at odds with a black male perspective on what would enhance African American existence. They address society's dehumanization and oppression of black women. Finally, they resist grand narratives...with obfuscate particular realities and then to universal experience form the dominant group's perspective. (p. 175)

Womanist theology also becomes a way to examine and interrogate religion's influence in all spheres of life and institutions, even the church.

A womanist theology provides a workable frame for exploring issues in educational leadership. "Religion is something that educational theorists tend to speak about as outside observers" (Warnick, 2004, p. 345). By examining the stories of Black female principals, these insiders to their own religious spirituality can exist as the primary voice for their own meanings concerning educational leadership. One important outcome of this work is that research relating to religion is no longer relegated to specialized arenas or niches. As more work is done in the area of religious spirituality, it is given a chance to challenge essentialized concepts of educational leadership. Warnick (2004) suggests that education *must* engage religious thought or it risks becoming extraneous to the field and alienating those to whom religious thought matters. A large number of people look to their religion for meaning and guidance, and education is not exempt. This import includes critiquing religion from the inside, exploring tensions of faith, and examining whether there are resources concerning an individual's religious spirituality that can offer education and leadership.

Black Women's Spiritual Narratives

In the past twenty years, there has been a movement to explore African American women's auto/biography as a vital part of literary history. Mostly in the form of slave narratives, these stories of the nineteenth century have chronicled the history and lives of slaves and the mining of them has interrogated the atrocities of the Middle Passage and slave life. These early slave narratives showcase a strong religious faith that mirrored these women's (and men's) refusal to be silent or silenced. As Stacey Floyd-Thomas (2006b) asserts:

> A recurring theme in the slave narratives is an assertion of how these enslaved women understood that their resistance and survival were contingent on their action as guided by their personal relationship with God. (p. 118)

When Africans first arrived in America as slaves, they brought tribal and religious practices that were a vital part of their culture (Lincoln, 1999). The rich tradition of oral narrative, or telling stories, originated in Africa and was brought to American shores with slavery (Gates, 1991). Birthed from the tradition of storytelling and oral history, the slave narrative became a way to make known their lives and was a dominant form of telling the Black Story (Mullane, 1993).

During this same time, much of the religious experience for African Americans was located within Christianity's "conversion of the savages" movement, situated in the slavemaster's Christian justification for slavery, and as a manipulative tool to control (Cone, 1997; Townes, 1995). Nevertheless, slaves re-appropriated Christianity to interpret and make sense of the bondage in which they found themselves and ultimately to make meaning for the whole of their lives (Moody, 2003). Rather than a means to marginalize, religion became a way to ease marginality and often found in the Bible liberation stories (Cone, 1997; Townes, 1995). Religious belief offered comfort, coping, and happiness but also set in motion resistance and rebellion (Williams, 2000). The whole of their religious lives manifested itself in slave and spiritual narratives.

Black women in the nineteenth century may have lacked the skills to inscribe their narratives, but not to organize or authenticate them (Moody, 1997). What was most significant was that these were recorded by the women themselves since the white establishment at the time would not record them. However, works by Harriet Jacobs (1861/1987), Elizabeth (1863/1988), and Sojourner Truth (1851/1993) found their way to the forefront of Black published works at the time. In spite of deprecation of the Black reality as "primitive" and "African," these stories showed Africans' capacity for learning and for addressing patriarchy, and showed the Bible as an authenticating text for their lives (Houchins, 1988). In each of these works, there was the story of an "incontrovertible faith that they were divinely ordained, each woman's absolute that God had established a relationship with her personally" (Moody, 1997, p. 33).

Many historians, archivists, researchers, and womanist and feminist scholars name the inherent political importance of spiritual narratives and auto/biographies. Nineteenth- and twentieth-century works of this nature encourage effective leadership and personal, institutional, and structural creation and transformation (Martin, 1998). In theorizing these auto/biographies, researchers have explored the over-feminizations of religion (Mitchem, 2002), challenged notions of the essential Black churchwoman (Moody, 2003), examined the role of religious spirituality in naming oppression and seeking abolition (Sanchez-Eppler, 1992), and examined the erotic/exoticization of the female religious experience (Carby, 1998; Lorde, 1984). However, this theorizing also tends to downplay the strong, religious meaning for those who believe that is in these same texts. Religious spirituality is still almost ancillary to historicizing the times and contexts in which slaves lived and these texts are also generally seen as part of the larger works in literary theory, history, and theology.

The Case for Black Women's Contemporary Spiritual Narratives

We are only beginning to examine the notion of contemporary spiritual narratives. However, most of these are still limited specifically to theology or self-help (Tisdell, 2003). The work of veteran Black women scholars and theo-ethicists Katie Cannon, Jacquelyn Grant, and Delores Williams have applied theology to current feminist scholarship and treat religious spirituality as a vital aspect of studying women's lives. Even works by literary greats Zora Neale Hurston and Alice Walker are often called spiritual narratives because "religious language, religious practices and religious issues help resolve these plots" (Moody, 2003, p. 175). Much like the literary text, real lives contain characters, plots, and subplots. Womanists such as Emilie Townes, Toinette Eugene, Cheryl Townsend Gilkes, and Jacqueline Grant use religious spirituality as a hermeneutic to explore the "plots" of ordinary Black women's lives and theologies. In spite of these efforts of womanists and other researchers, contemporary spiritual auto/biography remains largely tied to theology and the literary tradition or subsumed as a part of the larger plot of Black feminist concerns.

It is only recently that scholars have begun to focus on notions of Black spirituality, yet those studies still treat spirituality as a peculiar phenomenon of the urban school or as a framework of social justice. While religious spirituality does serve as an informant in these areas, it does not stop there. "African American women leaders grounded in a religious tradition traverse the religious and sociopolitical spheres...and interrogate the seamless web of complex interlocking issues in society" (Martin, 1998, p. 51). Much like earlier religiospiritual narratives, contemporary narratives can serve to highlight Black Christian women's life discourse and reflections and the significance of the effects of spiritual conversion and spiritual preservation upon life and work. Womanist scholars have taken great strides in exploring pre–nineteenth-century Black women writers. However, these examinations can serve to enlarge the scope of these works and give way to modern-day spiritual narratives that inform our lives (Martin, 1998).

> We not only learn from the life stories of our ancestors, but also to live our lives in ways...that will allow for the construction of new narratives to be appropriated by future generations. Autobiographies offer the best models for encouraging the construction of narratives...that makes individuals...aware...of the meaning that their lives have...Narratives can provide...access...to the values that we want to uncover and examine for their reappropriative potential in the contemporary. (Denard, 1998, p. 92)

Current research surrounding spirituality does not specifically mine religion and even backs away from it in favor of a more acceptable or ambiguous form or apologizes for its existence (Floyd-Thomas, 2006b). Current information remains limited concerning religious spirituality in the professional arena. My research attempts to "testify" to the African American religious experience through the "narratives of divine interaction with ordinary life" (Ross, 2002, p. 13). Contemporary spiritual narratives can help to discover the values and beliefs that are being portrayed, an opportunity to examine these beliefs within context (Denard, 1998, p. 93).

The Black Church

In light of women's spiritual narratives and the historical slave narratives that form a foundation for them, we should examine African Americans' newfound space in Christianity during the nineteenth century. "In order to counter the predicament of the slaves' acceptance of Christianity, White Christian slave owners decided to officially offer Christianity to Black slaves in the form of segregated worship space" (Travick-Jackson, 2003, p. 23). With the Civil War culminated a two-hundred-year struggle for Blacks to worship in their own Christian services. "Afro-protestant" (Foster & Haywood, 1995) denominations and governing bodies were formed. These Black denominations were versions of "Protestantism unique and fitting to their own experiences" (Foster & Haywood, 1995, p. 19). The Black Church emerged with an emphasis on social activism and the well-being of the Black community. Any attempt to discern the meaning of African American women's faith and action would be incomplete without reflection upon the Black Church (Williams, 1993, p. 204).

While Blacks do not possess one body of doctrines that defines their religious identity, they do have a common stock of religious experiences from which the notion of the Black Church is formed.

> The Black Church escapes precise definition...Some believe it to be rooted deeply in the soul of the community memory of Black folk. Some believe it to be the core symbol of the four-hundred-year-old African American struggle against White oppression with God in the struggle providing Black people with spiritual and material resources for survival and freedom. Others believe it to be places where Black people come to worship God without White people being present. I believe the Black Church is the heart of hope in the Black community's experience of oppression, survival struggle and its historic efforts toward complete liberation. (Williams, 1993, p. 205)

Although considered symbolic, the Black Church refers to the social and religious collective realities that African Americans experience (Mitchem, 2002; West & Glaude, 2003). From this hermeneutical and epistemological reference, one can study Black spirituality without apology (Noel, n.d.). The Black Church became and remains a pillar in the Black community and often represents more than just a place of worship. Lincoln (1999) states that "to understand the power of the Black Church, it must first be understood that there is no distinction between the Black Church and the Black community. The church is the spiritual face of the Black subculture" (p. 96). The church all at once provides political, religious, social, educational, and cultural activity (Cannon, 1988).

In our efforts to understand and explore spirituality, one cannot trivialize the role that organized religion and denominations play in cultural, racial, ethical, moral, and philosophical understandings, politics, and activism. The Black Church has also served as a valuable symbol to Black people that they could manage the structures of civil society (Murphy, 2000). Opportunities for leadership, not given anywhere else in society, served to train Blacks in leadership opportunities and to provide a space for affirmation, recognition, service, and demonstration of ability. In light of this, any attempt simply to secularize spirituality and ignore the importance of organized religion is unreasonable and disingenuous. In fact, Bolman and Deal (1995) offer that the many basic principles and tenets of spiritual teachings and religions are surprisingly similar.

The National Baptist Convention, USA

Although the symbolic nature of the Black Church is considered "invisible," denominations are "visible" representatives of the church. However, to speak of denominations as representative of the Black Church at large is a fallacy (Williams, 1993). In spite of this, there have been moments in Black history "when denominational churches have been effective instruments of freedom, survival, and positive quality of life" (Williams, 1993, p. 209). Black denominations have founded schools, delivered the civil rights movements, provided community activism, and nurtured many great leaders such as Martin Luther King, Jr., Harriet Tubman, Medgar Evers, and others (Williams, 1993). Indeed, the Black Church has been influential in the local and world community.

One such denomination was the National Baptist Convention, founded in 1895, not to be confused with the Southern Baptists, a white Baptist denomination. Prior to its founding, Black Baptist denominations were in existence as early as 1834. In the South there were some independent Black Baptist churches, but they were a part of larger white associations. At first, attempts to form all Black churches as denominations were not allowed. But as early as 1840, Black Baptists sought to develop a cooperative movement beyond state lines. Baptists in New York and the Mid-Atlantic states formed the American Baptist Missionary Convention. In 1864, the Black Baptists in all regions of the United States began to form consolidated conventions. Yet the Consolidated American Baptist Convention was rife with regionalism among Black Baptists. This continued regionalism and other factors caused the decline and eventual demise of the Consolidated American Baptist Missionary Convention.

Leaders in Black Baptist Churches believed that the demise of the Consolidated American Baptist Missionary Convention created a void in mission work, especially for African missions. This seemed to be a unifying answer to Black Baptists across the United States. Even while unifying, Black Baptist denominations still maintained three separate conventions. However, in the American National Baptist Convention, the National Baptist Convention, and the Foreign Mission Convention merged in 1895 at the Friendship Baptist Church in Atlanta to form the National Baptist Convention of the United States of America (NBC-USA). The heart of the organization of the NBC-USA was that the three former conventions served as the three boards of the convention: Foreign Missions, Home Missions, and Education.

During its history, the NBC-USA has offered opportunities for Black ministers to publish their own works by creating a publishing company, the National Baptist Publication Board. It was given the right to supply National Baptist churches with all of their church and Sunday School supplies. In a short time the publishing house became the largest Black publishing enterprise in the world. The NBC-USA also served as one of the leaders in civil rights activity. The NBC also became incorporated, naming itself the National Baptist Convention, USA, Inc. Shortly thereafter, NBC-USA built the Baptist World Center, which provided a headquarters for the convention. According to the current president, William Shaw (2007), the goal of the convention has been and strives to maintain its legacy of integrity and to make the convention a leading organization for Black people in the nation.

Women have played an important role in the building of Black denominations, including the Baptist tradition. Baptist women have been recognized as "elocutionists, lecturers, field secretaries for the Women's Conventions, missionary workers, teachers, writers, training school directors, and orators" (Carpenter, 2000, p. 101). Although women gave great time and energy to the Baptist Church, information about them remains sketchy. One famous Baptist woman, Nannie Helen Burroughs (1968), was a brilliant lecturer whose motto was, "Do ordinary things in an extraordinary manner." She was a political and religious leader and was the first to encourage the Woman's Day observances in churches. Burroughs took a keen interest in the causes of Africa and did much to get Blacks to vote in the United States. Burroughs' activist and leadership roles in the church, community, and schools laid an important foundation for women in the Baptist Church and other denominations.

What's Educational Leadership Got to Do with It?

A presumption still exists that organizational and most institutional culture is inhospitable to spirituality and religion. While empirical studies on religious spirituality in educational leadership are growing, it still remains an apprehensive topic. Even more interestingly, most of the current research seems intent upon highlighting spirituality as separate from religion and existing without religion (Fullan, 2002; Rogers & Dantley, 2001). While spirituality does not always denote a connection to religion, spirituality linked to religion does exist for some. In attempting to stay true to the separation of church and state, religious spirituality often gets overlooked in favor of a more neutral position.

Part of the reluctance to explore these topics could be due to the lack of a cohesive definition of spirituality and the notion that religion and education are mutually exclusive (Shields, 2005). Much of the literature on spirituality and leadership includes the authors' own peculiar definitions and treatments of spirituality (Bolman & Deal, 2001; Houston, 2002). Many of the definitions of spirituality describe it as connection to a higher power, yet they do not include proselytizing or converting others (Thompson, 2000), being present to the realities of one's world (Starratt, 2005a) and forming a commitment to life truths that one finds most important (Gottlieb, 2003). Many of these seminal works have begun to explore the inner realities of leadership, but have disengaged religion from this conversation. By remaining in this state of scholarship, spirituality is only partially explored if we attempt to over-secularize or under-spiritualize the concept.

Educational Leadership and Spirituality

A prevalent theme found in the literature about Black women and leadership is the issue of spirituality. Religion and spirituality have been found to be important to coping and making meaning for African Americans (Dantley, 2003). Spirituality has been found as central to Black scholars' research and teaching (Dillard, Abdur-Rashid, & Tyson, 2000). In her study of Black female educational administrators, Jones (2003) found spirituality was described as a way of life. Murtadha-Watts (1996), in her study of Black women superintendents, discussed spirituality as a source of sustenance, survival, and resiliency. Although some research exists concerning spirituality and education, upon closer examination, many do not, in fact, examine educational leadership and religious spirituality. These studies explore spirituality in educational leadership, as they are located in the perspectives of principals in urban schools.

Educational leadership research highlights a gap in educational leadership research surrounding the issue of religious spirituality in schools. However, these precursive works in spirituality provide an important base from which to investigate and privilege religious spirituality in educational leadership. Educational leadership research also highlights the trend of treating religious spirituality as an urban construct or one limited specifically to religious schools. Yoder's groundbreaking work underscored how spirituality matters to the whole of educational leadership practice (Yoder, 1998) and my dissertation research adds to the growing body of that literature.

Educational Leadership: Moral Imperative or Technocratic Ideal?

In 2005, the University Council of Educational Administration promoted a new social justice agenda for the organization. One of the current challenges in educational leadership has been how to institute socially just understandings and how to transform these understandings into everyday practice. Current national standards in educational leadership are being reformulated to better prepare educational leaders as moral and ethical agents of social justice. As the educational leadership literature moves toward a social justice framework, administrative practices become a focal point in analyzing how administrators engage in the process of social justice. By examining school leaders' decision-making practices and the unique frames of reference that inform them, we may better understand how to engage leaders in social justice in schools.

This move toward social justice highlights the continued emphasis on the ethical and moral responsibility of educators. In many districts, a morality clause was a vital part of gaining and maintaining certification, and that trend still exists (Fullan, 2002). Educational leaders are considered champions of this morality in schools and must adhere to a code of ethics or maintain strict policy behaviors. The educational literature has only scratched the surface of maintaining that personal values and priorities impact the principalship by informing critical, reflexive, and socially active leadership (Dantley, 2003). Something on the inside acts as a support for the actions (Terry, 1993).

This same literature on morality and social justice in educational leadership focuses on the reductionistic practice of relegating moral, ethical behaviors into a set of skills to be mastered. The purpose of this dissertation research is not interested in creating a social justice framework or "12-step approach" to socially just leadership practice. It is concerned with exploring whether and how principals' moral, ethical, and social justice values are informed by religious or spiritual beliefs. This research can deconstruct and critique the silence surrounding the spiritual and religious roots of these values. Dantley (2005) states:

> Reflection, deconstruction and the making of meaning are three spiritual components that must enter the educational leadership discourse…School leadership that is grounded in spirituality will push for transformation in education. Those who lead from a spiritual center will be dedicated and committed to changing schools because they are compelled to do so by their very deep sense of mission, calling, care and need to make meaning. (pp. 23–24)

Educational leaders must investigate the values, assumptions, and beliefs through which they interpret schooling and leadership and how these lead to social praxis. There *is* a body of work that highlights the interrelatedness of religious spirituality, social justice, and education (Comenius, 1990; Freire, 1996; Purpel & McLaurin, 2004; Wolterstorff, 2006). This idea of social praxis was echoed in a study by Capper and Keyes (1999) in which participants indicated that their mission for social justice was motivated by their spirituality. In the case of Black female leaders, Collins (1998) indicates that Black women have uniquely experienced inequities based upon their race, class, and gender and that this may compel them to be particularly concerned with issues of oppression or injustice. She states, "Even though Black women's concern for justice is shared with many others, Black women have a group history in relationship to justice" (p. 244).

In our corporate society, initial ideas of spirituality and leadership emerged from the business world (Covey, 1994; Jones, 1995). However, a by-product of educational leadership's kinship with the business world has been educational administration's attention to spirituality (Ah Nee-Benham & Cooper, 1998; Dantley, 2005; Shields, 2005). Managerial agendas and technocratic skills do not often leave room to explore cultural or religious cores that are important to administrative practice. There is an uneven worth placed upon these skills and one that fails to acknowledge spirituality's role in schools such as helping students to succeed (Hoyle, 2002) and making teachers more responsive to school leadership (Khanna & Srinivas, 2000). In fact, while educational leadership has often referred to school leaders as CEOs, some researchers have likened the role of educational leaders more to that of a minister than to the "business" leaders the field promotes (Houston, 2002).

In this age of accountability, the achievement gap, and an outcome, bottom line–based leadership, religious spirituality may seem irrelevant, ancillary, or escapist to the "real" issues of school leadership (Soder, 2002). "It is difficult to reconcile the work of leaders as strictly managerial when so much of it deals with the aspirations and dreams of people; when so much of it denies their very essence" (Houston, 2002, p. 1). However, Soder counters these notions by acknowledging that religious spirituality must be given legitimacy and thought of as a way to engage schools and leadership critically and ethically. Overemphasizing technocratic ideals leaves little space for exploring the subjective beliefs of diverse individuals and spiritual ideals characteristic in educational leadership (Starratt, 1996).

Spirituality: Why Does It Matter? Ontology and Epistemology

What role can spirituality—often considered deeply private—have in the very public realm of school leadership? Solomon and Hunter (2002) discuss this issue by perpetuating the highly contested interpretation of separation of church and state. They do this by suggesting that spirituality and religion are "acceptable" when understood as meaning systems. While many may not agree with debating constitutional rights, the authors provide insight into emerging scholarship in educational leadership. The authors state, "Meaning systems provide a relatively unified…framework for making sense of and interpreting one's perceptions and experiences…Most people need to know that their work can fit into their meaning systems" (2002, pp. 1–2).

Spiritual meaning systems are legitimate ways to conceptualize and frame leadership (Solomon & Hunter, 2002). Carolyn Shields (2005) posits spirituality as a valid epistemology to be considered in educational leadership along with other epistemological stances such as women's ways of knowing (Belenky, Clinchy, Goldberger, & Tarule, 1986), indigenous perspectives (Smith, 1999), and the host of "endarkened" epistemologies of people of color (Dillard, 2000). Rather than treating spiritual or religious epistemologies as ways of *not knowing*, we treat them as powerful counter-narratives to traditional knowledges in educational leadership, schools, and society (Shields, 2005, p. 611). Other literature echoes spirituality as a meaning-making lens through which people interact with their world (Brummett, 2000; Sayani, 2005).

Spirituality and religion have been linked to and concerned with the nature of being (Bowe, 2003). As educational leaders, one must be able to bring the totality of their existence into school space as well as allow students and teachers to do so as well (Shields, 2005). Failure to investigate various epistemological frameworks in educational leadership reproduces totalizing ideas of leadership and threatens to silence the voices of those to whom spirituality and religion matter (Dantley, 2003; Dillard, 2000). Religion and spirituality

> Are not simply a belief system but the expression of the ways in which we understand and live our lives, ground our identities, and relate to the world outside ourselves. Spirituality...as epistemology and ontology cannot be negated by educators—either because of anxiety about coming into conflict with those who misunderstand the legitimate boundaries circumscribed by legislation, or because (after decades of historical and systemic neglect) we do not know how to open up spaces in which spiritual perspectives and deep meaning may become central in public education. (Shields, 2005, p. 612)

Even in the wake of current literature calling for reinterpretation of educational leadership, we still do not know to what extent spiritual beliefs or religious upbringing influence practice in schools or inform commitment to social justice (Capper & Keyes, 1999). Research in this area can serve to reduce the overemphasis of traditional norm of leadership and "fixed ontologies" inherent in the field.

> Ontology can be said to study conceptions of reality and, for the sake of distinction, at least to the extent to which its counterpart, epistemology, can be represented as being a search for answers to the questions "What do you know?" and "How do you know it?", ontology can be represented as a search for an answer to the question "What are the knowable things?" ("Ontology," 2007)

Emerging notions of educational leadership can challenge traditional leadership ontologies. New research can contest currently accepted knowledge that is worth leaders knowing currently posited by technocratic skills and what leaders need to be or become as posited by leadership traits, personalities, and abilities (White, 2007).

How do these notions of epistemology and ontology fit into the context of religious spirituality and Black female principals? Collins (2000) and Stringer (1999) define epistemology as the way one knows reality or a knowledge frame reasoned by what a person says or does. However, Collins takes this a step further by defining epistemology as it relates to Black women. In these most silenced experiences, the starting point of these "standpoint epistemologies" is the lived experience of Black women and their representation in their own voices. Denzin (1997) echoes Collins' idea that standpoint epistemologies "attempt to recover and bring value to knowledge that has been suppressed by existing epistemologies" (p. 58). The personal experiences of the participants serve as the foundation for the interpretation of the research.

Challenging Traditional Educational Leadership: Religio-Spiritual Leadership

The field of educational leadership has many leadership styles that have been generated over the years. Among these are transformational leadership (Leithwood, 1992), transactional leadership (Judge & Piccolo, 2004), facilitative leadership (Conley & Goldman, 1994), instructional leadership (Blase & Blase, 2000), visionary leadership (Starratt, 1995), ethical/moral leadership (Sergiovanni, 1992), situational leadership (Hersey & Blanchard, 2007), autocratic leadership, participative leadership, laissez-faire leadership (Lewin, Lippet, & White, 1939), and servant leadership (Drake & Roe, 1999). However, much of this leadership promotes narrowly prescriptive ideas of the skills, characteristics of what is necessary for the principalship (Smith & Piele, 1996). All of these styles have found space in the educational leadership research and scholarship as valid epistemological viewpoints with their own ontologies. This trend is problematic in that it fragments spiritual and religious leadership, rendering religion as insignificant.

Joseph Rost (1991) gives a historical overview of the term *leadership* and its definitions in his book, *Leadership for the Twenty-First Century*. He examines how problematic defining the term is and looks at issues of conceptualizing and practicing leadership. Rost outlines that leadership was not used until the turn of the century and was not connoted as it is today and is purely a twentieth-century construct. Rost argues that the term does not account for the complex nature of leadership and the intersecting realities of enacting the term. It is problematic that *leadership* and *management* have been treated as synonymous and merely denotes holding the position of leader, possessing certain traits, or implying that leadership is purely about the leader and not the relationship to others (p. 45). Dantley (2003) argues that even many of the preparatory materials for training principals "accept labels such as administrative or management science as descriptors of educational leadership practice" (p. 182). An examination of leadership has important implications and insights for educational leadership scholarship. The field tends to pay little heed to conducting research on female leadership and certainly leadership by females of color, when the field desperately needs to do so (Bass, 1981). Dantley writes:

> The field is being challenged to consider a cacophony of voices that dispute the normative discourse of hierarchical and bureaucratic syntax, empirical and positivist idioms, and expressions of efficiency and productivity that have been borrowed from the classic business discourse. These new voices are communicating and language, spirituality, libratory praxis, and democratic dialogue... Essentially, educational leadership is being challenged to engage in a broader conceptualization of its purpose. (p. 182)

In keeping with the notion of religious spirituality, what of an ethical leadership style that is grounded in a religio-spiritual tradition of Black women? The aforementioned prescriptive ideas of leadership also have implications for women and principals of color and their acceptance, socialization, and effectiveness in the principalship (Blackmore, 1993; Eagly, Karau & Johnson, 1992; Enomoto, Gardiner, & Grogan, 2000; Shakeshaft, 1999; Tillman, 2003). Current educational leadership research still reveals a tendency to identify "leadership" or "administration" as male in spite of studies that show that women use different leadership styles than men (Blackmore, 1999; Shakeshaft, 1987).

> When the annals of Eurocentric history generally define leaders as male and of non-African descent, and when the annals of...history focus mostly on white women leaders, what of the (in)adequacy of scholarship, research,

and instruction devoted to Black women leaders...in society? And what are the methodological implications for...traditional categories of constructed leadership behaviors to be assessed in light of the complex nature of Black women's lives and history? (Martin, 1998, p. 56)

New paradigmatic research must be undertaken that challenges descriptive criteria, conceptual categories, and taxonomies that define leaders to account for counter-narrative (i.e., gendered, contextual, political, social) influences upon leadership.

Current scholarship concerning religio-spirituality has been largely explored in the psycho-social and medical fields and run the gamut across religious traditions (Marx & Seldin, 1973; Mitchell & Romans, 2003; Sakar, 2001; Sutherland, Poloma, & Pendleton, 2004). These studies are gaining traction but are still limited. In light of this movement of religio-spiritual culture in these fields, educational literature can benefit from exploring the validity of a religio-spiritual leadership style. An example of this possible style in Black women grounded in a religio-spiritual tradition is theorized by Riggs (1998). These leaders will exhibit the following characteristics:

1. *These leaders will be interpreters who exhibit moral courage.* They will be social-analytical interpreters of the context and knowledgeable about counter-hegemonic narratives and traditions as resources for interpretation. They will be morally courageous in that they know that moral life is an act of imagination, depending upon which images are presented as central to it.
2. *These leaders will be facilitators who are guiding a process of mediating differing ethical positions so as to engender creative moral responses.* The leadership style will be more that of consensus building (educating, persuading, seeking to mediate the tension and conflicts) than that of crusader or commanders. They desire participatory democracy.
3. *These leaders have committed but not absolutist morals, leaving themselves open to transformation in and through the very process of mediating the moral debate and agency that they are seeking to facilitate.* (Riggs, 1998, p. 43)

Religio-spiritual leadership goes beyond "solitary leader development" in favor of "more sophisticated approaches that challenge value-free presuppositions inherent in definitions of leadership...and argue for adaptive, relational, and interactive models of leadership" (Fluker, 1998, p. 11).

Black Female Principals and Religio-Spirituality

The spiritual and religio-spiritual convention of Black women is manifest in their participation in religion, education, and social reform. This is best characterized as socio-religious because of the interrelationship of a religious worldview and the conditions of society and institutions (Riggs, 1998). One of the most dominant tendencies among those who study female spiritual narrative and auto/biography is the notion of the Black spiritual/religious woman as irrational, self-sacrificing, emotional (Campbell, 1994). Tendencies such as these limit the cultural, spiritual, private, professional experiences of these women. Even womanists and womanist theologians can tend to portray religious Black women as "nurturing" and lose the strength of religious spirituality as a vital base for Black history.

In the same vein, current school scholarship concerning spirituality among Black female principals tends to treat this as an exotic or urban phenomenon, even though a spiritual worldview has been found to undergird the leadership experiences and practices of Black and African women (Jones, 2003; Murtadha-Watts, 1999; Reid-Merritt, 1996). Researchers such as Alston, Jones, and Murtadha-Watts who studied Black women leaders found that a profound spirituality imbued their leadership experiences and consistently appeared as a source of resiliency amid structural sexism and racism. Spirituality also informs and permeates the teaching and research of Black women scholars (Dillard et al., 2000). Murtadha-Watts (1999) referred to the participants in her study as spirited sisters, Black women leaders for whom spirituality was a constant source of inner strength, divine direction, and courage under fire.

There is reason to write about Black women's religious spirituality. It provides intellectual and practical space to discover the value that comes from Black women's lives. With Ross (2006), I agree that it

> involves uncovering and explicating life-giving norms embedded in Black women's moral practices, especially by exploring Black women's activism and attending to the pragmatic way many Black women...engage religion.... I see a complex working out of what it means to be Black and Christian, a working out that involves not only engaging the meaning-making

power of religion, but also interrogating religious traditions and practices while assessing functional uses of religion for shaping social action. (p. 115)

Nellie McKay (1989) makes a strong argument for including Black women's spiritual writings in scholarly activity. "In a racist and sexist society, the concept of a woman empowered by God is doubly radical" (Tate, 1992). Researchers often subsume and consume the religious and neuter and fragment the professional and spiritual, in the process dismissing what is significant to women about their own lives (Campbell, p. 63). This almost nonexistent body of work on religious spirituality in educational leadership snubs its importance for reframing leadership narratives, enacting social justice, working at decision making in schools, and bridging the gap between church and state in schools.

Summary

Religious African Americans have long been proponents of educational privileges in the community (Murphy, 2000). Education was seen as being of chief importance in the moral and social advancement of the Black community. The Black Church, womanism, womanist theology, and histo-graphic and contemporary spiritual narratives can serve as a bridge to examining this long-standing tradition in current research concerning educational leadership. My literature review represents an intersection of concepts, research, scholarship, and theory as they relate to providing context to reframe traditional notions of educational leadership, Black women, and religious spirituality.

Chapter 2

Womanist Theology as Methodology and Method

> *There is something about African American culture that compels oral history and narration.*
>
> (Cone, 1997, p. 6)

It is not customary to include an entire chapter devoted to methodology in a work such as this. However, I wanted to highlight the crucial nature of womanist theology to this undertaking. Theology in this context is not homogenous because of the varied ways in which people interpret or validate their experiences (Frederick, 2003).

In my quest to give voice to the principals in this study, I employed narrative analysis that sought to deconstruct quantification by exploring meaning (Vaz, 1997). Narrative inquiry and narrative analysis of lives have gained popularity in recent years. Narratives often take the form of first-person accounts. Other genres of "stories of experience" (Merriam, 2002, p. 286) include life history, oral history, life narrative, and autobiography. Professional practice in educational leadership tends to silence certain narratives regardless of what these narratives could teach us. Narrative research commands particular and historical significance for expanding and transforming knowledge about Black women (Vaz, 1997). Martin (1998) states:

> The interweaving of Black women's religious, biblical, theological, and sociopolitical thought and reflection as it often emerges in autobiography, biography, and other narrative forms, documents processes.... wherein one can

chart the evolution of the Afro or Afra-American self evolving from the more "private" citizen to the more "public"…leader. (p. 57)

Theological, spiritual, and religious concerns of Black women are located in their varied life experiences (Mitchem, 2002). For this reason, I refer to the stories of the Black female principals as spiritual historians and their stories as spiritual narratives. In this section, I also refer to these principals as narrators and myself as the researcher for further clarification concerning method and methodology. This is not to say that all Black women are religious; however, there is a historio-cultural communality among the experiences of Black women that allows examination of religio-spiritual matters with an intersectional locus. Roger Betsworth (1990) notes that narratives of culture differ from ordinary stories told in that particular culture. All stories are contextual, set within a world. Thus, what we think of as the narrative of culture sets the stage for the context in which the ordinary story makes sense. In the case of this research, the context of Black religio-spirtuality informs people's narratives in which they set the stories of their lives. In applying these ideas to spiritual narratives, "the history, scriptures, and narratives of a culture, the stories told of and in family and clan, and the stories of popular culture" (James, 1902/1982, p. 15) articulate, clarify, and give knowledge and meaning to the ordinary narratives people tell. "Unlike most of our research methods, which abstract dimensions, sort out variables, and name factors, narrative works the other way pulling seemingly disparate things together" (Roof, 1993, p. 4). Because of the intersection of contexts, identities, and the master narratives of society upon the individual, it is important for the focus of this research to explore the intersection of these socio-cultural narratives and multilayered meaning systems (gender, religion, race, educational leadership, social justice, and schooling) through the lens of the religio-spiritual stories of Black female principals.

What follows serves as a womanist theological methodological approach that moves spiritual narratives from solely literary and theological traditions and brings them to other disciplines as well. The particular nature and components of narrative research provide a link to womanist theology. Womanist theology promotes the tenets of radical subjectivity, traditional communalism, redemptive self-love, critical engagement, appropriation and reciprocity, and Spirit-love. By appropriating the basic ideas of womanist theological theory, my research methods, creation of the spiritual narratives, themes emersion, analysis, discussion, and implications provide a theoretical context for this qualitative research and exploration of the religio-spiritual.

A "New" Narrative: From Life History to Spiritual Narrative

"Life history and narrative approaches have emerged as important research over the last decade…and offer exciting alternatives for connecting the lives and stories of individuals to the understanding of larger human social phenomena" (Hatch & Wisniewski, 1995, p. 113). If one were to ask different researchers to define life history, one would likely receive varied interpretations. Atkinson (1998) describes life story as "an autobiography, with one person having guided another through the telling of the story" (p. 2). Tierney (1993) defines life history as a story that "revolves around questions pertaining to one's life" (p. 1). Life history has also been described as "the history of a life, a single life, told from a particular vantage point" (Lincoln & Guba, 1985, p. 115). However, rather than focusing on a definition of life history, unifying ideas of life history may be achieved by focusing on the purposes or philosophy behind examining lives. Most researchers agree that the basic premise of life history lies in examining "how individuals talk about and story their experiences and perceptions of the social contexts they inhabit" (Goodson & Sikes, 2001, p. 1). Because of the religio-spiritual nature of this narrative research, I name my work as *spiritual narrative*.

To free spiritual narrative from being largely situated in the areas of literary theory, history, and theology and to provide a link to education, I conceptualize my research this way:
  I. Qualitative Research
     A. Narrative
        1. Life History
           a. Spiritual Narrative.

For my research, I view life history as a type of narrative. To distinguish life history from other narratives, Foster (as cited in Hatch & Wisniewski, 1995) suggests the term autobiographical narrative. This definition seems limiting and fails to recognize the various reasons life history is employed. Instead I draw from Goodson and Sikes' (2001) ideas on the three reasons for researchers to employ life history:

1. It explicitly recognizes that lives are not hermeneutically compartmentalized…and that consequently anything which happens to us in one area of our lives potentially impacts upon and has implications for other areas too.
2. It acknowledges that there is a crucial interactive relationship between individuals' lives, their perceptions and experiences, and historical and social contexts and events.
3. It provides evidence to show how individuals negotiate their identities and consequently, experience, create and make sense of the rules and roles of the social worlds in which they live. (p. 2)

The three points above recognize the intersecting contexts and identities that make up individuals' experiences, the communality among people and groups, which is what makes narrative research so rich. To add to the three points, I would argue that life history also acknowledges that lives and their stories are not hermeneutically compartmentalized and recognizes diverse ontological and epistemological positions and standpoints. For this reason, many of the life history definitions are lacking for me in their theoretical location and leave little room for methods and methodologies that embrace the broader meanings of narrative and the diverse nature of individuals.

Research methods and methodologies often depend upon what a researcher wants to know (Goodson & Sikes, 2001). However, this book not only examines the distinctiveness of each individual principal, it also examines the ways in which religion and spirituality reflect communality of experiences, culture, and worldview and the ways in which religio-spirituality is reflected in the women's work.

Inasmuch as life history narratives are the stories of people's lives, spiritual narratives are the stories of people's spiritual lives. This book highlights that spiritual narrative can be seen as a usable research genre or derivative of life history, particularly when examining the multi-defined, multi-storied, and multi-historied nature of leadership, religion, and spirituality.

Spiritual Narratives

Historical spiritual narratives in the form of slave and conversion narratives informed much of my research. At first, I sought examples of narratives by Black women who particularly had ties to education. However, from exploring these narratives, I quickly found that the "work" of life was not simply located in a profession or lack thereof; rather, works often transcended boundaries and communities. Moreover, I found that the womanist ethos also transcended the boundaries of autobiography to extend to contemporary fictional works by authors such as Octavia Butler, Alice Walker, Zora Neale Hurston, and Maya Angelou. Some of these fictional works contain religio-spiritual themes and are often included among the genre of spiritual narratives. Some historical memoirs highlight resistance, such as that by Elizabeth (1863), a slave, which recounts her resistance in a doubly oppressive society by traveling as a woman preacher. Jarena Lee (1836) and Zilpha Elaw (1790), preaching partners, both chronicle their conversion experiences, lives, and work as evangelists. Sojourner Truth (1878/1992), spiritual leader, orator, and abolitionist, often chronicled the unique experiences of Black women in her writings. These works began to offer a foundation for many contemporary scholars of color, especially when examining religion and spirituality. For many, the written work of Virginia Broughton (1850), a Baptist teacher and missionary, has been largely regarded as the precursor to womanist theology. A leading advocate for women's rights, Broughton believed there was biblical support for women's equality (Houchins, 1988).

Early spiritual narratives often helped to confirm and strengthen the individual's own faith; it also was important to teach, edify, persuade, and exhort. Even though some of the first spiritual narratives expressly focused upon doctrinal issues such as communion, by the mid-nineteenth century, these narratives became more autobiographical in nature (Lincoln & Mamiya, 1990). For instance, early spiritual narratives and "white" spiritual narratives rarely discussed the writers' lives or discussed the self or God's relationship to individuals. In particular, Puritan and missionary writings were often written to convert others and to make sure individuals followed the "rules" of religion (Moody, 2003). There was clear presentation of doctrine, scripture, and literal interpretation of the Bible (Caldwell, 1983). For example, a public confession was considered the standard for admission to the church. Jonathan Edwards (1738), a staunch defender of Puritanism and leading eighteenth-century religious thinker, demanded that each person give an account of his or her own faith before gaining admission to the church or taking communion. These testimonial presentations of faith became some of the earliest spiritual narratives.

The spiritual narrative eventually evolved through the narratives of people of color as a means of self-examination and a way to examine society and the world. Furthermore, historical spiritual narratives were as concerned with identity as much as they were with doctrinal and theological concerns (Gates, 1991). Many authors of the spiritual narrative began to write about and contest the conditions in which they lived, their relationship to God and people, and their racialized, gendered, and religious roles and identities. Ida B. Wells-Barnett (1892), before becoming the editor of *Free Speech*, began her career working for social change initially to call others to the faith. However, she became a leader in ending lynching in America. In her seminal speech, "The Requisites of True Leadership," Wells-Barnett discusses her vision for social change and calls the community to show leadership in mobilizing others for social change. In subsequent writings, instead of merely recounting her own faith journey, she called upon others to critique institutional religion. She wanted others to strive to interpret their own faith as exhibited in their life and work. Sarah Dudley Pettey (1870) was a Christian worker "endeavoring to lead men and women… Heaven-ward" (Culp, 1902, n.p.). Still, her spiritual writings discussed her desire to see women move beyond uplifting people in their personal households to those of the entire Black race. These women and others reacted on "spiritual impulse" (Townes, 1993b). The spiritual narrative began to move beyond simple testimonial of conversion and the theological mandates of Christianity, to what Christian spirituality meant in terms of living the whole of the "Christian life." By sharing the spiritual narrative, the spiritual historian affected the entire community by speaking of trials endured, victory over those trials, interpretation of the Bible, mandates to service and social justice, and the power and privilege held as children of God. These spiritual narratives were no longer just about the "language of God," but the actual "working of the Word" in daily life and practice.

While spiritual narratives told much of the life history, there was a particular focus upon the life as it was lived now by faith, after conversion, and based upon God's historical and cultural connection to African Americans. As stated in the literature review, certain white narratives were intent on highlighting sinfulness and often overapplying this sinfulness to the African American. What was important about the African American slave and spiritual narratives is that they reconstituted and re-appropriated the spiritual narrative for themselves and as it related to their lives. The spiritual narrative became a new way to read Christianity and to make Christianity one's own. Much like historical spiritual narratives, this research seeks to add to the narrative research umbrella by examining the various ways religio-spirituality is personally defined and the ways in which it influences daily practices and outcomes.

Qualitative researchers have imbued the term *narrative* with a variety of uses and meanings. Narrative can be seen as a story or as interview data as told to the researcher (Atkinson, 1998); the societal structures and discourses in which the story is situated (Tierney, 1993); the way in which the story is told (Hendry, 2007); and the "end-product" of the research text itself (Clandinin & Connelly, 2000). In my research, individual life and spiritual stories and episodes provide the data of religion and spirituality as lived experience. These data as solicited by interviews provide the basis for an endproduct of a spiritual narrative and are analyzed by attending to various factors such as the way the story is told, omissions in the story, and the larger societal and historical narratives that construct society. "That narrative includes both process and product, phenomenon and method, and is emphasized throughout the narrative literature" (Hatch & Wisniewski, 1995, p. 126). The work of spiritual narratives commands a holism (Mitchem, 2002) of all of these elements. Atkinson (1998) states:

> The role of life history [narrative] is primarily to pull together the central elements, events, and beliefs in a person's life, integrate them into a whole,

> make sense of them, learn from them, teach the younger generation, and remind the rest of one's community what is most important in life. (p. 19)

In this same way, the spiritual narrative can provide a way to better understand and pull together the varying and various aspects of the human experience and the integrative and intersecting functions of religion and spirituality in the life story. The next few sections illustrate how womanist theological tenets of radical subjectivity, traditional communalism, redemptive self-love, critical engagement, appropriation and reciprocity, and Spirit-love outlined in the literature review and the concerns of life history and narrative inform this research.

Radical Subjectivity: The Need for Narrative

Radical subjectivity has been described as the "anecdotal evidence of Black women's lives" (Cannon, 2006, p. 16). Radical subjectivity denotes the ability of Black women to name their own subjectivity in light of intersecting oppressions that they face. What does it mean to discuss and "prove" the ordinary spiritual realities when they cannot be proved in a scientific manner? Many researchers acknowledge "the power of life history and narrative to go beyond scientific and empiricist standards that they believe continue to dominate other qualitative methodologies" (Hatch & Wisniewski, 1995, p. 119). The premise of this research rests in its ability to apply a womanist theological, theoretical, and methodological approach grounded in the experience of Black women, culture, and narrative. The tenet of radical subjectivity seems to need what the autobiographical nature of narrative has to offer: an ability to name oneself in narrative while applying theoretical and identity frameworks that allow Black women to become a part of the greater religious, spiritual, professional, political, and other socio-cultural narratives of society.

> The goal of Black autobiography has never been just an attempt at an objective reconstruction of an individual's past or a public demonstration of the qualities of selfhood or a private meditation on the meaning of a life of struggle. It has also sought to be discursive. (Houchins, 1988, p. xxix)

The goal of Black women's spiritual narratives existed and exists as a way to understand and read religion and spirituality into and as their own story, in light of a feminist-style hermeneutic (Houchins, 1988; Morton, 1985). In the case of my research, a womanist theoretical framework is understood as a way to do this.

Womanism recognizes itself as a standpoint of Black feminists or other feminists of color (Walker, 1983). This research is explored through the frame of an African American Christian female perspective. Womanist theologians preoccupy themselves with the everyday "stuff" of women's lives to spin narrative and give voice to the many facets of history, culture, and spirituality of Black women and these facets' effect upon their lives. Narrative is a process and a means by which to do this. Lee, Rosenfeld, Mendenhall, Rivers, and Tynes (2004) state that "narrative is a powerful tool that . . . unfolds and acts in culturally specific ways" (p. 39). Narrative research is cross-disciplinary and varies in its definition (Chase, 2005; Riessman & Quinney, 2005). "All talk and text are not narrative" (Riessman & Quinney, 2005, p. 393). But what seems to be unique is that it engages micro- and macro-level themes and allows individuals to move beyond a naturalized discourse. Rather than viewing experiences as natural (thus opening the door for stereotypes and misappropriations), individuals can "construct who they are and how they want to be known" (Riessman & Quinney, 2005, p. 394). Rather than be constructed, individuals can construct and contest forced identities and meanings.

Narrative also does not mean merely illustration (Roof, 1993). Narrative has a much broader practice and function. More than just stories as illustrations of an idea, narrative is motivated by a search for meaning (Roof, 1993, p. 2). While narrative research does not require an explanation of what it is not in comparison to other research methods, it was important to me that my topic and modes of study illuminate the participants, their stories, and meanings (Munro, 1991). For this particular research, "narrative is a crucial conceptual category for such matters as understanding issues of epistemology...depicting personal identity and displaying...convictions" (Hauerwas & Jones, 1989, p. iv).

Radical subjectivity also draws similarities to "being positioned" and "positioning self" (Baumberg, 2004, p. 136). This research claims the importance of privileging the sense-making processes of the participants and their particular identity claims (Baumberg, 2004; Stanley & Billig, 2004). Researchers of narrative are "interested in the way people do narrate our lives, not the way they should" (Goodson & Sikes, 2001, p. 16). Narratives are always rooted in the sense-making systems of individuals and how these systems affect individual and collective life (Lincoln, 1995). In particular, the ways that the stories are used takes on particular importance. In this research I focus upon spiritual narratives as a form of the life history process by exploring religio-spirituality and its significance to the principalship.

Narrative inevitably tends to work well with sensitive topics (Goodson & Sikes, 2001). Lee and Renzetti (1993) suggest that sensitivity in research may occur when "research intrudes into the private sphere or some deeply personal experience or where researchers are investigating religious practices, articles or beliefs, subject to profanation" (p. 5). This makes the spiritual narrative a good support for researching the lives of Christian Black female principals. Narrative becomes a way to explore intersecting realities such as race, culture, gender, and religious differentiation in a way that other qualitative methods cannot and also to become emancipatory and empowering (Giroux, 1991).

"Narratives, short stories, and autobiographies are valuable…because they make specific use of narrative form which is the most basic form of comprehension" (Denard, 1998, p. 86). While spiritual narratives told much of the life history, there was a particular focus upon the life as it is lived now by faith, after conversion, and based upon God's historical and cultural connection to African Americans. Narratives, by nature, are "unapologetically subjective" (Ayers, as cited in Hatch &Wisniewski, 1995, p. 118). Womanist theologians' interpretation of radical subjectivity enables the research process to make use of the spiritual narrative to "read" the religious narrative and make it its own.

Traditional Communalism: Data Collection Methods and Researcher Self in Story

Traditional communalism recognizes the relational bonds among Black women (Floyd-Thomas, 2006b) and the hybridity of Black women's experiences (Stewart, 2005). Traditional communalism is taken from the ways that Black women have nurtured and supported other Black women. Traditional communalism recognizes the uniqueness of the individual, but connects seemingly disparate experiences and identities among the individual and others (Mitchem, 2002). In this same way, it affected the way I initially positioned myself as the researcher and co-spiritual historian, and the way I collected data. Traditional communalism in womanist theology encourages researcher and participant field interdependency, researcher involvement with and immersion in events and situations, personalizing phenomena and encouraging a lack of distance from topics and subjects (Smitherman, 2000, p. 87).

What I perceived as the troubles in my methods turned out to be the strengths of them as well. Particularly, I wanted to maintain close connection to the spiritual historians, have them "control" processes as much as possible, and support them in the struggle to tell their stories rather than check off my list of procedures for the research. A large part of narrative inquiry and womanist theology connects in a way that moves what is perceived simply as a data collection procedural process to each step in that process becoming deliberate and meaningful. For example, in completing research concerning African American women, Peterson (1997) recognized that theoretical perspective and the who, what, and why of research are important to the ways in which we conduct research. The researcher's philosophies and standpoints, what she deems as important, determine the process. My commitment to traditional communalism and narrative research required me to recognize mutuality in the researcher/narrator relationship. Each principal was interviewed in an initial interview and follow-up interviews totaling a minimum of three hours and a maximum of seven. The women were interviewed at the site of their choosing and control, but one in which an uninterrupted block of time could be maintained. An open-ended, in-depth interview process was used (McCracken, 1988). This process is not solely about a pre-determined list of questions but more about supporting what the participant has to say in her own words. Open interview (Patton, 2002) questions were asked so that room was left for spontaneous questioning by the researcher and so that the voices of the spiritual historians were heard as much as possible. Paying attention to communalism in my research served to link womanist methods through connecting with participants in conversational interviewing rather than embodying phenomenology's call for researcher restraint (Bloom, 1998). Interviews were tape-recorded and then transcribed as quickly as possible after the interviews (White, 1997). Notes were taken in a journal to record "anything that transpires" (White, 1997, p. 117), but particularly as a way to reflect upon the research process and exercise reflexivity (Vaz, 1997). This journal allowed me to record researcher thoughts and analyses, method changes, new interview questions, and nonverbal events and to evaluate my personal commitments and the ways I identify myself and their impact on this research.

I, too, consider myself a Christian Black female and once occupied a principalship. While not engaging in an auto-ethnographic method per se, because of my relationship with each principal, I have been able to share my own story with each of them. I believe that a commitment to a womanist methodology and traditional communalism necessitates and obligates me to engage with this research in a way different from traditional positivistic research. Traditional communalism allows one to see the self in the other and the other in the self (Floyd-Thomas, 2006a). While collecting the stories of others and reflecting upon them, one is able to examine and balance individual narratives in light of the narratives of other spiritual historians and socio-historical texts (Hatch & Wisniewski, 1995; Peterson, 1997). Rather than being a call for researcher restraint and objectivity, womanist and feminist research "involves weaving the stories of both the researcher and her respondents" (Cotterill & Leatherby, 1993, p. 67). Womanist theological research also involves a particular attention to the stories and identities of others in the research process and what we can learn from them (Cannon, 1988). More important, a weaving of stories and the researcher's own experiences can serve to problematize traditional modes of research and can serve to engage the researcher in an even greater level of ethical behavior and reflexivity.

One such concern of this research was the construction of narratives, the analysis of those narratives, and the authenticity of the research. What did it mean for this research that I was so closely connected to it? What did it mean when it became apparent that my spiritual story and its significance to my principalship was so deeply a part of the research process? "Writing the self into the research reports enhances the authenticity of the research" (Ezzy, 2002, p. 154), and all data can be a part of the reflexive process, including the researcher's story (Stanley, 1993). Even so, my first-person-by-proxy stance, the style of my writing, and the liberties I took with time and tense, fiction and nonfiction, and filling in gaps of story in construction of the narratives troubled me. Narratives are often thought of as co-constructions among the narrator and the context and culture; and as joint constructions between the researcher and narrator (Gergen, 2004). Moreover,

> It might be said that the narratives revealed in a research study are themselves by-products of the relationship of researchers to respondents. The mutual gaze, subtle signs of agreement or disagreement, silences, smiles, frowns, and comments related to shared or diverse experiences all lend shape to the story being told. If the storyteller is the same age, race, and/or gender as the listener, certain assumptions of similarity may lead to embellishments on themes that might be avoided were the listener someone completely different and vice versa. (Gergen, 2004, p. 280)

While the above quote can lead to an over-preoccupation with issues of authenticity and validity, radical subjectivity and other womanist theological tenets highlight the values of stories and the researcher's position. Stories are the closest we come to experience as we and others tell of our experience (Clandinin & Connelly, 2000, p. 415). There must be a constant co-creation of the narrative (Munro, 1998). To interpret another's religious or spiritual experience carries an obligation to nuance it and respect it. The effectiveness of this relationship impacts the telling of these stories.

Redemptive Self-Love: The Aesthetic and the Authentic

The womanist theological tenet of self-love also highlights communality, yet it is also committed to individual expression and the aesthetic. My interpretation of self-love for my research makes the claim that there is a beauty and a worth in the Black woman and her experiences without measuring them against societal norms. Self-love serves communally and is reconciled with the dominant culture, yet it is also in protest to a culture that systematically and institutionally assaults the worth of Black women (Gilkes, 1993, p. 239). Black women are called to love themselves and value their own experiences and interpretations in spite of contrary circumstances and intersecting oppressions. Self-love is a reaffirmation of Black womanhood and knowing "that it is all right to be Black and female" (Douglas, 2006, p. 142).

I could have easily used my spiritual historians' narrative interviews and simply "coded" them. However womanist theology's self-love aesthetic can seek to reaffirm Black women's experiences in any form in which a research text is presented. Beyond my personal interest in spiritual narratives, the question that kept coming to mind was, "What does creation of narrative do that simply coding my narrative interviews does not?" Much like teachers, I believe that principals' knowledge is derived from the aesthetic, personal, emotional, and moral aspects of experience (Clandinin & Connelly, 2000). Just as important, I believe spirituality and its import on practice can be understood in the same way.

If womanist theology and the tenet of self-love give way for the affirmations of the history, humanity, customs, and aesthetics of Black women (Floyd-Thomas, 2006a, 2006b), then spiritual narratives can serve the same purpose. It has been said that self-love means to acknowledge oneself but also respect the paths and contributions of the ancestors (Settles, 2006). By examining slave and conversion narratives as a resource for this research, I honor the self-love commitment to history and also allow my spiritual historians' works to be a part of the ongoing process of "writing Black women...into history" (Floyd-Thomas, 2006b, p. 106). Black women's historical spiritual texts have had a transforming presence on society, institutions, and individuals. Moreover, I believe that "new" spiritual narratives need to be created to continue to add new voices and insights in spiritual, cultural, and educational thought. Womanists' redemptive self-love is expressed in scholarship that rescues Black women from caricature and produces new paradigms.

All of the appropriate (if they can be described as such) steps to ensure validity, reliability, and authenticity of the research have been taken. However, I believe on some level these things to be limiting to the overarching goals of narrative and difficult for the narrative researcher. Even so, validity of findings was attempted by "member checking," reviewing with participants the data, narratives, and the researcher's interpretation of data. This consisted of sharing transcripts and narrative drafts with the spiritual historians for feedback and accuracy before creating and presenting these narratives. It also included allowing the spiritual historians to engage with my interpretation in light of the literature and my own story. I was also able to examine through conversations and readings of the text with the spiritual historians and highlight how my story and interpretation presented themselves in like and different ways. School and district characteristics are included in Chapter Four along with the past and current life and societal contexts to paint a more complete picture of the analysis.

I remain fairly convinced that a loss can take place in our validity/reliability conversations. As a Black female Christian, my insider status compels me to tell the story. Because of this, I remain committed to overcoming the academic community's temperance of certain research with its constant calls for trustworthiness. As a researcher who considers herself an outsider based upon my own notion of religio-spirituality and as an academic, I struggle to un-other the narrator by the telling of their stories. However, this double-conscious nature (DuBois, 1994) also compels me to examine the story more closely, instead of simply the purposes for which I want to tell the story or why the story should be told at a certain time.

The duality of my insider and outsider status becomes one that completes or propels the research. A religious criticism approach (Warnick, 2004) guides much of this research. Warnick believes that when working with issues of religion and spirituality, there are two basic assumptions. One must have a basic attitude of "respect toward the tradition—its stories, texts, revered heroes, and traditional interpretations" (p. 347). Also, one using a religious criticism approach should have a deep knowledge of the religion and spirituality herself. The two ideas presuppose that there is worth in the researcher coming from inside her arena of religion or spirituality. Zora Neale Hurston (1990) suggests that any hermeneutical interpretation can at best give us only partial truths, religious criticism and the womanist methodology I have set up moves me to view the truths of the stories not as partial, but as more complete by my participation in them. Instead of truths, insider/outsider status is one that completes or at least keeps me moving around, in, and through the hermeneutic circle. My own religio-spiritual background helps me ascertain my research in a deep way as an insider, yet also to examine the research in a scholarly and critical manner. Despite popular opinion in some research circles, these examinations are not and do not have to be exclusive of the other.

Hendry (2007) has said that the narrative and the telling of it should be considered a spiritual act, one in which we have faith in the story. I would also argue that we have faith in the storyteller, but not because researchers are such great tellers. There needs to be a suspicion in this telling that keeps reflexive praxis at the forefront of what we do. However, with our constant calls for non-navel-gazing, there is an erasure that can take place for the researcher of color. A majority of researchers of color write about issues that are close to them (Stanley, 2007). Some of the issues surrounding narrative research and research in general can serve to stifle methodologies and methods committed to people of color and by people of color. There has to be a resistance for the scholar of color but not a "folding" to empiricist project of research. Instead, I want to promote this notion of faith in process. My research is not about merely telling my own story, but about walking alongside the women I participate in research with and sharing their stories and indeed my own with the world. For when else and by whom would, could, and should it be told? The matter for me as a researcher is that it is told at all. Instead of a crippling concern with reifying practice, critics of narrative and the process itself reify for the researcher of color and thus their participants when they attempt to over-manage the research. My own commitment to redemptive self-love requires that I redeem the story from traditional stances of research and promote those that "demystify the lives of Black women" (Floyd-Thomas, 2006b, p. 10). This demystification occurs by using methods, methodologies, and analyses that honor the peculiarity of the lives of religio-spiritual Black women.

There were times when the research "glitch" happened—the moment when my ideas did not line up with the spiritual historians', the moments when the interview seemed to "get away from me" and take a turn that I did not expect, the moments when some "fact" did not seem quite right. The glitch offered moments not to over-examine rigor, truth, method, or facticity. The glitch served as an opportunity to attend more closely to the story, the "authenticity" of religio-spirituality for the spiritual historian, and the opportunity to honor the womanist theological locus for the research that I set up. This is one that does not require "authenticating" to be published as many historical slave narratives did, but that honors the rich narrative, storytelling heritage of the spiritual historians as they tell what they know and how they know it. As the researcher, I recognize the need to "make space for negotiation and meaning...for a new epistemology and methodology" (Goodson & Sikes, 2001, p. 49).

Critical Engagement: A "Nitty-Gritty Hermeneutic" of Categorizing, Collecting, and Presenting Stories

Critical engagement as conceptualized by womanist theologians requires that one "recognizes the poignancy that characterizes the Black woman's intellectual positioning" (Copeland, 2006, p. 208). Critical engagement offers a "nitty-gritty hermeneutic" (Harris, 2006, p. 54), one that seeks to interpret and unpack the realities of everyday life in society and how we present those realities to others. This includes taking Black women's stories and everyday experiences, without "sugarcoating" oppressive realities, and naming them as valid epistemologies. Black women can "outwit, outmaneuver, and outscheme" (Copeland, 2006, p. 228) dominant social systems and structures, which involves "debunking, unmasking, and disentangling" (Cannon, 1996, p. 138) dominant ideologies. Hermeneutics is closely related to interpreting narratives (Lichtman, 2006), and "hermeneutic interpretation is embedded in African American culture" (Peterson, 1997, p. 157). It shuns reductionism. Theological perspectives, which provide important frames for this study, rest on hermeneutical, interpretive principles. Because this research seeks critical engagement, this affects the analysis and interpretation of the spiritual historians' stories.

"The forms that narrative representations take are related to the purposes for which their authors use them and the audiences to which they are directed" (Rosiek & Atkinson, 2007, p. 504). However, it may be that these alternative forms of research texts allow the reader to empathize, understand, and "know" the "truths" more adequately than do traditional research texts (Rosiek & Atkinson). The researcher always has to concern herself with remaining "true" to the voice, representation, truth, and experience of the narrators (Clandinin & Connelly, 2000; Hendry, 2007; Tierney, 2007; Vaz, 1997). "Overall in the academic arena, disenfranchised groups, which include women, women of color, and poor people, are othered in the telling of their stories" (Johnson-Bailey, 2002, p. 325). I did not want the spiritual narrative to be simply clever posturing (Atkinson, 1990).

There is a general political and moral implication of writing about others, naming their experience, and analyzing narrative. One such way to ensure the voice of the participants was to refrain from line-by-line, micro-level coding. In contrast to narrative analysis, more traditional types of research rarely examine the individual as a whole (Ezzy, 2002). "Whether we conceptualize the subject as unitary constituted through direct experiences that are linear or knowable, and representable or as nonunitary constituted through language and discourse, the subject is still viewed through narrative" (Hendry, 2007, p. 490). The oft-used "coding" process can detract from what is being conveyed in the story (Chase, 2005). For narrative inquirers, the analysis process is more than a micro-level, reductive practice:

> Narratives are primary and irreducible. They are not imperfect substitutes for more sophisticated forms of explanation or understanding, nor are they unreflective first steps along the road which lead toward the goal of scientific or philosophical knowledge. The meaning-making at which stories aim is a primary goal. (Mink, 1970, p. 557)

For narrative researchers, "the meaning is in the story and the interpretation of the story by the researcher" (Lichtman, 2006, p. 165). Because of this, the totality of the generated stories has been examined as data, yet the production of narratives functions also as a part of the analytic process.

"The narrative method requires that the story be told, not torn apart in analysis" (Mitchell & Lewter, 1986, p. 8). In spite of this, as the researcher, I did not merely present raw transcripts to the reader in constructing the spiritual narratives. When I researched historical spiritual and conversion narratives, patterns and themes for constructing them emerged. Viewing data as narrative is a valuable approach in analysis and counteracts the culture of fragmentation (Atkinson, 1992) that is prevalent in coding and categorizing. The womanist theological ethic stresses that knowledge is constructed out of experience first; it is from lived experience that theoretical inferences can be posited and tested. "It needs to tell without much tampering" (Floyd-Thomas, 2006b, p. 72).

Narratives "do not present neat, chronological accounts of women's lives" (Munro, 1998, p. 12). Spiritual narratives are also rarely neat (Coles, 1998). Moreover, spiritual narratives do not present neat accounts or categories of spirituality. Womanist theology is highly self-critical of categories of spirituality and religion and methods of analyzing as well. The womanist theological "hermeneutical suspicion" (Floyd-Thomas, 2006a, p. 208) is ever present in interrogating the intellectual and identifying space it occupies and the methods by which one analyzes.

Critical engagement's hermeneutic of suspicion required that the narratives not be treated as offering "fixed" ideas of themes and interpretation. Johnson-Bailey (2002), in what she described as culturally distinctive analysis among her work with Black women, offers that the data collection and analysis process always attempts to keep the story as the central locus. In applying these ideas to my womanist theological method, a handling, revisiting, and filtering process of the data was constant. Data were initially transcribed and unpacked for broad themes. Data analysis remained ongoing, open ended, and deductive (Riessman, 1993). In addition to basic demographic questions, interviews focused initially upon participants' definitions of spirituality, spiritual background, school leadership, and issues of social justice. However, as interviewing continued, these questions were expanded upon for clarification, particularly as it became clear that my ideas concerning data and my "theme-anticipation" did not align with the spiritual historians' actual stories. Because of this, data were analyzed throughout the study and themes were revisited. Data were coded and recoded until initial themes emerged from each spiritual narrative. After initial themes emerged, each spiritual narrative was analyzed according to narrative-specific elements. Individual narratives are explored in Chapter Three. Further "thematizations" (Wolff, 2002, p. 97) were completed to bring initial themes into broader ones for cross-narrative interpretation that is explored in Chapter Four.

Appropriation and Reciprocity: Lives and Literature in Action

"Womanist approaches to religion and society have not only been invested in knowledge production and reconstruction only for themselves and their mainstreaming disciplines but also for other scholars...and those who remain on the margins" (Floyd-Thomas, 2006b, p. 11). Womanist theologians are also committed to appropriating other scholarship and maintaining a constant reflection and interpretation of historical figures and events to continue to advance their cause. Even in the dialogic process, there is also a commitment to the everyday "vernacular" (Phillips, 2006, p. xxiv) of ordinary life and the ways in which individuals describe it. Appropriation and reciprocity recognize the intertwining nature of things: narratives, people, ideas, and what has "gone before," including history and previous scholarship. The use of narrative methods allows this research to place a focus on the intersecting realities of Black, female, religio-spiritual principals.

First, the literature review has formed a basis for exploring the often-difficult task of narrowing the overlapping and intersecting terms such as *beliefs, religion, faith,* and *spirituality* and what they mean in light of education, and specifically educational leadership. The task of operationalizing these terms into one overarching idea for this study has been arduous, as I have attempted to do what these spiritual historians in this study do not do. The spiritual historians do not treat these terms as contested ones nor attempt to operationalize them for clarity's sake. I do this for them, even though it is important for research participants to define and be defined in terms that are meaningful for them (Gold & Bogo, 1992). In their own ways of knowing, truths, and narratives, these terms make sense to them and are not solely, to the exclusion of others, products of the denomination to which they belong, the churches they attend, or the experiences they have had. These terms and their meaning and ideas are lived cross-institutionally, cross-situationally, and cross-experientially. My use of the term *religio-spiritual* seeks to honor the "overlapping perspectives and paradigms" (Denzin & Lincoln, 1994, p. 2) of spirituality for the spiritual historians.

Second, this research has a strong connection to my own positionality, identity, and perceptions as they relate to religio-spirituality and educational leadership. Through this process, I was able to examine more fully my standpoint regarding these issues and how they informed my life and my leadership. I came to my work prepared to examine the finer points of Christian religio-spirituality from a theological perspective as if there were just one. I needed to understand religio-spirituality as it is understood and lived by these women. This proved to be a difficult task as my own grid informed so much of my own personal hermeneutic and not just the communal hermeneutic of Black women principals. The fact that religious faith is personal and makes one vulnerable for those who live it and believe it, there was no way to completely distance myself from this research. From a narrative perspective, the researcher never stands completely outside of the hermeneutical circle (Ezzy, 2002). Hurston (1990) suggests that any hermeneutical interpretation can at best give us only partial truths. However, the womanist methodology I have set up moves me to view the truths of the stories not as partial, but as more complete by my participation in it.

There were moments when my literature review threatened to overtake and compress my narrative. Early attempts at a literature review explored topics and issues that I thought would be important to the exploration of the Black women, the principalship, and religio-spiritual concerns and traditions. However, as data were collected and analyzed, certain emphases in the initial literature review needed to be under-emphasized and certain ones needed to be highlighted more. As a part of the analysis process, attention was paid to cultural themes of religio-spiritual traditions such as references to race, the Black Church, and other spiritual rhetoric, community consciousness, and cultural reference (Smitherman, 2000). Existing research and literature served to provide an analytical framework for the story. "The lens one chooses provides a criteria of rigor that insures that the construction of the narrative illuminates the rich context, content, and tensions of ideas and actions about a particular or set of phenomena" (Ah Nee-Benham & Cooper, 1998, p. 2). The narrative plus literature approach can help to explore, examine, and reveal linkages between silence and voice and the dynamics of race, ethnicity, class, gender, and other human diversities such as religion and spirituality. Appropriation and reciprocity demand that the womanist theological process is always dialogic across disciplines, beliefs, genders, methods, theories, and histories. Appropriation and reciprocity form an "intentional and concomitant effort of other to participate in solidarity with and on behalf of Black women" (Floyd-Thomas, 2006a, p. 250). This effort also extends from Black women to other women of color and marginalized and oppressed members of society. History and the narratives of African Americans serve as a scaffold for this effort. While this research makes many references to the communal and historical nature of spiritual narratives, this was not a historical investigation per se. I began reading collections that highlighted slave narratives, which served as the earliest examples of African American spiritual narratives. In particular, the Schomburg Library of Nineteenth-Century Black Women Writers series housed at the Schomburg Center for Research in Black Culture at New York Public Library provided me with invaluable information. I also collected anthologies, autobiographies, and narratives of early twentieth-century Black women compiled by scholars spanning various disciplines such as theology, literary theory, and history. I want to be clear that I was not looking for a particular structure or essence in historical narratives. "It clearly would be unproductive merely to examine large numbers of narratives—whether or not derived from interviews—in order to demonstrate that they have the same underlying structure" (Coffey & Atkinson, 1996, p. 61).

Secondary sources were helpful in that they helped me "to analyze the primary sources effectively" (McCluskey, 1993, p. 194). Because I had collected so much information, I narrowed my attention to the resources based on the themes I set out to research: religion, spirituality, and educational leadership. Many of the anthologies, compilations, and commentaries contained information about Black women but I focused my attention on those that specifically highlighted each woman's spiritual and religious perspective and how that perspective affected the ordinary realities of her life perspective on education. Rather than relying too heavily on commentaries, I focused upon compilations and anthologies of actual speeches, letters, and personal documents written by nineteenth- and twentieth-century contemporaries and framed my ideas around my research questions in examining their commitments, actions, and thoughts on religion, life, education, social justice.

Spirit-Love: Spiritual Historians and Religio-Spirituality

For this research and the womanist theologian, my idea of Spirit-love places an emphasis upon religio-spirituality and its interaction in Black women's lives (Mitchem, 2002). This last tenet of womanist theology serves as a unifying idea of this research. In Walker's definition, love of Spirit seems to be ambiguous. One does not know if she means religion, spirituality, or even the notion of a Christian God. Love of Spirit by Walker's (1983) standard is not intrinsically religious or Christian. However, this tenet was added due to the role that Walker's definition has offered womanist theology. The definition has affirmed for Christian Black women their rights in society and the religious community. "Womanist theology is informed and inspired by traditions of Black women working with religious thought in new ways" (Mitchem, 2002, p. 55). Womanist theology "affirms Black women's connection with both feminism and with the history, culture, and religion of the African American community" (Martin, 1998, p. 56). Womanist theology begs a response to questions surrounding religious spirituality and its impartation to the lives and work of leaders, educational and otherwise. More than just denoting the journey of one Black woman literary genius or a scholarly trend or fad, womanism has become an answer for many Black women scholars in studying religious spirituality (Floyd-Thomas, 2006b, p. 7). Womanist theology is meant to transcend denominational Christianity through a collective and inclusive standpoint (Cannon, Johnson, & Sims, 2005).

Four participants were gathered through the use of purposeful sampling (Patton, 2002). Although this number may seem small, "The representativeness of a small number of interviewees can be high...Narrative interviews provide in-depth information...that gets its significance from its thickness" (Hoopes, 1979, p. 27). Methods are employed that capture the in-depth experience of a few. A womanist theological perspective is willing to give up the "assumption that legitimate analysis is derived from a broad spectrum of a large sampling of women whose perspectives are reflective of a consistent pattern or thought or belief system. Instead, the researcher privileges a method that captures the in-depth perspectives of a few" (Floyd-Thomas, 2006b, p. 92).

I have a personal or professional relationship with each spiritual historian. However, through variation I chose principals in different parts of a southern state and at different career junctures, different school levels (elementary, secondary, etc.), and levels of education. Two of the participants, Bobbie and Pattie, are in the same district and one in which I worked. This allowed me to have a continuation of the deep, vivid dialogue that had already been established. Two other participants, Toni and Avery, are both in another district, and I possessed rapport with these through graduate courses and consulting, respectively. Ultimately, since religious spirituality is considered by some to be very private (Lei & Kyburz, 2005), these principals were selected based on their willingness to discuss how their religious spirituality influenced the principalship. Both of the school districts in which these women work are located in one southeastern state. Each district is characterized by its own demographic characteristics and district culture.

Each of the women is at a different career juncture. Using pseudonyms, brief descriptions of these spiritual historians follow. During the time of initial research, Bobbie was in her thirtieth year in education. Her career is unique in that she was an assistant principal for three years, a principal for two, and has now transitioned back as an assistant principal. Pattie was in her eighteenth year in education and her seventh year as a school principal after having been a central office administrator. Toni was in her thirteenth year in education and her second year as a school principal of a prestigious magnet school. Avery is in her tenth year in education and is a third-year principal.

Spiritual Historian	Bobbie	Pattie	Toni	Avery
Education Experience	30	16	18	10
Admin. Experience	10	7	2	3
Educational Attainment	Ed.D.	MA	Ed.S./ABD	Ed.S./ABD
School Info.	MS	Primary	Elementary	Elementary
Religious Affiliation	Baptist	Baptist	Baptist	Baptist

All of these principals are religiously affiliated with the Baptist denomination, part of the larger Protestant denomination of the National Baptist Convention (NBC).

Although spiritual narratives are rooted in early nineteenth- and twentieth-century writing, this research suggests that current inquiry delve into the idea of contemporary spiritual narratives. Hine writes (1994):

> It is not enough simply to uncover the hidden facts, the obscure names of black foremothers. [What we need is] the development of an array of analytical frameworks that allow us to understand why black women of all classes behave in certain ways, and how they acquired agency. (p. 12)

Researchers can use spiritual narratives to focus not only upon accumulation of data, but also upon how certain knowledges and truths for the individual lead to certain choices (Floyd-Thomas, 2006b). Particularly for womanist theologians, spiritual narratives become a means to examine the "testimony and witness" often inherent in them. Testimony and witness becomes a workable process whereby Black women can recount stories of their personal religious experiences and daily practice to highlight how these beliefs affect all areas of their lives including their work.

Religious belief and practice are not merely an idiomatic Black religious experience. These narratives are not meant to generalize the religious experiences of Black women principals, but can serve to shed a broader light upon the principalship. However, examining spiritual narratives of Black female principals, "the interweaving of Black women's religious, biblical, theological, and sociopolitical thought and reflection as it often emerges in autobiography, biography, and other narrative forms" (Bellah, 1985, p. 27) allows the story of religio-spirituality and leadership to develop and become more legitimated in the broader field of educational leadership. The multiple stories of spirituality and leadership then become a part of the larger narratives that shape our work as researchers and school leaders. In other words, the religious context of "[spiritual narratives] is not viewed as separate from the social, and professional is not divorced from the personal...[They] are active...with life decisions" (Mitchem, 2002, p. 59).

Womanist Theology in Analysis: A Hermeneutic of Suspicion

Just as it is not always clear what counts as narrative, it is sometimes just as difficult to explicate how one does narrative analysis (Daiute & Lightfoot, 2004). According to Mischler (1995), there are three types of narrative analysis. Narrative analysis can be done by examining reference, function, or structure (p. 90). Reference describes the analysis of the relations between events and their presentation and representation. In particular, reference examines the relationship "between what was told and the interpretations and actual texts that they mean to interpret" (Chandler, Lalonde, & Teucher, 2004, p. 253). Function describes the reasons for which a story is told, what it is meant to do, and why it is told at a particular time (Coffey & Atkinson, 1996; Hendry, 2007). Structure concerns itself with formal, structural properties of a story involving matters such as sociolinguistics, story organization, and literary elements (Labov, 1982; Riesmann, 1993).

Viewing analysis in an either/or manner seemed counterproductive to the womanist theological exercise. The womanist theological story claims many identities including ones that embrace Blackness and femaleness and claims the right and agency of the Black woman of faith in the telling of her own story and in its interpretation (Floyd-Thomas, 2006b). The womanist theological story is one that varies in its function, but one that always seeks to transcend oppressions and quandaries (Floyd-Thomas, 2006b; Mitchem, 2002). Womanist theology honors African American rhetorical and structural traditions (Cannon, 1988; Floyd-Thomas, 2006b; Smitherman, 2000). I used a method that allowed me to consider all three types of narrative analysis. The hermeneutic of suspicion (Williams, 1993) of womanist theology allows multi-units of analysis and honors no one "right" way to interpret narratives. Hermeneutics rest on the tradition of interpretation that acknowledges the collaborative, engaging, and dynamic principles of narrative (Williams, 1993). Within womanist theology, there is a resistance to any "right way" to interpret. Because of this, the womanist hermeneutic becomes the lens, posture, and position from which to interpret.

The Nitty-Gritty of a Womanist Theology: The Womanist Way of Interpretation

Hermeneutics traditionally deal with interpretation of texts, and a consideration of how they make and communicate meaning informs the task. Ricoeur (1976, 1995) stated that narratives are a part of discourse and a reality for the narrator that cannot merely be reduced to the sentences that make up the narrative. So for instance, in interpretation, the researcher has to examine how religion and spirituality influence and are influenced by other aspects of the human experience. Ricoeur (1976) recognized the danger of the interpretive act of the researcher "understanding the author better than he understood himself" (p. 23). Maybe at best we can only "guess the meaning of the text because the author's intent is beyond our reach" (Ricoeur, 1976, p. 75).

Religion and spirituality may be best explored through the use of stories (Healey & Sybertz, 1996). Sometimes the story is so compelling that standard social science formats do not fit (Gilgun, 2004). This idea is echoed by leading scholars of narrative theology. Narrative theology begins with the narrative stories, myths, proverbs, and sayings (Healey & Sybertz, 1996). Narrative theology is based upon actual and everyday spiritual events and life experiences of people, whether in written or oral form. In the case of narrative theology and this research, actual biographical or autobiographical texts, rather than simply responses to research questions, can serve to present a "thicker" story of spirituality and religion. This relatively new theological construct highlights the impact of the narrative and storied nature of the Bible and its historical characters and religion as it is played out in the lives of individuals. Narrative theologians posit that these texts make it difficult to conceal gender, class, race, and other important socio-cultural issues by not claiming a universal religious or spiritual experience (Gibbs, 2007). In its overlap with womanist theological commitments and those of narrative research, these narratives tell and analyze the religious story by

1. Starting with experiences or issues in context and the implication for people in that context.
2. Having the principal locus or source for theological reflection in life experience.
3. Examining issues from the particular perspective of the Christian faith.
4. Orienting one toward understanding, but also transformation and practice. (Gibbs, 2007, p. 6)

In interpreting and appreciating the multiple informers in a religio-spiritual person's life, one cannot interpret THE meaning. Religion and spirituality cannot be removed from the larger world. Ricoeur (1976) seemed to require that the researcher be suspicious, in a sense, and consider larger units of society as well.

In applying a womanist hermeneutic of suspicion, Williams (1993) states that "another truth must be articulated" (p. 188) than the dominant one that society dictates. The hermeneutic of suspicion determines how we read and interpret the narrative. As womanist theologians are suspect of the traditional lens with which we view religion and spirituality and the daily existence of Black women, so this research does away with traditional lenses of school administration. They take seriously and reject the assumption that the only narratives of value or worthy of interpretation are male, androcentric, and European. A hermeneutic of suspicion recognizes the dynamic, complex nature of religio-spirituality; the constant re/framing of identity; and the historicity of Black women, religion, spirituality, and culture. A hermeneutic of suspicion allows the researcher and the researched to engage in an ongoing work of writing and rewriting life in light of their worldview. Even in the interpretive process, one recognizes that the interpretive possibilities are still open.

What did it mean for me to apply my understanding of hermeneutics and the hermeneutic of suspicion? The womanist method of "theming" (Floyd-Thomas, 2006b) served as an important method for analysis. Although themes are a part of qualitative research, African Americans often have "topic associative" (Michaels, 1981) stories and historical spiritual narratives to bear witness to this. However, the emphasis on the "topics" of religion and spirituality are not separated from the rest of a life. Because of this, I found I could not simply highlight the religio-spiritual elements in the narratives, as I originally thought. Just as the Bible is sometimes thought of as having a non-linear plotline (Gibbs, 2007), so these historical spiritual narratives and the lives of the Black women traditionally defied any one structure. "The structure and content of narratives vary by specific historical periods and cultural traditions" (Nelson, 2004, p. 93). The womanist theological way of hermeneutics is

> one that is focused on Black women and the ordinary theologies that operate in their lives...The communal dimension of Black women's experiences often inform the ordinary theologies, especially those regarding...social activism. The scope of womanist theology demands the creative use of multidisciplinary methodologies. Ethical and social analyses of all forms of oppressions [are explored]...Ongoing dialogues with other perspectives are constitutive and take on particular intensity when internal to the intellectual traditions of Black communities. (Mitchem, 2002, pp. 105–106)

The above quote also illustrates how the womanist hermeneutic connects back to the womanist theological tenets outlined earlier.

Particularly helpful to my research was Bruner's (as cited in Nelson, 2004) position that "narratives consist of a landscape of action organized around a theme or problem or trouble with respect to the way that things are expected to be, as well as a landscape of consciousness that specifies goals, motivations, emotions, and beliefs of the actors that instigate the action" (p. 93). My own experience with religio-spirituality and life consists often of the individual episodes of my life that happen and are often recorded in my journals. Through my personal experience with journaling, I tended to view my life through a serious of episodes and events and also on the causal relationships (my religio-spirituality makes me do this) of people and the events of my life. I tended to view the spiritual historians' lives in the same way. However, this was insufficient in getting to the nitty-gritty, everyday realities of what their narratives had to say. As with my own chronicling, emotion, motivation, goals, thoughts, beliefs, interpretations, musings, and reflections all make up the landscape of a religio-spiritual story. In echo, Floyd-Thomas (2006b) believes that the researcher's interpretive thoughts in examining spiritual narratives can be organized by:

a. Theo-ethical Analysis—Reflecting upon events, resources, and discourses that have been influential in shaping faith and ways one has and can reconcile disparate issues that emerge.
b. The Past—Attending to past and historical events, people, constructs, contexts, and how these impact one's values, feelings, reasonings, and concerns
c. Causation—Examining the religio-spiritual narrative in light of cultural context and social location of current situations, religious heritage, social action, and vocation and purpose in life.
d. Ethic of Liberation—Asking the question of how the religio-spiritual can help resolve the dilemmas of the privileged and the othered in society. (pp. 166–167)

In addition, broad themes were produced by identifying repetitive refrains, rituals, resonant metaphors. All of these, helped to scaffold my thinking in the process of my analysis.

It has been said that the Bible is God's biography, the story of His encounters with people (Yancey, 1999). By examining the stories and the lives of others, one can find his own (Yancey, 1999). Much like the autobiographical accounts and narratives in the Bible, the contemporary spiritual narratives in this research can serve as windows into the workings and outcomes of spirituality in the lives of individuals. "There is a power and persuasive nature of faithful lives, and…biographies, autobiographies, and memoirs of spiritual people" (Gilmour, n.d.). The hope is to better prepare principals to deal with their own and others' religious spirituality in their careers.

One of the things that I had to remember during narrative analysis was that the story remained the central focus. Since interviews indicated that religion and spirituality formed a personally defined enentity, it was important that the participant's representation of that spirituality be maintained. While reviewing documents about historical slave and spiritual narratives, I attempted to find a framework for creating the narrative. It was important to me to unite and integrate methods to my narrative process that were not only culturally but also spiritually distinctive. Since creation of the narrative serves as data and analysis, I used culturally (Etter-Lewis & Foster, 1996; Vaz, 1997) and spiritually distinctive tools in creating and analyzing the narratives. This was hard to do in light of the fact that the spiritual life "is an individual matter and general formulas do not apply" (Yancey, 1999, p. 38).

My very act of finding a spiritual narrative framework seemed counterproductive to the individual process of explaining and defining spirituality. Although researchers propose alternative research texts, there is still the general idea among narrative researchers that we move away from essentializing frames (Daiute & Lightfoot, 2004). Even so, there had to be some method. Through the use of Johnson-Bailey's (2002) "sans questions" technique of removing all questions from the interview transcript, I was able to initially envision the interview as an autobiographically written narrative. Rather than moving to initial coding as one would expect, I carefully reread the sans questions narrative as if it were written by the participant herself. I then divided up the narratives in categories based upon major life events, reflections of the participants, and gaps or interruptions. These ideas are based upon Denzin's (1997) biographical analysis. In womanist theology, the idea of "testifying" and "witnessing" became important also in analysis. Ross (2002) describes the terms as follows:

> Testifying occurs both as an interpersonal narration of divine interaction with everyday life and as a formal portion of worship wherein believers share in community what God has done in their lives...Testimonies require the presence of witnesses, persons who also have seen or experienced God's work and who are able to certify or attest to the truth of it in testimonies they hear. By identifying as witness, a believer asserts that she has personally experienced God's provision or other intervention. Moreover...the term

witnessing has arisen as a complementary way of naming the believer's ordinary moral practice—way of living—as religious practice. (p. 14)

These terms became important as I looked for testimonies and witness in each story. Testimony represented areas in which the individual, God, the church, family, community intersected with other parts of the life and religio-spirituality. Witness became a way to identify those particular actions that the individuals identified as religio-spiritual.

If the story seemed incoherent or left "gaps," these were areas where I identified follow-up questions. Subsequent answers were added to the narrative and reread. This process also revealed a recurrence of terms. As I reviewed historical and contemporary spiritual autobiographies and biographies and resources concerning them, I began to highlight basic characteristics and themes in them. I began brainstorming a list of spiritual narrative elements that emerged for me. These elements were less about any one conversion experience than those elements of the narratives that held ordinary, everyday salience. These everyday experiences in historical narratives were often illuminated through the use of metaphor. "In everyday use, [metaphors are] an interpretive framework that guides social meaning and serves as a mental map for understanding the world" (Stepan, as cited in Collins, 1998, p. 278). Paying attention to and understanding the metaphors used in the participants' narratives became an important part of analyzing and presenting their stories.

For the spiritual historians in this research, I found that they moved beyond my narrowly defined scope of the research. Although they all located within a Protestant, Judeo-Christian orientation, their spirituality transcended simple boundaries of their Baptist denomination and/or a traditional Christian viewpoint. Their belief systems contained what I call a mixture of spiritualities and ones that were influenced by self and affiliations with other groups. In addition, I wanted to explore the notion of public and private religio-spiritual realities. What impact was there upon their lives and particularly their work? Was there a difference in these realities and if there were, how did they negotiate them privately and publicly? Was there anything in these narratives that highlighted congruence or discordance between the formal school environment and religious identity? In what ways does religio-spirituality affect how the principalship is experienced or performed, and vice versa?

Also, a parallel issue was religious identity and how that was developed or how it had changed over time. This was an emerging theme in the narratives as interviews revealed a fluid process of shaping and reshaping of the religio-spiritual identity. More important, I began to see that my religio-spiritual identity and my own "outerworkings" of that identity differed from my participants in key respects. Their interests were not my interests and their commitments were not my commitments. How could I convey their stories without coming across as if I knew their story better than they did (Delpit, 1995)?

Meditations

As much as this research is about examining religion and spirituality in the lives of others, it is also about a gender-cultural and spiritual way of doing research. Much like feminist or Black feminist methods and methodologies, this is my effort at a new methodology and method by synthesizing womanist theological scholarship in creating a womanist and religio-spiritual way of conducting narrative research.

This chapter has highlighted the creation of womanist theological methods. This chapter shows how I draw upon womanist theological tenets and from "traditional disciplinary approaches and transform them in order to understand those very people whom normative disciplinary approaches render invisible" (Floyd-Thomas, 2006b, p. 3). How I interpret my research methodology and methods through the lens of womanist theology and my own religio-spiritual story informs the processes and procedures I undertake. Mitchem (2002) states

> Methodologies are not benign: scholars have commitments in their work. Generally the commitments of womanist scholars include, among others: centering black women's experience; social analysis;...exploring the authentic shape of African American religious life; deconstruction of all oppressions that stunt human growth. Reaching this level of commitment does not happen accidentally; arriving at this place becomes a part of the methodology itself. Therefore, as part of the method, womanists will often spend time

> stating portions of their own autobiographies. This disclosure names their formation processes. (p. 77)

What follows is each spiritual historian's spiritual narrative. Many narrative researchers have a natural tendency to present stories chronologically. However, many spiritual autobiographies were written as dialogue that directly addressed the audience or the reader. Much in the same way, the spiritual narratives in this research mimic earlier ones in this regard and in that they were often dictated to others (Moody, 2003, p. xiii). However, one way in which some of the narratives in this research differ from historical ones is my removal of all identifying markers in the narratives. Pseudonyms are used for each spiritual historian and all references to other individuals have been changed to more generic statements such as "my husband" or "the superintendent." All names of cities, counties, schools, and states have been removed. The participants wanted to be able to speak freely and their privacy was very important to the telling of the story.

Each spiritual historian's narrative begins with an introduction to the text and an example of a text that serves as a model for it. Each narrative has been presented as a different research text in a different format similar to historical spiritual narratives. The format used for each text was determined by the nature of data collected by each spiritual historian. I did not initially set out to do this! Since this was a deviation from what I initially discussed with the participants, I conducted follow-up sessions to discuss their "new" narratives and gain their insights. To my delight, each participant expressed excitement. When discussing with one participant how I interpreted her narrative as a poem taken from her favorite Bible verses, she commented, "Wow, I always knew I was poetic!" This process was fearful for me, however; I had become so emotionally attached to each participant and each sentence that had been transcribed. By this time, I held each woman in awe and their words had earned my affection. Working out their narratives became a labor of love. To be sure, each narrative uses the participant's own words, was reviewed by the participants and granted "approval," and assembled. This was not an artistic endeavor on my part, but an attempt to honor the rich aesthetic heritage of the spiritual narrative in all of its forms.

While laboring over transcripts, I noticed that some transcripts and accompanying notes and follow-up were longer than others. I began to think that some data were not as rich or "thick" as others. As I continued the interviews, I became a better "questioner" and listener. For instance, Bobbie's transcript filled a file folder, while Pattie's was not as lengthy. However, I began to change my focus and approach to my data. My commitment to the womanist theological framework forced me to refuse to see any of my data as lacking in any way. A deficit model of research would not serve my purpose. Instead, I saw the different nature of my data as I did the different nature of historical spiritual narratives. As much as spiritual narratives are diverse and tell the stories of the individuals that told them, so are the narratives in this research.

Comstock and Mayhall (2004) view narratives "as a specific kind of literary form, the form that uses plot and character" (p. xvii). Others contend that narratives always follow a temporal frame and pattern of events and contend that they differ from other forms of language such as poems, sermons, and speeches (Polkinghorne, 1988). However, there are those that disagree. MacIntyre (1984) promotes the idea that narratives are simply our ideas and thoughts about ourselves. Anthony Paul Kerby (1991) follows up this idea by saying that narratives represent our "best" and most "privileged" way of giving voice to our lives and the stories therein.

The best and most privileged way of giving voice to the lives of others lies at the heart of this research and the creation of narrative. African American cultural and literary history claims a fuller dimension and characterization of what counts as narrative (Houchins, 1988). My research adds to the contested notions of what counts as narrative and the appropriate forms of them. The African American way of giving voice to life has resulted in volumes of fiction, poetry, autobiography, biography, essays, speeches, and sermons, among others, that have become a part of the rich tapestry of narrative. What some scholars label as spiritual narratives have taken some of these same forms.

These historical works have formed a link and foundation to current works by contemporary authors such as Alice Walker, Zora Neale Hurston, Jamaica Kincaid, Audre Lorde, and others. "Literary works configure into a tradition not because some mystical collective unconscious determined by the biology of race or gender, but because writers read other writers and ground their representations of experience in models of language provided largely by other writers and writings to whom they feel akin" (Houchins, 1988, p. xviii). Although this is true, there is still a tendency to treat historical spiritual writings as canonical, with little room for new works. Were it not for a group of researchers committed to preserving the heritage of African Americans, there had been a danger of losing the writings of the Black women from the eighteenth and nineteenth centuries (Houchins, 1988). However, we are also in danger of losing the history that is "still being written" (Burk, 2007) by failing to create new narratives. Historical narratives are the narratives of ordinary women and the ordinary experiences of their lives. This research also seeks to add new ordinary narratives to the depository of narratives of Black women.

Very few scholars engage in research that explores the lives and narratives of people of color, much less know much of the large history of Black women and their writings (Houchins, 1988). This research can add to the current research in the area of educational leadership as well as add a new dimension to the genre of spiritual narratives. These narratives were created by ordinary women to chronicle the stories and meanings of their lives. Just as their predecessors' writings did, these contemporary literary forms challenge what counts as life and narrative, but also challenge what counts as research and the research texts that result. African American women's spiritual auto/biography espouses an "exceptional theology" (Moody, 2001, p. 20).

> Just as important, the texts express the women's Christian identity and their spiritual life as they believe they should live it. It is no fortuity that the oldest extant prose by Black women in America are sacred writings. To read African American women's writings one must have regard for their significance-political, social, and cultural significance...(Moody, 2001, p. 20).

Earlier literary and cultural studies of early African American narratives insufficiently attended to their discourse. Let the current study not repeat this. Some of the narratives have been divided by using as headings the themes that are most prominent in them. Although themes were identified, these themes were interpreted, analyzed, and conceptualized using religio-spiritual imagery and meta-metaphor as an alternative way of conceptualizing the principalship. Some of the narratives are read as longer and more detailed text. Some narratives have been presented as shorter, more philosophical, aesthetic pieces, and/or oratorical pieces such as poems, sermons, or speeches. Analysis will reveal how each narrative lends itself to the particular manner in which it is written. Many spiritual writings in the nineteenth and early twentieth centuries were written in the manner that best emphasized certain points and realities in them. "The aesthetic value of the spiritual narrative is not determined by its imaginative departure from convention" (Moody, 2001, p. 149). However, the spiritual narrative was and is at its best when it authenticates the religio-spiritual experience for that individual (Moody, 2001).

Chapter 3

Testimony:
Presentation of Narratives

Take time to share your story, share your story, share your story.
(Hambrick, 1997, p. 81)

Testimony is described as the "willful assertion of divine intervention in ordinary circumstances" (Floyd-Thomas, 2006b, p. 132). Testimonies are "verbal affirmations of belief and narratives of divine interaction with ordinary life" (Ross, 2002, p. 14). For this reason, this chapter is called "Testimony: Presentation of Narratives." This chapter represents the spiritual narratives, and indeed the testimonies, or religio-spirituality in the lives of these Black female principals. Each spiritual historian's narrative begins with an introduction to the text and an example of a text that serves as a model for it. Each narrative is presented as a different research text in a different format similar to historical or contemporary spiritual narratives. The format used for each text is congruent with and determined by the nature of stories of each spiritual historian. Each narrative represents the most salient, overarching themes illuminated in it.

Meditation has been described as spiritual reflection and/or prayer. Each participant actively talks about the Bible and its application to her life. The Bible states:

> Study this Book of Law continually. Meditate on it day and night so you may be sure to obey all that is written in it. Only then will you succeed. I

command you—be strong and courageous! Do not be afraid or discouraged. For the Lord your God is with you wherever you go. (Joshua 1:8–9)

Each participant has a strong commitment to the Word and its power and "success" in her life. For this reason, each narrative ends with a meditation. Each participant has a strong commitment to prayer and reflection. Each woman believes that direct communing with God is the key to her life.

Some details that would have made their stories even richer have been deleted because of the need to protect their identities. Because context is important in narrative (Merriam, 2002, p. 9), there is uneasiness in "removing" so many details from their stories. Narrative research is always concerned with the individual lives first (Bloom, 2002), yet there is a way to remain contextual without trying to itemize, specify, identify, or detail facts, figures, faces, and places. Contextuality can be found in the ways the teller "reads" the world around her, how the teller contends with the social world in which she lives, and how larger social structures are seen "through the lens of the individual" (Bloom, 2002, p. 311). Their stories highlight how their religio-spirituality impacts their lives and work, although parts of their stories concerning the principalship are examined in Chapter Four, which looks at their stories across cases.

BOBBIE
THE JEREMIAD

My soul became filled with a holy indignation. I complained.
(Maria W. Stewart)[1]

Bobbie is a fifty-two-year-old, self-described "warrior." Her story recounts portions of her life and work as she narrates events. Her story "reads" as a jeremiad. The Black jeremiad identifies the form of spiritual narrative named for the Hebrew prophet Jeremiah who warned Israel that it would be destroyed for deserting its covenant with God. Jeremiads, such as those by Maria Stewart, rely on deep feeling, social

---

[1] M. W. Stewart (1835/1988). "Productions of Mrs. Maria W. Stewart." In S. Houchins (Ed.), *Spiritual Narratives* (pp. 1–80). New York: Oxford University Press.

justice, and a sense of passion while being deeply critical of oppressions, institutions, and the community and/or society. It is the holy complaint. Like some spiritual narratives of the seventeenth and eighteenth centuries, Bobbie's narrative has been divided for readability by headings taken from her initial interview and from the themes that are portrayed most prominently in each section. From her interview, Bobbie's story often moves between two lines: first, her family, church, and community as initiations and cornerstones for her faith (getting churched); and second, her school experiences while growing up and as an educator (getting schooled). Written in two parts, Bobbie's story carries the themes of legacy and warfare and makes for a modern-day jeremiad of her life, work, and religio-spirituality.

Getting Churched

Family

> It seems weird to talk to you about dates and brothers and sisters and all that. I am the youngest of three children and I am fifty-two years old. I grew up with both my parents and a strong sense of family, community, and purpose. I suppose my story starts with my family and how I grew up. I grew up in a small rural town in the Black Belt. My father was a farmer until the civil rights laws started to change, when we were given opportunities to have good jobs. He started working for a major company there in town. He had a job, when they first started hiring Blacks into these big companies. They made them work outside, like in the yard doing janitorial cleaning. At some point, the plant moved him inside. He got a better position because he began working in the lab at the company and worked there until he retired. My mom worked at home until I started school. After I started school she went to work. When I went to school, she was a substitute teacher and then she worked at a sewing plant. After a while, the plant where my dad worked started hiring women into the company. It was a big plant where they made paper towels. They ended up having a very lucrative life. I guess you could say we were middle class. At least we were middle class during my childhood than when my sister and brother grew up. It was a different story for them. Growing up, we lived like five miles outside the city limits in my hometown so we had our own little suburb. Actually the city limits were not as nice as where my family lived. Black people had nice things. Because of the industry that had come to town, all the Black people I knew had nice homes. I think this always made an impact on me to make me aspire for the bigger things in life. My family owned our own home and most

people did in our neighborhood. And people owned land. In many cases, a relative had land and they gave it to the children when they grew up and got married. Everybody seemed to have their own. Land was a big thing and everybody was trying to buy up land in the county.

Passing It On

Even from an early age, believing in God was just like something I knew I had to do. I joined the church when I was nine years old but I believed even before then, it was just, you know how those old traditions are, that you have to confess and they have you out there seeking God for a week or two, praying. I had to go through the ritual. There were always church people saying, don't you get up there on that bench until you know for sure. I guess I always felt a little stubborn or defiant or whatever it is, but I knew early on that this doesn't make sense. They'd have me out there praying all day in a room by myself, yah know doing revival, and I was thinking, "I already believe. What else am I supposed to do?" I felt like a fool listening for this voice and looking for a sign to show me I really believed. People tell you about all this stuff happened when they believed: "A bird flew across the sky when I asked the Lord to give me a sign that he was there." I already believed! I had been taught from as early as I can remember. Things were always God, God, God…That is all I knew. Daddy was very spiritual, but he was real quiet with it until it was church time. In church, he shared his testimonies, but he was always in the Bible and everybody knew him as always being in the Word. I spent a lot of time with my grandmother. When I spent time with my grandmother, I got more of it from her even than I got at home. Grandmother was always singing a hymn or something when I was at her house. I used to sit on the porch at my grandmother's house and she would piece quilts and sing hymns all the time. Needless to say, my family was a big influence on my faith in God. All I heard was what Lord wanted me to do as a child, and how He wanted me to love everybody and treat everybody right. Following the Ten Commandments was really emphasized when I was growing up. I had to memorize them and I had to know them and try to live by them. My parents would also discipline me with the scripture by saying, "Now what does the Ten Commandments say? What does the Twenty-Third Psalm tell you?" Even when I had my own children, I found I did some of the same things. My husband and I tried to raise our kids like our parents raised us. Never underestimate the power of crisis either. During the time my daughter went through her abuse and divorce, that is the time my son really became real spiritual. He was like I was when I was little. You grow up hearing this stuff and you know this is what you are supposed to be and you believe it. But none of it becomes real until you see that you need it or people around you need it. Crisis even had an impact on me and my husband. When we were going through all of that stuff with her, we got closer, more involved and more in prayer over that situation and trying to deal with it. It also gave us an opportunity to talk to our son about it. My son was hurt, he was crushed himself and we were worried about how to help him deal with it. He just couldn't understand why things were like they were. We got with him and we encouraged him to read his Bible more and my husband got him a Bible with a guide in the back where you could outline how many verses he read. My son read until he finished the Bible. Then he would have questions about it and he would come to us. He is still that way. If he's got questions he is going to come to us even though he is twenty-five now; he is still coming to us with it.

At that time, my husband and I were buying a lot of Christian books. My son began praying about his own life instead of us just praying with him. He began to pray about school and what he wanted to do with his life. At his high school, so much was going on. We told him to pray about school. We told him often, "You can't fight this stuff. You can't say what you want to say, you're just going to have to pray about it and ask God to help you with it." He got in college, and you know how stressful college life can be and all the decisions you make. My husband would buy him books about the makings of a man, what a man is supposed to be. My husband always shares stuff like that with my son. My son developed his own spirituality and made it what he wanted it to be.

He's very spiritual. All of his decisions, they are spiritual. Before he makes a decision he's going to God with it. We tell him, "You go to God with this; go to God with it. You pray about that and don't you do that unless you have prayed about it." My son had his own business started a year after graduating from college. He met someone at his first job who paved the way for it, so we know it was a God thing. Even in college, one of his main professors used to talk to my son a lot and tell him how there was something special about my son. The professors always talked to my son about the things that he was going to do in his life and how he was going to be able to affect the lives of a lot of people. This professor's influence was important because the professor was very spiritual. He would always talk to my son about paying attention when you hear this little voice in the back of your mind telling you different things. He told my son that this is God talking. My son had that kind of relationship with this professor, which I think really impacted him a lot in his spirituality. My son now has a different outlook on life and he is real mature for his age. He's twenty-five and always says he's going to date somebody who is thirty or older.

Protest

The neighborhood where we grew up was very into civil rights. A turning point came because jobs really started opening up for all people in that county and then Martin Luther King came to our area. It was great! He was larger than life.

The churches during that time held all the civil rights meetings. Civil rights meetings rotated from church to church throughout the county. During those meetings, there was a time when they decided the children wouldn't go to school. This was decided by the SCLC [Southern Christian Leadership Conference] working together. The civil rights leaders were trying to force desegregation among other things. Many families were afraid that if we did not go to school, the teachers would give us failing grades. So while we boycotted school, we met in the churches and adults from the neighborhood taught us. They didn't want us to think that education wasn't important.

My family personally was very involved in the civil rights movement. My mom participated in all the marches, all the meetings. My granddaddy was one of the main leaders with the SCLC and I guess the real militant side of me came from that because all the young people in my family learned to fight. We learned to fight for what we wanted. I grew up listening to everyone advocating for change. I can remember singing freedom songs. Even after that first year of integration in schools, we still boycotted. Integration certainly did not solve all of the problems. We just walked out of school once because it was so unfair how the white kids would push us into the walls, spit on us, do anything to us and nobody would do anything to help. There were not that many Black teachers. There were a few Black teachers brought over. I'll never forget *ABC News* came down during this same time, when a girl was run over by a car and was murdered. A boycott of stores was organized. That boycott lasted a few years.

Times were very dangerous. It was at the point that Blacks couldn't go anywhere at night. Many Black civil rights leaders would change cars all the time because white people in the town threatened to kill them. There was a lot of protesting going on at that time. My mom and dad weren't too keen on me being out there doing that. But the young people during that time were fearless. We had a strong conviction to get out there and march and protest and fight. One of my mom's white friends said, "Don't let her be out there involved in that. Aren't you afraid something is going to happen to her?" I do remember one young girl who was out marching with us and she fell in the street. She couldn't get up really fast and a white man ran right over her. I'll never forget that. One of my friends grabbed me by the arm and pulled me onto the sidewalk because that man was driving through the march. You know, nothing ever happened to that man. He didn't go to prison. He wasn't even questioned. He still lived in that town and everybody knew where he lived. All the kids wanted to go get him. But the adults wouldn't let us. We didn't do any violence; there was no violence to be committed. Even still, because of the march, we were put in jail for a week. In meetings at the church when we organized this march, they had already told us in the meetings that if the police stopped us, do not resist or fight back.

There were so many of us so they took us to a National Guard Armory and put us in a yard with a chain-link fence around it and locked it. It was like a pen sitting down on the ground because there was nowhere to sit. They would bring water and food, but we decided we wouldn't take food or water. During the day it was so hot. One day, I had something in my hand and I can't remember what I had in my hand at that time, but I dropped it on the ground. When I reached down to pick it up, a police officer hit me in my stomach with his night stick. The men guarding the women did things that were not decent. They would shake their private parts at us and they would do all kinds of nasty stuff.

There were over one hundred kids there. They did mug shots of us. I know this white friend of my mom's son was in the National Guard. He called his mother and told her that I was being locked up and his family called my mom. This family offered to get me out. My mom and my dad went along with the civil rights leaders who told us that if we get locked up to let us go and not get us out. Some parents did get their kids out of jail but mine didn't. I didn't want to leave anyway. I was down for the fight! After a couple of days, the police shipped us off to a jail in another city. We were down there for a week with no change of underwear. There were three or four of us in a cell. There was a shower, so what we wore during the day, we washed at night. The water fountain was right over the commode. We had no privacy. At night we had to take sheets from the bed and put them up over the cell so we could have some privacy to change our clothes or at least get out of some of what you had on. The food was atrocious. All the kids would just sit in there talking or some were crying to go home. We couldn't have any visitors. They did allow some of the civil rights leaders to come. But we were getting pretty smelly so our families could bring clothes. They couldn't bring us any food or anything, only clothes. Once a day they would take us out to a place called the bull pen and we could walk around for a while.

We prayed a lot this whole time. That was something that was part of the civil rights movement because they always prayed and always told you to pray about it. We did. I remember everyone saying their prayers at night in jail before we went to sleep. Some kids would get really ugly with the guards and stuff. Some of us would remind them that God was watching them. After one week, on a Sunday evening, we got to go home. The guards put us back on that school bus and drove us to a place, to a church. That's where we were picked up. Somehow I think that was appropriate.

I don't know why I just thought of this. My mother had some really good white friends because my grandmother worked for one of the doctors in town. Granny had worked for different white people during that time and so white people thought highly of Granny and our family. I used to go over to their houses and play with their kids while Granny worked. We had some of the white people who were like on our side a little bit. That kind of helped us through some of these hardships.

I have always stood up for what is right. Even when you are young you know what is right and what is wrong. I was young but I knew that when you had to go to the doctor, there was a door that the Black people went in and there was a door where the white people went in. You could go at the crack of dawn in the morning, but they were going to see everybody on the white side first. It didn't matter if you were dying, you were gonna be there all day or until they saw all the white people before you. I knew that wasn't right. My mother was real strong-willed and she would stand up for anything. Nobody could run over her. I take after my mom in that regard. She was and is that kind of person. She is a take-charge kind of person. My daddy was always real passive, patient and quiet; a real compassionate and loving type of personality. Daddy was just so sweet and he really believed in turning the other cheek. But my mother was not like that. Maybe I take after her or maybe it is God. Whatever the case, I am who I am.

The Church

Growing up, my family had always been Baptist. My dad was a deacon and mom taught Sunday school and sang in the choir. After I left home and got married, my husband and I were Baptist for a while and then we started going to a Methodist church. We left because we weren't getting what we felt we needed in our Baptist church, and the only other option where we lived was to go to the Methodist church. The Methodist minister had some education. I don't necessarily think that education makes a big difference when it comes to God, but this minister organized the church and opened up some new ideas. I learned new things and I wasn't stuck in simply the old way of our grandparents. When we got to the Methodist church, we were able to get involved in a lot of different things our old church didn't have. Once my husband and I moved here, we went back to a Baptist church. My husband and I immediately got involved. My husband became a deacon and an officer in church because he watched his dad do that. I taught Sunday school, sang in the choir, and served as an usher. I grew up knowing that these were important parts of my faith.

The Baptist church I am in now is quite different from the Baptist church in which I grew up. The head and associate pastors in the church I attend now were very traditional. BUT then the head pastor was struck with a serious illness. A woman in the church prayed for him and he swears he was healed. I know it has changed his whole perception of spirituality and the way he conducts things in his church. We now have women ministers in our church. I like this. Ever since I began reading some books by T. D. Jakes and other ministers and watching TBN, I knew that we needed something different in our church. We follow all the Baptist rules and stuff but the way we conduct church is quite different. You would think we are a Pentecostal church. If you walked in, you wouldn't know we were Baptist. This is a good thing, too. I was becoming dissatisfied with a traditional notion of church and the way they did services. I needed more. A woman preaches on Friday nights and Sunday 8:00 a.m. service. A woman never preaches at the 11:00 service. The traditional folks would have a heart attack! It's weird, though. Some of these traditional people don't have a problem with deliverance and healing services. Women are really involved in those.

My daughter attends a Pentecostal church. After her divorce, she didn't feel secure and up to par with everybody else in our church anymore; she felt less than them. The church she attends accepts the brokenhearted. There were a lot of young women there with bad marriages and who had been through abuse. There were a lot of guys with substance abuse including alcohol or some other kind of trauma in their lives. I suppose in that kind of setting she was comfortable. It didn't matter what your life had been; they welcomed you in just as you were. We were very leery of this church when she began attending. My husband and I would visit sometimes just to see what she was getting herself into. It has been good for her and she is happy there. Her life has changed and I guess that is what matters.

The Supernatural

I get feelings about things. I get like a strong feeling or something like a thought that sticks with me and I can't dismiss it. My sister is the same way. I can see something going on and I usually I tell my husband, "Something is wrong with that. That's just not right. That shouldn't be happening." I can just be so against it. He thinks I'm crazy sometimes but I know when something is not right. I've always been like that. When I was really young I could tell when something wasn't going to work and I would feel real strongly about it not working. People would come back later and say,

"You were right. How did you know?" I just knew. Prophets in the church have often commented on how I know things. I don't know how I know or why I know but I know things. I guess, I can assess a situation because I pray for spiritual discernment a lot. I pray for that a lot. My mother says she is kind of like that, she has always known things before they happen and my daughter is like that too.

When my daddy had his eightieth birthday he was up talking to people at the party. We had it at church in the fellowship hall and he was telling his testimony about how he had recovered from illness over and over. He's had cancer for the majority of his life that I know of. When I was in eleventh grade was when we found out the first time. That first cancer was healed, as well as two others in different parts of his body. He got this prostate one and then it spread to his bones and but yet at his party, he was sharing his testimony. After the party was over, my daughter came to me and she said, "The Lord just showed me" and she said she had a vision and she said he will not live to see his eighty-first birthday. I wasn't really sure about it and asked my daughter if she was sure. All if this was in September. Right after that, I can't remember what it was called, but the levels of it were going crazy, it just got out of control and the cancer kept growing and spreading like crazy. By the spring, I guess about around February or March, I talked with this doctor and the doctor told me that if my dad had any type of a bone break he wouldn't overcome it. Anyway, daddy messed around and let the lawn mower back off the truck and it hit him. Daddy didn't tell anybody, but the mower broke his hip and he walked around for a while with a broken hip. We ended up having to go to the hospital to repair the hip and when the doctors got in to operate, they saw the cancer was just everywhere, all over him in there. Daddy didn't die from the cancer though. His heart stopped. Oh, he came through the surgery fine. My family called us and said he's okay and the doctors were closing up. The next thing I know, they called me back and told me his heart had stopped. My daughter knew all that day that he was dying. That morning when I called her to tell her daddy was going into surgery, she had been crying all morning long. My daughter told me how she had been crying all morning long and didn't know why. When the Lord is dealing with her, she gets stomach problems and she had been sick all morning. When I called my daughter and told her that daddy's heart had stopped and they had him on life support, she told me that she knew that. She said that God had prepared her for it, that God had told her that's what it was. And my sister too, she knew, and it hurt her but she was already prepared for it, she knew even before I called and told her. She was on the road, she travels a lot with her job, and she just knew, she just kind of took her own time getting into town, because she already knew. One thing about my sister though, she won't tell you. She knows things but she won't tell you anything.

It's interesting how God deals with you. I have had some episodes in my house where I felt there was something in this house, a spirit or something. My friend said well it's some kind of spirit; somebody has been in your house and has brought some kind of spirit into your house. We prayed all over our house and I think it is gone, but I do not sleep with my lights out in a black room no more. My husband does not understand because he does not have these encounters. I always have these strange encounters, and he doesn't have those encounters. I know they are real because I know that I am wide awake when this stuff happens.

Warfare

My daughter has a prayer room and she doesn't allow anybody in her prayer room and nobody goes in there but her. She lets her son in there, but other than that, nobody goes in there unless she has prayed about it and feels she can let someone in. I'm scared to go in there. I just don't know what might happen. With some of the experiences that she has told her she had in there, I know I don't want to go in there. She deals with things. She really has to fight things sometimes. And it's like the more spiritual you become, the more attacks you get with that kind of stuff.

My pastor is always talking about that too. My grandson swears that he sees angels and stuff. He has been saying for years that he sees angels. Sometimes, he will get up in the night and tell my daughter that there is somebody in the room with him. He won't go back to his room unless she goes in there and prays. Sometimes my daughter goes into my grandson's room and lies down in the room with him. She has had dreams where she has felt like she needed to get up and rush into my grandson's room. My daughter's pastor told her that my grandson is going to experience a lot of stuff like this because my grandson has a real calling on his life and the devil wants to take that life. It's heavy, it's heavy. It's deep.

When you deal with spiritual warfare it is, it's something. My pastor has healing services at church. I have seen people come in with diseases and leave healed. Have you ever seen those services where those people fall out and stuff comes out of their mouths, foaming, white stuff, I've seen black stuff. We have had deliverance services where people have been delivered. And if you are not strong spiritually or if you don't feel like you are up to par, you know they tell you to leave the service and go on home before you know you catch something. It's interesting. It's interesting to see those kinds of things.

Being Schooled

Community

Growing up, it seemed everybody in our community went to church. It was a way of life and we didn't know anything different. I also remember sharing everything. This was in a time when you had to buy your textbooks and every family couldn't afford textbooks. I had textbooks and when it was time to go to the next grade, my books went to my cousins or someone in the community. Kids from the neighborhood would come to my house to use my books. It was kind of a family thing, everybody worked together during that time.

That sense of community served me well when I was a principal. It is such an important part of being a principal. I always believed that I needed to connect with those who I was serving. I tried to become a part of the life where my students lived. I stopped going to my regular beautician and I got a beautician in the community where my school was. I still go to that salon even though I have been moved to another school. The kids and the parents come through there, they got to see me, they got to know me, they go to talk to me and that they go to see I'm just like ya'll.

That first year, if it had not been for my own spirituality and a couple of the Black ministers, I would not have made it. The central office in the school district gave me no support. The Black ministers in that community really helped me. When the teachers couldn't control discipline, I just went to the community. I remember going to a ministerial alliance meeting. I was asking for male volunteers to come into schools and help monitor the halls. One of the pastors and his deacons partnered with our school. This helped to improve a lot of things in the school. They even did a lot to help beautify the school. I really appreciated these volunteers. They prayed with me and for me. I had different ministers come in and bless my school. My own pastor would come and pray with me during the day in my office. He would always say, "I can't do counsel with your kids but I can counsel you and I can come pray." Christian women also came. They were more behind the scenes, but they would come over after school and pray with me. They often called me to check in and see how things were going. Having support and my spirituality helped me go on.

The State of Church and School

School when I was growing up was more church-oriented. The school was predominately Black. We had church at the little school. First thing in the morning you had devotional services. We learned to sing. We learned to pray, to recite scriptures, sometimes a whole chapter like the Twenty-Third Psalm, One-Hundredth Psalm, Sixty-Third Psalm, all those kinds of things. The first book I ever read was the Bible because the teacher that I had would give us something like the Twenty-Third Psalm, like the first two verses and tell you to go home at night and get somebody to teach it to you and she meant you needed to know the next day and you were fearful not to know it. So, before we got Dick and Jane, we had the Holy Bible to read. I was exposed to this up until the third grade. And then when we moved to a real public school we still had devotions in school because religion was still allowed to be discussed. We still did devotion in our class. Unfortunately for me, the lady that I had for first, second, and third grade followed me to the next school and she was my teacher. I was so tired of her I was ready to get that woman out of my life. She was my Sunday School teacher at school and I could not get away from her. But that's just how it was back then. And she moved on to that next school until they moved us to that predominately white school. She stayed in the elementary school still so I didn't get to see her anymore. So, let's see, I went to a two-room school the first three years of school. Then after the three years at the private school…Well I think of it as a kind of a private school, but it wasn't really a private school. It was just where Black people had to go to school. After those years they built a school on the other side of town, which took me almost an hour to get there since I was bused.

Middle school was nothing real exciting, but I remember middle school being the most difficult academically. Socially, it wasn't that bad, but academically it was hard. My parents had really prepared me for difficulty though. And education was big on their list of priorities. They always told me I had to study harder than anybody else. They would not allow me to bring home anything less that a C. It's funny, because at one time, no matter what Black students did, all we were gonna get was a C. I remember one of my friends was so smart. She was always a straight A student, was retained once in middle school. So my parents and other civil rights leaders were always on us to study. Eventually, the grades we were given caught up to the superior level of work we were doing.

I liked high school a lot because it seemed as though white and Black students were beginning to get along. The adults were another issue. There were still white parents who didn't want their kids going to school with us. Other than our classes, we rarely had time to be with the white kids anyway. Black students were not allowed to do many extracurricular activities. You either played sports, sang in school choir, or band. The first time I tried to get into band, I couldn't. Some excuse was made as to why I could not join. I went home and told my mom and my granddaddy. My granddaddy spoke with some of the civil rights leaders in our community. The next day, the principal pulled me from a class and took me down to the band room. I was the only Black person there. The band director gave me all of these almost impossible criteria to meet. My parents went back to the leaders in the civil rights movement and told them about all this stuff and that man dropped his supposed "criteria." The band director let me and two other Black students in the band. We could go to the football games and play in the stands but you couldn't play on the field. The band director said that we (the Black students) were not intelligent enough to be able to march and do the precisions and play at the same time. Once again, I told my family. The next Friday night, we were on the field.

I graduated with honors from high school and it was time for me to pick a college. I always wanted to go to a Christian college. That was always in my head for some reason. I don't know why, but I just felt like I needed to go to a Christian college. But it was expensive to go. I remember my momma saying that the banks didn't allow Black people to get loans. A white family that my mom was friends with were wealthy and owned a majority of the town. They helped my family get a loan so I could go to college.

College was kind of like home in a sense. You had to go to church or chapel. You had to sign in for chapel and one of the professors was responsible for keeping up with chapel attendance. It was kind of like your mother being over you all the time.

Paths and Callings

As you know I eventually went into education. I did not always want to be. When I was in tenth or eleventh grade I wanted to be a social worker. I remember the teacher telling me that I wouldn't make any money with that. Then, I wanted to become a commercial artist. My English teacher that year was a minister and he had us do research on different jobs. I realized quickly that the starving artist idea did not appeal to me either. My momma didn't want me to do that anyway. I thought about modeling, but she said no to that too. She gave me a long speech about how all of those jobs can put you in situations where women are abused and men take advantage of you. When I got to college I still wasn't entirely sure what I wanted to do. I still wanted to do art, because I love that. When I met my husband, he was an elementary education major. At the time, he was completing student teaching and I got involved by helping him type his lesson plans and units. I got so involved in what he was doing and I liked it. I decided to change my major to education. So, in my junior year, I pledged a sorority AND changed my major. My sorority was always raising money for different causes in the community. I am the only Greek in my family. My husband was also in a fraternity. I always wanted to be Greek because of the Black female teachers I had growing up. They were all in sororities and thought that was so great.

I soon graduated and frankly my first teaching experience scared me. I grew up in a close-knit, rural area and when you come to a city like this, it is a culture shock. One of my professors got my student teaching assignment changed. When I drove over there, I mean it was an old neighborhood, I had never seen anything like that, I guess you call that kind of like the ghetto, I guess that's what you would call that during that time, and I hadn't seen anything like that.

My first job was as an extended substitute. A lady was having surgery and she was going to be out that first semester here in the district. This was the school in which I had interned. I had my classroom and everything set up, but two weeks after that I got called to another school because they needed a Black teacher. During that time the district was not fully integrated like most towns were. I feel like this city has always been late. There were a total of five Black people in that school when I went there. Well, this is not counting custodians and cafeteria folks because they were Black. I tell you, it was as if I was praying from the minute I stepped my foot into the system, until the present. There was so much racial discrimination. The schools were predominantly white. All I knew to do was just pray.

One of the hardest things about my first teaching experience was the parents of the students. I had one family who really tried to get me moved out of that school the first year I was there. Some parents had written a letter to the superintendent to get me removed from the school. I remained at this school until I got another job at another middle-class school that was THE school at which to teach.

Even when I graduated with my undergraduate degree, I was already looking toward the future. I had already enrolled into the master's program before graduation. After I got my master's degree, I took a break from getting degrees. After I had taught seven years, I knew I needed to do something different and I wanted to go into supervision. I ended up getting a certification in supervision and administration. After that, I got a certification in physical science. Eventually I went on to get my Education Specialist degree and my Ed.D.

In between all of this, I went to the university and was a teacher-in-residence at the university. I had to leave the school where I was because my principal did not like that I was getting all of these degrees. After my three-year stint teaching at the university, I went to another elementary school as a teacher. There was no way for me to advance at my old school. I wanted to go into supervision and my old principal knew it. When I did my internship in supervision, my supervisor came up to check up on me. He assigned me to intern at another school because my principal told my supervisor that I didn't need to be in that program because I wasn't going to get a job in the system. My supervisor told me this. I talked to someone in the State Department of Education and she allowed me to shadow her to get internship hours.

Obstacles and Obstructions

It's funny, but when I was like a regular classroom teacher, I did not feel as much of a need for my spirituality. Don't get me wrong, there was a lot of discrimination going on, but this total reliance on God did not come until later. I think I got more into more of a spiritual mode during my time at the university because I really began to feel a lot of pressure being at a university. I then had the pressure of returning to the school district after having had this opportunity and that did not sit well with some people. In either setting, being a Black woman didn't help either. I began to rely heavily on God to help me. I found myself constantly in prayer about what was going on. I was always asking Him to change people's hearts and minds about things. My principalship certainly kicked up the spirituality thing a notch.

What I think was the hardest was people putting obstacles in my path that I felt like should be supporting me. Other Black females took issue with me, and were so competitive. It did not matter if it was the teachers in my school or the people throughout the district; I had very few other Black female allies. Other white women, including my superiors, often tried to discourage me from progressing. I think there was a lot of resentment that I was this Black woman and I wouldn't stop and sit down, I kept trying to go higher. My principal when I was getting my supervision certification told me that I did not need another degree. She actually told me that. When I was working on my Ed.S., my superintendent told me that I needed to focus on my daughter and how to help her rather than get a degree. Here was a Black woman who had gotten all the way to the superintendency and she wanted to discourage me from doing anything myself?

I guess some of my trouble with other women and with the district comes from the fact that I am just not seen as all that nice. I think I am nice and other people who know me think that I am, too. But I guess professionally I am all about business. I do what I have to do. I fight when I need to fight. I try to treat everyone like I should. I try to do what I think that Jesus would have me to do. Sometimes, that's not always pretty. This job isn't pretty. You cannot please everyone. I just try and make sure that God is pleased.

The Principle/al of the Thing: What Would Jesus Do?

My first principalship was very hard. Maybe it was, but so many people seemed to have these preconceived ideas about me. It just seemed that many people had problems with me and they did not even know me. They even had problems with the way I dressed. They had problems with me because I came in and I made some changes. They didn't have any set procedures in place so I had to go in and put some rules and procedures in place for the students and the teachers. Teachers would write me up all the time and send e-mails to the board. You would think I was just horrible.

I have so many stories and many that would take a long time to tell. In addition to all the crazy things that were ever done to me or said about me, a time period involving my faith stands out. Someone, I never knew who, accused me of having a prayer meeting, because they knew. Maybe that is the downside of people knowing that I was a Christian. We allowed the students to participate at a "Meet Me at the Flagpole" event. Even after this event, students began doing this frequently with some area ministers. It was all student-led but the students liked the ministers there. One particular morning it rained and the kids still wanted to have prayer. I allowed them to have it in the gym. We also had students in the gym who were early arrivers, so not everyone in the gym was a participant in the prayer. I made an announcement and informed those students who wanted to participate to simply go to the center of the gym. Those who did not want to participate could continue to do what they normally do every morning. I always participated in the prayer time. Later that day, I received e-mails from the central office that said that I made the kids stay in the gym and participate in the prayer meeting. I felt my spirituality was being attacked. It did but it didn't stop me from letting the kids do the prayer at the flagpole.

Shortly after this, things got really interesting when we had a group of students who had gotten into witchcraft. They were checking out books from the library on witchcraft and some of the kids had done a whole lot of reading and research stuff. These kids were trying to practice witchcraft on other kids in school. Some of the kids were sent to my office about it. I talked to the kids about it and told them that they couldn't tell somebody what to worship. Even I could not tell them what to worship and what not to worship. I had to explain to them that they could not threaten to put spells on other kids. They were scaring some students to death. A big issue ensued about religious rights. I was constantly asking the Lord, "Why am I going through all this?" I hadn't asked to work there. The superintendent sent me to that school without me even applying for it, so I thought this was where God wanted me to be. I couldn't figure out why my time there was so hard.

Even in spite of so many things that happened, while I was there I did believe I had a mission and that I was on a mission. I was removed from that school and I sued the school system to get my job back. I won the suit and went back, so I really believed in what I was doing. The second time things were a little different. The second time I went back I really noticed. A lot of the evil that I sensed and felt the first time had been removed. Even my relationship with the teachers was different. As various people would come into the school and they often commented that things felt different, things were calmer. God did intervene.

I had a lot of compassion that I had for that school, the community, and for the children. They all needed someone who was compassionate and who cared about them. That's the simple principle of the thing. I couldn't help what I inherited. I could only decide what I would do while I was there and how I left it. My principalship was so rough and so hard that I feel like if I had not been a spiritual person I could have possibly have had a nervous breakdown. Had I not been, I think I would have cracked.

In a lot of ways, I don't feel like I really had a principalship, but I feel like I did a lot of good. It was and still is constantly a fight, but I am doing a lot of good. As long as I've been in it, I think so. When you are a spiritual person, you are very compassionate and you have this desire to want to help somebody. I feel like I do a lot of good and not just with academic stuff. Not many people have the courage or the guts to speak up or stand up for what is right. I do.

I am of the mind that Jesus should show up in everything I do. I should do what he would do. I think that the way I carried myself, handled situations, and my relationships showed my spirituality. Then again, it could have been the Bible on my desk or some of the wall hangings in my office. But, I think people can tell and could tell that I was a spiritual person and that I had very strong religious convictions. I don't think I was ever out there trying to make a big, open show of my faith. I still don't.

The older I get, I recognize how more deeply involved I am in my spirituality. I am at a different level. Earlier in my life, I knew it was the right thing to do. My faith has always been a part of my life and not just an isolated part. It has always been all I have ever known to do. I went to church. I believed in Jesus. I did know Him, but I knew nothing about advancing. Through my principalship, I think I learned that one's faith has to reach another level and it has to take you to another level. I rely on that as my main source of strength and guidance. It really is what keeps me going and keeps me focused. I almost feel I have to be totally drenched in it. I don't know how people, much less any principal, survives without it.

I guess no amount of schooling can ever really prepare you for the principalship. I think I got a lot of skills maybe but not all the other stuff. I don't think any course anywhere really prepared me for the on-the-job, day-to-day operation of being a principal.

I could have retired several years ago. I have been in education for thirty years and in administration for ten. I could walk out of the school today and get full retirement. But who am I to retire myself? God hasn't retired me. And I still have work to do.

Bobbie's need for anonymity prevents me from discussing much of our history. Her protection precludes my ability to discuss some of the rich details and history surrounding her story and those that define the cities and district in which she lives and serves as an educator. I first met Bobbie in my senior year of college. She was the first person of color that I had during my undergraduate education as an instructor or professor. There were only three Black students in this class. We were the only students of color and we were all female. We would stay after class almost every day just to talk with her. During classes, she often talked about her family and particularly her daughter who was the same age as the three of us. Even then, I felt a connection with her and she served as a de facto mentor to me.

After I graduated the next semester, I got a job and we stayed in touch. I would often ask her about her family and school. Bobbie always gave great advice. We both gained district and state consulting experience in different areas of curriculum and this served as one more link in building our relationship. As each of us moved up the ranks from teaching to state and school leadership positions, our relationship easily moved from professional colleagues to friends.

The relationship that Bobbie and I had was further cemented when she became a principal and began her doctoral studies. During this time, I finished an administrative certification and was placed on a short list for prospective assistant principals and principals in my district. Bobbie would often discuss the difficulties of her job and the major political plays and players involved. During these discussions, Bobbie would always discuss her deep faith in God and how it sustained her personally and professionally. For this reason, I always knew that she would be one of the women I would one day "study" after becoming convinced that spirituality was important in examining the principalship. Throughout our personal and professional relationship, spirituality remains a strong part of our conversations.

While "formal" interview data with Bobbie took a total of six and one-half hours, this does not include all of the informal and anecdotal information that are central to this book. At the time of the initial discussions, Bobbie was the principal at an all-Black middle school. Foster Middle School[2] (FMS) was in another year of successive identification by the state's Department of Education as "low-performing" and is classified as a Title I school. Schools are identified as Title I if they have 40 percent or more of students on free and reduced lunch and if a certain percentage of students are low achieving. FMS is located in an area of town characterized by low human and fiscal capital, few capital improvements, and a majority of students who qualify for free and reduced lunch.

Subsequent interviews and conversations were held during a period of intense unrest in the district over what Bobbie describes as discriminatory practices by the local school district administration and the school board against the schools located in her particular part of town and against Black principals in the district. Bobbie was initially hired for the middle school and was terminated after one year. Bobbie sued the school district and won and was returned to her school for one year, and, as she puts it, "demoted" to her current position as an assistant principal. Bobbie frequently spoke of her actions to achieve what she considers "right" outcomes for her students and her community and that this is what "got her in trouble."

Legacy

Bobbie is the youngest of three children and, she indicates, was the "surprise" baby after her sister, who is six years older than she. Bobbie's narrative supports the claim that family relations serve as a primary factor in passing on cultural norms (White & Parham, 1990). Womanist theology takes this idea further by focusing on stressing traditional communalism and the "priority of collectivity" (Hopkins, 2005, p. 82). Indeed, we all are born in to community (Hopkins). From her very inception, Bobbie was born into a family that influ-

---

[2] Pseudonym.

ences her and shapes her influence on her own children, her school, and her church. This reality for Bobbie translates as *legacy*.

"People require sociality for sustenance; no person can infinitely provide food, clothing, shelter and spirituality for himself or herself alone" (Hopkins, 2005, p. 84). Hopkins highlights the notion that spirituality is indeed one of the things that is provided for an individual and is indeed passed down. While this is true, this reality does not negate the womanist idea of radical subjectivity that allows one to change and name her own reality. Bobbie's narrative sheds light on her attempt to create her own faith system, in spite of the "material, aesthetic, and spiritual legacies" (Hopkins, p. 84) provided by her family.

Spirituality and religion comprise a collective of beliefs, values, and rituals (Tisdell, 2003). This collective extends to people and communities outside of the immediate family unit. Bobbie indeed connects to individuals in her church and community and these entities form her circle of influence. However, her family remains the main influence upon her notions of spirituality. Womanist theology emphasizes community and communality; however, it sometimes does so by reducing influences such as immediate family. In an attempt to emphasize more global bonds such as the Black Church or culture, the true significance of the family can be lost when examining spiritual identity development.

Although the church is a large part of Bobbie's religio-spiritual development, her narrative presents a type of familial spiritual legacy that shapes her religio-spirituality. In some research, images of spirituality are resigned to the "domestic base" (Eugene, 2000, p. 435) of the church rather than the true domestic base of the home and family. According to development theorist Carol Gilligan (1982), individual Black women and men largely live their lives according to a system of relationships and familiarity with others in the community. Bobbie's story does highlight the interconnected network among family, community, and the church. However, her story and many other historical and contemporary spiritual narratives can sometimes fall silent regarding the strong connection to immediate families in religious and spiritual development and sustainment.

Bobbie's own description of her introduction into the church extends beyond simple induction rites of the church body as is sometimes typical in the Baptist tradition. Bobbie's narrative of herself at a young age shows some disdain and rebellion for the confessional/conversional process,[3] which represents ritualism to her. Bobbie's own experience is one that is deeply personal and grounded in her own interpretation of what it means to "believe." Bobbie's own experiences and thought processes determine how religio-spirituality is interpreted and understood. These processes also determine how Bobbie provides a religio-spiritual legacy for her own children. Bobbie's idea of who she is and her definition of religio-spirituality lies in the formation of it by her family as well as the church body and denomination.

Bobbie's church, and indeed her denomination, is one through which her legacy of protest has developed. Black clergy and the churches in the Black community have always been central to the "project of seeking change" (Sawyer, 2000, p. 297). For the historical Black Church, the idea of "social justice and religion seemed inseparable" (Raboteau, 2000, p. 290). When independent Black Churches were first founded, Black people could worship God and be treated as humans, and their issues of oppression could finally be engaged (Frederick, 2003). When the first major Black denominations emerged, they were Baptist or Methodist. The very existence of these churches was and remains rooted in the idea of protest. Paris (1985) points out that

> the growth of Black churches is both significant and inspirational. In its history lie the stories of countless men and women...in humble economic stature, completely lacking in social status. Under paralyzing conditions...a multiplicity of Black churches emerged. (p. 85)

---

[3] Many seventeenth- and eighteenth-century American churches had a standard for admission to the particular church body they wanted to join. An oral testimony had to be given before the church assemblage to show a true conversion experience (Caldwell, 1983). After this testimony, one was then eligible for water baptism and thus could obtain full fellowship in the church. This idea has been maintained well into this century and is one of the tenets of the National Baptist Convention, the denominational body of Bobbie's church.

The historical Baptist Church was often a site of slave rebellions and other revolts protesting enslaved conditions. All the while, the Baptist denomination and others often believed in the idea that protest was inspired by God and freedom (from slavery to sin and of man) was at the heart of the Christian church (Frederick, 2003).

Churches and parachurch organizations (not traditional places of workship, but spaces out-of-church that influence spiritual development) such as the National Association for the Advancement Colored People (NAACP) and the Southern Christian Leadership Conference (SCLC) were also a big part of Bobbie's religio-spiritual development. "Parachurch organizations are vehicles by which Christians work collaboratively outside and across their denominations to engage in social welfare and evangelism" ("Parachurch," 2007, para. 1). Although ecumenical, organizations such as the NAACP and SCLC were historically associated with Black churches and denominations for "consciousness-raising and protest" (Sawyer, p. 299). This protest and the involvement of the church begin Bobbie's ideas about her early educational narrative. Schools became sites of protest. Bobbie's description of her school years illustrates schools as sites of protest. This protest occurs well after the 1954 Supreme Court decision of *Brown v. Board of Education* in which legal segregation in schools was outlawed. However, the district in which Bobbie went to school, like others in the South, had not been desegregated. Bobbie's story represents her pastor and members of the church body as leaders for progressive social actions, while not forsaking their pastoral duties of converting the masses and making sure that current believers remain faithful. Even though the church had tremendous influence in the community and upon the civil rights movement, one sees from Bobbie's story that her family still played a primary role in her life and even served as the conduit for her participatory action in the civil rights movement and in her church.

Raised as a Baptist in the NBC tradition, Bobbie indicates an early indoctrination into what I describe as *denominational identity*. This identity forms a basis for her personal religio-spiritual identity. When asked about her spirituality while growing up, Bobbie couched her spirituality within her Baptist church. Even during a brief absence in which she left a Baptist-affiliated church, she still framed her

Christian life by the denominational tenets of the Baptist Church she first embraced. Bobbie offers somewhat competing narratives as she very much retains traditional Baptist beliefs, but attempts to make sense of these beliefs in light of "new ideas" and the situations in the Methodist church she embraced for a while and much like the situation she confronted with her daughter.

Bobbie is also heavily influenced by Christian authors and televangelists. The traditional rules of her denomination are blurred for her as she reads books by Christian authors and watches religious programming on popular Christian networks. For instance, women serving in leadership roles in the church are a source of tension for her. Although Bobbie made it clear that she does not necessarily challenge the issue in church or to members of the church leadership, it impacts her when some of these traditional roles begin to change. From her narrative, it is clear that there is some tenuous dynamic between "trying new things" and remaining faithful to what she believes are true tenets of the Baptist denomination—one in which women rarely serve as pastors. She quickly pointed out that she "still follows all the Baptist rules" but changes the way "they do some things." There is still a need to have her identity rooted in Baptist traditions. It is interesting that she juxtaposed some of the changes in the worship at her Baptist church and compared the preaching to Pentecostalism. Incidentally, the Pentecostal denomination is considered one of the first to grant leadership roles that extend beyond traditional bounds of church "woman's work," such as children's Sunday School leaders. These roles in the Pentecostal tradition extend to preaching and teaching by women (Gilkes, 2001). Pentecostal churches also enjoy the characterization of being more charismatic, emotional, and demonstrative. This style of worship is characterized by some as more "authentic and freeing" than the more traditional worship of the Baptist Church (Frederick, 2003).

Bobbie clarified that she applies to her spiritual frame "whatever speaks to her and her situation," while measuring it against God's Word. Spirituality is all at once key for her personal well-being but also pragmatic and useful in professional spaces. Bobbie is still able to do this by retaining her denominational identity, and doing so by *enlarging* the tradition that she embraces.

Warfare

In as much as legacy illustrates Bobbie's narrative, so does the concept of *warfare*. The Bible is rife with the themes of spiritual struggle and "battle." Some of these struggles include those between Light and Darkness, but also struggle with humans' personal nature and the nature of the "new creatures" that God wants to make them by giving them a new nature. According to Murphy (1996),

> Some speak of [Spiritual Warfare as being] the struggle between good and evil. Others talk of the battle between right and wrong, or between light and darkness. Still others refer to the conflict between the positive forces which seek to preserve life and order in the universe and the negative forces which tend to disturb and even destroy life and order. From a biblical perspective, however, this dualism is revealed to be an ongoing conflict waged on two fronts: God and His angelic kingdom confront Satan and his demonic kingdom, while the children of God contend with the children of Satan. (p. 13)

Bobbie discussed what some may believe as being psychological or ambiguously "in the spirit realm"; she regards warfare as literal and tangible supernatural manifestations of spiritual warfare in her life, the lives of her family, and those of her church members and friends. But for Bobbie, the term *spiritual warfare* is not merely a figurative battle among good and evil, but a very real one "against the evil rulers and authorities of the unseen world, against those mighty powers of darkness who rile this world, and against wicked spirits in the heavenly realms" (Ephesians 6:12, New Living Translation). According to Bobbie's narrative, evil can be overcome by prayer and by direct communication and power from God. Bobbie spoke of evil spirits when she discussed some supernatural events involving her daughter in her prayer room and discerning events before they happen. She also spoke of supernatural occurrences when her pastor was fighting his own illness, but also during "healing services" at her church. Bobbie also spoke of an incident in her own house in which she awoke to sense the presence of something in her bedroom.

Whether others believe Bobbie's accounts of these events or not, they are very real for her. Belief in supernatural occurrences and spiritual warfare is something that Bobbie indicated began at a young age for her. Bobbie hinted as this being a heritable trait by indicating that her mother, Bobbie's sister, and Bobbie's daughter all have these same spiritual tendencies that have been passed along because of their familial connection. It is interesting that she did not attribute this "gift" to any male in her family other than her grandson. Also within the community or church, her pastor's thinking regarding spiritual warfare changed after a woman in her church "introduced" him to these phenomena by "healing" him. In all of these accounts, Bobbie spoke of a very real connection by which God speaks to individuals, works through them, protects them, and helps them fight these forces of darkness. Through it all, prayer becomes center stage in the battle.

Even so, Bobbie's narrative also symbolically portrays the theme of warfare. In her narrative, Bobbie often used "war words" to describe her life. The word *fight* appears eight times throughout her narrative. She used it when discussing the many struggles she faced as a child, particularly during the civil rights movement. This word was used as a verb but also as a noun, as the civil rights movement was often seen as the *fight* for civil rights (Mullane, 1993). The word *fight* seems to have peculiar meaning to her when discussing the response to particular oppressions during this time. The word *fight* returns yet again when Bobbie narrated her experiences as a principal, and the word becomes a metaphor for her experience as a principal. She spoke of countering her professional issues as a principal with battle metaphor. She used this metaphor again when describing events of achieving justice for her students. Bobbie used fight symbolism yet again when religion and the school collided, as seen in the incident in which Bobbie was accused of proselytizing. Indeed, spiritual warfare can be said to be a theme of her life as she has attempted to navigate intersecting realities of her life as a Black woman and a school administrator.

While many commentaries concerning historical spiritual narratives have much to say about struggle, ironically they have little to say about warfare. In a key word study of fifty books related to womanism, theology, and/or Black women, not one table of contents or index examination yielded the term *warfare*. However, this term seems to be apt in describing a theme related to that of the justice she attempted to achieve in her life while becoming an adult and in the principalship. This sense of justice was undeniably bestowed upon her by her family but the church played a big part as well. Bobbie's early experiences with her family and with her church provided a foundation for leadership in her school and in her life. Early family and church experiences had a direct impact upon her leadership development. Her family modeled participation in church but also influenced how she interacted with the church and the community. The church, Bobbie's family, and her own school experiences framed for Bobbie early on that the spiritual was not separate from other parts of life and in fact informed what their daily activities would be.

Through Bobbie's whole schooling experience, the church and community played an important role in school and education. As an elementary student, high school student, and college student, the church remained a steady influence in her choices and in her ability to rise above her circumstances. Going to college was her first schooling experience away from her community and home, yet it still "felt like home" because it was a Christian college and those same traditions of church and community were able to be maintained. Recreating this same experience became a priority for her when she became a principal. Frequent involvement from the church, parachurch organizations, and community members became a priority for her. Indeed, her story highlights how her personal relationship not only to God but also to these other entities sustained her during the principalship.

Bobbie's story squarely places her in the noted position of both segregated and newly integrated school environments. In her early school years, this was a reality as she went from an all-Black, Christian schooling experience to a more diverse, integrated secular situation. As we see later in her story, she was uniquely positioned in this same way in her school district as a teacher. Her principalship was marked by a re-segregation process with the onset of neighborhood schools after a more than thirty-year desegregation order. Bobbie was then placed in a middle school that had once housed all middle school students across the district to become a neighborhood middle school located on the "Black" side of town. This school was 100 percent African American and more than 60 percent of the students were on the free and reduced lunch program. The school was also considered "failing" owing to low achievement scores in every subject. This school had become her new battlefield and the social justice in this school and surrounding neighborhood had become her new fight.

Getting Churched and Being Schooled: Bobbie and Womanist Theology

Small-town Christian communities often denote a Christian from a non-Christian as the "churched" and the "unchurched," respectively. To be churched means to have a religious affiliation ("Unchurched," 1978) or to go to church regularly (Hong, 2000). The churching of women also refers to a blessing given to women by the Catholic Church to purify a woman after childbirth (Shorter, 1982). "Getting schooled" means to be taught something or "taught a lesson the hard way" (Shaneo, 2003). In either instance of being churched or getting schooled, there is the implication that something has happened to the person in question and that they have been "fixed" or indoctrinated (Johnson, 2006). These phrases highlight two strands of Bobbie's life.

During the eighteenth and nineteenth centuries when independent Black churches were emerging, there was still an adoption of the theological frameworks of their white parent churches (Ross, 2006). In spite of this, one of the lasting legacies of the first independent Black denominations is the emphasis on other streams of thought. This emphasis upon critique was original in its opposition to the monolithic Protestant denominations of the time and caused these independent denominations to separate from white church bodies initially. This opposition consistently examined the pragmatics of religion, the contribution of African peoples to Christianity, and faith considering the everyday realities of their lives. While Bobbie may not have had this historicity specifically in mind, she sought to ask the same questions of her denomination as these early independent churches did. Part of womanist theology demands that we not only walk spiritually, but that we serve to critique it as well. By being critically engaged in her own religio-spirituality, Bobbie honors her commitment to her denominational beliefs but also draws upon other works and life experiences to complete her circle of meaning.

Bobbie's story seems to suggest a situational religio-spirituality that delineates from any one way of "doing" faith. Bobbie in some ways reshaped her denominational understandings of her faith to one that is more inclusive with her personal struggles and situations. For Bobbie her religio-spirituality translates into denominational foundations but with multiple "informants" to her worldview. Bobbie sustains her religio-spirituality and its meaning-making role in her life through her persistence in engaging in most of its practices but she "maintained and accented practical reasoning capacities in making choices about religious interpretations of social and political life" (Ross, 2006, p. 126).

The ideas of appropriation, reciprocity, and traditional communalism are evident in Bobbie's narrative. Her story emphasizes a strong family base with a dominant family member (Brown, 2000). In many African American families this dominant family member sets the tone for spirituality and is often a grandparent. Bobbie's story highlights her grandmother particularly at whose feet she learned about God. Extended families such as church members and friends also provided models not only for belief in God but also for early leadership behaviors.

These family structures often promoted racial uplift (lifting others as you climb) and a duty not just to yourself but to the entire community. Bobbie was taught by example that it was her responsibility through "right acts…to uplift those who had less or were without educational, economic, and/or occupational advantages" (Riggs, 1994). This uplift was particularly seen in her warring acts as she fought subjugation while attending school herself and leading one as a principal. Training for social change was also introduced in Bobbie's church and in the community in which she grew up and had a lasting impact upon how she performed the principalship. Bobbie's story illustrates that "agency is not subordinate to legacy" (Siddle Walker & Snarey, 2004, p. 10).

While appropriation, reciprocity, and traditional communalism focus on the intersecting realities of other women of color and men of color, Bobbie's narrative focuses on a connection to others as well. There is an idea behind these womanist theological tenets that one needs "fellow soldiers" on the journey to overcoming the sexist, racist, and classist tendencies of society. However, Bobbie's story recalls *white allies* in this struggle. Throughout Bobbie's narrative, she recalls instances of white individuals who assisted her and her family in direct instances of racism.

It is often hard to talk about the African American without discussing issues of racism, and indeed this was one of the foremost issues of the Black Church and its members (Wilmore, 1996). Although racism and sexism are recurring themes throughout her story, Bobbie never allowed these intersecting certainties to define her. In fact they even became a part of the larger "battle against evil" and one that she felt more equipped to wage. When asked about these issues specifically, she had little to say about them than that her faith and "her God" were always present in these battles. By demonstrating the womanist tenets of self-love and radical subjectivity, Bobbie was not limited by her realities as a Black female. However, the legacy and warfare skills that Bobbie learned helped her to "develop a sense of agency and sense of herself as a participant in the events around her; a sense of self-awareness, her true capabilities, and how her own intentions influence the world" (Brown, 2000, p. 47).

Schools can often be places of indoctrination of the status quo for adults and children. Bobbie did indeed "learn a few lessons" about the inequalities of schooling. Schools often did teach her some things. She was schooled each time she and her students were discriminated against. Bobbie did learn that policy matters and often following policy was key to determining whether she kept her job, which was a real concern. By examining her schooling through a womanist lens, one sees that Bobbie viewed "systemic injustices as simultaneously social educational problems" (Beauboeuf-Lafontant, 2006, p. 286). Bobbie understood that she has the responsibility to contest stereotypes. She also promoted the idea that it is her moral and ethical responsibility to prepare youth for "future leadership and…the enhancement of the quality of life for Black people" (Adair, 1984, as cited in in Siddle Walker, 1996, p. 206). Even though schools tend to limit the possibilities of children and adults, Bobbie refused to allow this. Bobbie saw it as her mission to educate the whole child through physical, mental, emotional, and spiritual nurturing. Even though Bobbie learned much about schools and the way they work throughout her own school years and as an educator, she was not indoctrinated by them. She took what she had learned and provided a little schooling of her own. Schooling became a site for "political clarity" (Beauboeuf-Lafontant, 2006, p. 286) and a way to subvert injustice.

Finally, Bobbie's story highlights Love of Spirit through what she believes in her personal connection to God and the power of prayer. The idea that one can personally speak to the triune God and appropriate His power is central to her narrative. "The label 'prayer warrior' runs deep in Black tradition" (Gilkes, 2001, p. 134). "Their faith in and prayers to God often focus on requests for pragmatic assistance in alleviating problems" (Black, 1999, p. 360). Bobbie's religio-spirituality helped her fight and cope with hardship. Through prayer, God was seen as fully integrated and concerned with individuals. Bobbie's prayer life and spirituality are grounded in family, church, and cultural legacy.

Meditations

Analysis of Bobbie's spiritual narrative has illuminated two major themes: legacy and warfare. It would have been easy to discuss a deficit model of the family, church, and community. There are many books highlighting the Black Church and community norms and their own reifying, hegemonic practices. However, no critique of the institutionalized Black Church, family, or community seems appropriate since Bobbie's story does not bear this out. Her narrative is one of spiritual nourishment that informs and empowers her as a Black woman and as an administrator. The story of *her* Black church experience is positive and contributed to her well-being, perseverance, passion, and piety in a life filled with many obstacles as well advancements. In Bobbie's case, her church and her religio-spiritual perspective was "educative and ego-building" (Brown, 2000, p. 47).

AVERY
TESTIMONY

We send forth this...as our contribution to the history of a race, whose true story must yet be told by members of the race would we give our young peo-

ple the needed encouragement to make their lives what they should be.
(Virginia W. Broughton)[4]

Avery is a thirty-seven-year-old self-described "missionary." The following is written as a testimony to a church body. Testimonies in church are often ways to explain what God has done in the life of an individual and given as an address to the church body. Testimonies often include reflections on the past, present, and future work of God and exhort others toward "godly" work (Floyd-Thomas, 2006b). Oral testimonies, even after conversion to print, used story to convey a message. Virginia Broughton was used as an inspiration for the following spiritual narrative. Broughton was a nineteenth-century Baptist educator and missionary who served for a time at a school in the same city in which Avery currently lives. Broughton often linked her work in schools with that of her work as a missionary and frequently gave addresses on the importance of young people. Broughton's piece, "Twenty Years' Experience of a Missionary," contains addresses to different audiences and includes stories she told about her time in these roles. Like Broughton, Avery spoke of her work as an educator as being divinely appointed. Her church plays a profound role in this work, as her church is an "adopter" of her school. Avery often gave her testimony and spoke to her church about her school. Avery's narrative holds the themes of mission, ministry, strength, and mothering.

> When I think back to my life I am amazed at what can happen. I am so passionate about my students because I see my own life in their lives. I am grateful for the support that I get from you to do what I have to do. So many of you join me in caring for my kids and I am grateful.
>
> My mother died at a young age and even before that I had a difficult relationship with my father I was often told that I wouldn't amount to much. I learned how to work hard and to get a good education. To this day, I often wonder how I made it or am still making it. But I know how I made it. I used to think that staying busy was the answer. I now know that God and having a good church home is what matters. The church has provided me

---

[4] V. W. Broughton (1850). "Twenty Years' Experience of a Missionary." In S. Houchins (Ed.), *Spiritual Narratives* (pp. 1–140). New York: Oxford University Press.

with accountability but has also given me encouragement. That is what I want to teach my students. As Christians we have to show these children that they can overcome their circumstances and have a future. I know that we can give them an education. But I believe that is all in vain if we don't teach them about God. We have to show them in how we live our lives that God exists. But we also have to show them in how we treat them. We have to be God's hands and feet.

I have to say that I am unashamed. I am unashamed to tell my students about God. I break the rules. Some of you know that I bring some of my kids to church with me and many people might not think that is normal. What is normal when there is nothing normal about the situation my kids live in?

I would like to tell you a story about one of my students. The little girl that I started taking home with me is Shay. She used to always ask me, "Can I come home with you? Can I come home with you?" In my mind I was thinking like a principal. I was thinking, "Why does she want to come home with me? I'm a principal!" I would say, "Sweetheart, you can't come home with me." She would continue to ask and so finally she just kept asking me and I thought to myself, "What is it that this girl sees in me that makes her want to come with me?" Finally I gave in and I offered to pick her up. I remember that first time. I had a meeting in another town and I called her mother and asked if I could pick her up and have her spend some time at my house. That was early in the year and from then to the end of the school year she came home with me almost every weekend. About a couple of months after she started coming home with me, I met another little girl. She was a new student and I didn't get to meet her when she enrolled. I introduced myself and found out that she was Shay's sister! I had never met this child at Shay's house. I found out that all of Shay's brothers and sisters had been taken by DHR and had been gradually placed back in the home. This little girl was just being placed back in the home. After a time or two she started coming home with me too and I started taking them to church and Shay joined the church and she was baptized in my church. She is an usher and they both participate in the youth program. Since then, I have another student who has begun coming with us too.

I have to tell you that I can teach my kids all day long about education and getting good grades and all of that. But this is about more than that. I'm looking at saving lives, not just educating bodies. I did not set out to be in education. Those of you who know my story know that I have had many jobs. I did many things before I got to the point where I could not escape. But the Lord has a funny way of dealing with you. I can see now where all the events of my life pointed me to where I am now. I have a responsibility. I have a mission.

Avery and I first met three years ago shortly after I left the principalship to become a graduate student. After only a few conversations, we bonded over stories about being in the principalship. Our conversations often centered on our schools but shortly turned to faith. Avery usually had a story to tell about the intersection of school and faith and I began to see much of myself in her. I remember asking her after only a short time of knowing her whether she would be interested in being a part of my research. She readily agreed and I began talking with her every chance I could get about faith and schooling.

Interview data with Avery took a total of four hours. However, this does not include all of the informal and anecdotal information I gathered and recorded in notebooks after one of our many professional and personal discussions. Formal interviews took place at her school during the summer months. Students and teachers were not present. Other discussions took place on the phone. At the time of the initial discussions, Avery was beginning her own process toward completing a doctor of education degree in educational administration. She was beginning the prospectus process and many of our conversations centered on this.

Avery has been a principal for three years at an elementary school of almost two hundred students with students in kindergarten to fifth grade. She is in her tenth year as an educator and has been a teacher and has held assistant principal positions. Avery's school has been identified as a Title I school and 98 percent of her students qualify for free or reduced lunch. Avery's school did not meet adequate yearly progress for the 2006–2007 school as classified by the state's Department of Education. According to Avery, this school is located in an area of town characterized by low human and fiscal capital. The physical structure of the school was built in the 1950s and has had few capital improvements since that time. The school district serves around 23,000 students, with economically disadvantaged students accounting for around 40 percent of the total enrollment in the district.

Strong Black Woman

I have always viewed Avery as a strong woman. As a former personal trainer, exercise television show host, and former member of the Army, she often hears other people call her "tough" or "strong." Avery walks into a room and others take notice. Avery has a quick energy that one observes while watching her. She moves from task to task very quickly and often thinks through situations at a faster pace than most of the people with whom we worked. During informal discussions, if a problematic situation is posed to her, Avery quickly finds a solution. Her words are often uttered with such a decisiveness and finality that no one seems to question her wisdom. While I find myself often lauding the historical and everyday strength of Black women, there are some individual women who elicit a declaration of strength that is uncanny. As a divorced mother, doctoral student, principal, and active church and social volunteer, Avery is one of those women.

Avery's narrative reveals her propensity for story. She often peppers informal discussions with stories and anecdotes to illustrate her thinking about a particular topic. Rather than being seen as merely discrete events, these anecdotes serve as parts of an important process in identifying the major themes concerning Avery's religio-spirituality. The themes of strength and mothering are highlighted throughout her narrative. Avery's discussions about God often come back to the strength of her faith, her relationships, and mission. She speaks about the strength she gets from her faith to do the job she feels she was "meant to do." Much of her actions in her personal and professional life stem from what can be characterized as mothering.

Over a period of one month, Avery and I had subsequent discussions over the phone. Our first face-to-face interview occurred at her school. During this visit, Avery revealed what she considers the defining story of her life: the murder of her mother by her father. One can hardly begin to discuss her story without beginning with this event. Italics shown in the following narrative denote areas or phrases with strong emphasis, in which she stopped speaking for a few moments, or cried before continuing.

When I was 18 my dad killed my mom. I'm still shocked. I mean, I don't ever talk about it and I feel ashamed and embarrassed. When people ask, I still say my mother died in a car accident. *I have never told anyone about this.*

Growing up there were five kids and I'm in the middle. I've got an older brother and sister and younger brother and sister. I was the baby until I was nine, so my younger brother is almost ten years younger than me and then my sister came about a year or so later.

I left home when I was eighteen. But growing up, my parents had an abusive type relationship. It was more verbal as far as I know, than physical, although I know for a fact that it was physical at times. My father was just mean, just mean. Even in hindsight I can see that. He drank early on but he stopped drinking. You know, even as a child, I always thought I would feel differently after I grew up but in hindsight my father was a mean man. I was the black sheep of the family. I never got in trouble or anything, but he used to tell me, "You're never going to amount to anything." I made straight A's and I did my chores. *To this day I don't know what it was that made him see me differently.* If we were being fussed at, I got the worst of it. It's weird because I look like him. Everybody used to say, "You are the spitting image of your father."

Mom the whole time just took it and put up with it. I don't know what it was, but as I grew up I developed a really close relationship with my mother. *Hmm… I don't know, I just became close to her.* My brother went into the army right out of high school. My sister went into the army right out of high school. We all were just trying to get away from home. That's why I got married so young. So, when my sister went into the army, I was a senior in high school and my mother and I had gotten really close. She would tell me that she wanted me to graduate high school and then she was going to leave my father. That's what she did. I graduated high school. I left to go into the army literally like a month or so after I graduated. After she left, my dad was following her around all the time. My mom had moved out and was living with her sister and he was stalking her basically. Stalking laws were not what they needed to be. Back then the police told her there was nothing that they could do unless he did something to her.

The night before my basic training graduation, I talked to my brother the night before I graduated and he said mommy won't be able to come. He said mommy was not feeling well. The next day after graduation was over the chaplain came and got me and they took me to the chapel and everything. My boyfriend was there. He and my mother were supposed to ride together. In the chaplain's office they told me that my boyfriend had gotten me a graduation cake and they had stopped to pick the cake. My father was following them. When my boyfriend went in to get the cake, he left my mom and my two younger siblings in the car. My boyfriend ran in and got the cake.

While my boyfriend was in the store, and my younger brother and sister were in the back seat, my dad came to mommy's side of the car and stabbed her twenty-six times. She was dead on arrival when they took her to the hospital. I had to testify at my father's trial.

Dad got a life sentence and he is still in prison as far as I know. My siblings and I *never* talk about what happened. It's there but we just never talk about it. I don't know if we have mentioned it since it happened. That's been over twenty years ago. We just do *not* go there.

By her own indication, this stands as a defining life moment. Avery described this moment by discussing within this larger story. Her emphases provide distinct story plots to follow and analyze. Careful attention is paid to emotions and agitations. Often during her discussions, Avery displayed heightened feeling and her voice became lowered. In keeping with the notion of metaphor in spiritual narrative, Avery's story contains "strong" words that are described further below.

Avery identified her mother's murder as a "family secret." Avery began her story by indicating her "different" relationship with her father and how that contrasts with those of her siblings and reveals the emotional abuse she experienced from her father. In her narrative, she correlated her performance with this abuse. As Avery continued speaking about her mother's murder, she provided context for the story by discussing events leading up to the day her mother died. She indicated the close relationship with her mother and that she could not understand why this relationship evolved the way it did. From Avery's story, it seemed that she and her mother were the two individuals on the receiving end of the abuse. When asked about this, Avery indicated that her other siblings had gone through this as far as she was aware. Avery admitted that a certain level of closeness could have occurred because of that fact. Avery pointed out, "I certainly understood what my mother was going through."

Avery also discussed her mother's "putting up with it," or tolerating the abuse. Avery discussed that her mother planned to leave as soon as Avery graduated from high school. At the time that her mother left her father, Avery's younger siblings were still in elementary school. When Avery was questioned further she revealed that none of her siblings or she discusses her mother's murder and none of them has ever been to therapy. Analysis of this event is not an attempt to psychoanalyze Avery, although during her interview she displayed great restraint. For instance, Avery's eyes would water, and she would shake her head as if shaking away the situation. After a moment or two, she would seem to muster new resolve or gather her strength and begin talking again. I remember thinking once again how strong she seemed as she began talking again, for I am not sure I could have been if faced with the same memory. She indicated that, "It was weird letting that out since I have never told anyone." This indicated a pain regarding this event, but more interestingly, the silence surrounding the abuse and the murder. Avery indicated that her mother did not discuss the abuse outside of the home and Avery and her siblings still seem to be trapped in their own silence surrounding the event. Avery discussed that she and her siblings talk about her mother but that they never speak of the event:

> We rarely talk about it. A lot of people don't even know my mother's not living, let alone how she died. When my siblings and I get together, sometimes we will talk about her, but we never talk about it. When we go home and we visit the grave, we take flowers but we really don't ever talk about what happened.

There is no way to fully mine all the meanings of this particular experience yet literature concerning abuse in the family may provide some insight.

The story of abuse and murder in Avery's family highlights the fact that there is often a silence in the Black community surrounding abuse (Collins, 2000). There is a silence in naming abuse; there is often difficulty in finding freedom from it as well (Simonsen, 1986). Richie's seminal work on battered Black women first posited the phrase *gender entrapment* to explain the connection between loyalty and racial identity. Richie posits that this entrapment keeps Black women ensnared in violent relationships. In many circumstances, Black women do not leave the abuse and do not obtain effective therapy (hooks, 2005; Richie, 1996). Refusing to report abuse often becomes equated with protecting the race or the community against racist practices in society. While Richie's work and other's provide important insights into abuse, what they fail to discuss are the ways in which women are trapped in abuse because of familial bonds or ideas of good mothering. Avery indicated that her mother kept telling her that she would leave once Avery had graduated from high school. Avery indicated that her mother had a need to keep what she considered an intact family. The notion of the ideal family (Collins, 1991) can entrap one in abuse as well. Black women have kept quiet "not solely out of shame, but out of a need to preserve the race and its image of family" (Pierce-Baker, 1998, p. 84).

As indicated earlier, Avery has always been called a strong Black woman. The strong Black woman or the superwoman is seen as someone who can do it all. Doing it all often means putting her needs secondary to those of her family and the community (Collins, 1991; Wallace, 1978). The strong Black woman often takes most of the responsibilities for the emotional, material, and spiritual realities of the home. While Avery did not make clear her parents' personalities, the idea of the strong Black woman seemed to have an impact on Avery. Some Black feminist and womanist theorists discuss the myth of the Black superwoman and the entrapment and silencing that occurs with this label (Lorde, 1984; Richie, 1996). However, when examining this label and Avery's story through womanist theology, a survivalist (Williams, 1993) theme emerges. One of the ways Williams discusses survivalism is in overcoming a particular hardship or oppressive event to improve one's quality of life. As a womanist theologian, Williams describes the role of faith and spirituality in this process.

Rather than simply being a silencer, the superwoman became a coping mechanism and a form of empowerment for Avery. Avery's father always told her that she "would never amount to anything." However, Avery's and her mother's abuse somehow served as an impetus for her success and her need to help others to succeed,

> It's hard, but I have to fight it. I suppose I fight it by staying busy in my career, I guess. My daddy telling me that made me work even harder. I have a strong church family that I know care about me. I won't go through what my mom went through. That made me realize what I need to do for my

family and the example I need to set for my daughter. I also got more involved with church. That is what I try to tell the kids I work with. Don't every let anyone tell you, you can't do something. I want them to be strong and to know that they can do anything that they want to.

Avery also uses this incident and her faith in God as a form of strength and resistance to other forms of oppression and violence in other areas of her life. Avery tries to encourage other children she works with and her daughter how to be "strong."

Traci West, an ordained minister, in her book *Wounds of the Spirit* discusses the religious and spiritual foundations of women surviving in and thriving out of violence. Although her faith and church are important to Avery, it is interesting that the arena in which she has thrived is not one in which she has chosen to break her silence. She described her church as her "church family," and her involvement in the church. Yet as with her own family, she has not mentioned this event. Faith can support women in thriving out of violence, but it can also be complicit in their silence. Black churches, which have been so outspoken concerning issues of race and class, are still largely silent on issues of sexism and violence against women (Frederick, 2003). Often the church and/or religious faith can be complicit in the silence surrounding abuse. The pressure to seem as though one "has it all together" or is a good Christian can hold women back from naming and resisting violence.

Avery discussed that neither she nor her siblings had ever been to therapy. When asked why this was the case, Avery simply said, "We just don't talk about it." When asked how she felt about this fact, she replied, "Maybe it is wrong, I don't know. Maybe I should have gotten therapy. I just found a way to deal with it. I just stay busy." The "busy" that Avery kept talking about seems to be the work that she pours herself into doing for others. Her work in her school and her work at church seem to be a way of coping. Womanist theology discusses the notion of "uplift" (Johnson, 2000) as a response to racism, sexism, and other oppressive conditions. One of the ways to promote uplift is to channel emotional damage into helping others. This seems to align with Avery pouring herself into church to help others since she indicated she "didn't have that growing up. It was very hit or miss." Avery ended the portion of the conversation concerning her mother's death by stating that she really wanted to show people what it meant to overcome hardship. Her frequent references to God and her faith seem to suggest that Avery equates being religio-spiritual with being strong. Showing others what it means to overcome hardship seemed difficult to do as Avery had not told anyone of her own struggle or sought assistance. hooks (2005) seems to offer one possible explanation for Avery's silence in the midst of being a strong religio-spiritual woman:

> Black women often perceive therapy as a sign that their faith is lacking. We need to understand that it is testament to the power of spiritual faith that we can seek therapeutic help. (2005, p. xxvi)

Mothering as Ministry

It became clear during discussions with Avery that she often refrains from sharing too much about her personal family, preferring to focus on her work at school. However, Avery's story also carries a theme of family and mothering. Avery described her church in domestic terms, calling it "home" and its members "family." Avery also described her church's involvement with her school as an adoption:

> I will tell you a story. You know what I like about my church. I joined a mega-church of 5,000+ members. Every piece of correspondence I received had Brother in front of my name. I called the church secretary and tried to let them know, but they didn't know who I was and nobody ever asked me. I was never involved so I never felt at home there. But the church where I am now, I mean, they adopted my school and on any given Sunday I'm speaking to them about various things and I'm involved with the kids. It has just been so different than going to the bigger churches where you just feel like you are just there. I visited this church with a friend of mine and I just enjoyed it. I came back several times and I just loved the closeness, it truly felt like a church family. You know, a lot of people use that terminology, church family, but this really did feel like a church family.

Avery described her relationship with her biological family only briefly; and her discussion of her own twelve-year-old daughter was just as brief. The one time when she did bring up her daughter, Avery discussed her while talking about the church and Avery's pride in her daughter participating in these activities:

> I'm actively involved in several different ministries and my daughter is secretary of her youth group and she ushers. That's my baby.

For Avery, the most important trait she wanted to pass on to her daughter was to "help her develop her faith." This idea of passing on faith seemed to have informed her work at her school as well.

Avery's conversation mostly centered on the role she plays with the students at her school. However, Avery's religio-spirituality plays a part in her principalship in that there is a blurring of lines between school and church. During her interview, I often would have to stop to ask when she was speaking about her students at school and when she was speaking about the children she worked with at church. Some of her students were church members, but it was how she viewed them. To Avery, they were just children, whom she was charged to "take care of." Her spiritual narrative highlights the fact that she openly proselytizes in schools. The principalship for Avery is a religious act and her ministry. Much like historical church mothers in the Black Church, the church mother often introduced individuals, helped others come to faith, and instructed them in the values for living the Christian life (Williams, 1993, p. 79). As a direct part of her ministry, Avery often participates in mothering activities in school and in church that lead others to a spiritual life and guides them. When asked if she was concerned about this in school, Avery replied:

> I think I work really hard to make sure all my children are taken care of. I try to make sure that I do right by all of them. I want all of them to succeed and have better lives. Some students I am able to really get to know and get to know their families and stuff. Those are the ones that I take to church and do things with.

While Avery works on behalf of all her students, she indicated special relationships with certain students. These special relationships are the ones in which she proselytizes. These students have accompanied her to church and have become active there. Avery equates the work of the principalship as a form of taking care of them in ways that their families are not and as being a proxy for some of the parents. Her role as a principal is considered a ministry and a part of her duty as a Christian:

> With this community and with my kids, I feel like this is a ministry in itself. I mean 98 percent of my kids live in poverty. I've got kids whose parents are on drugs. I know some of them are dealing with abuse, sexual and otherwise. Their home life is not what it should be. I know some of them are being neglected. It's like, you want to save them all, you know you say you can't save everyone you want to. I just honestly feel like without bringing God into the picture there is not a whole lot I can do. These kids are trying to survive. It's like you want so badly for them to somehow see that there is something else out there outside of these walls and what they see everyday out there. And in fact, I'm probably going to take some of them to Chuck E Cheese or something. They should have experiences like that. I believe that I am responsible for these kids in many ways. I always tell people that it's not just the parents who are raising kids. It takes all of us.

Avery had much to say about mentoring. Mentoring by the elders of the younger has always been a big part of the African American church (Collins, 1998). However, the literature surrounding mentoring in schools tends to focus on technical arrangements for professional growth (Ashburn, Mann, & Purdue, 1987) based on socializing one into a professional position (Grogan & Crow, 2004). However, Avery's mentoring relationships are more personal. While Avery indicated that she did not experience mentoring as a child herself, she considered it a big part of her duty to God. One can see from parts of her narrative that she views mentoring as another form of mothering and sees it as an extension of her work in the church:

> I work with the youth at my church and I mentor them. But I guess I also mentor my students at school too. I really think of mentoring as helping other people. That is all it really is. God simply asks us to love and help other people. I even do this for people in my district. If teachers or other principals need help, I try to help.

Although Avery considers spiritual success as the most important thing she can pass along, she also views student achievement as vital. Avery's religio-spirituality informs her goal of seeking academic success for her students. She discussed how making sure her students succeed is a part of her ministry to them. However Avery's narrative indicates that while student achievement is important, it was secondary to her students' emotional and spiritual success. Avery linked the cycle of poverty not only to a lack of educational opportunity but also to a lack of a "different life," which she considers a Christian life.

> We are always working on raising test scores. But I know it isn't all about that. The kids at my school may never be top achievers anyway by somebody else's scale. You know, too many come from backgrounds where education is not valued and as long as that is the case, that poverty cycle will continue to repeat itself. I do believe that education is key, but without that exposure to a different kind of life they are not going to understand it.

Avery also mentors others in her district, but receives mentoring as well. The mentoring she has with other principals is an informal, two-way process. This relationship also brokered other mentoring connections. Having a mentoring relationship also helped Avery cope in her early career as a principal and sustains her in her current position,

> I don't feel like I am formally mentored. I created my own mentorship with another principal, she and I have partnered our elementary schools, and we do our leadership training together; we did a retreat together and we just took a cruise together, both schools. We bounce ideas off of each other and we partner teachers from her school with ones at mine. I just met her and we just clicked that first year. She had been here for a year already and it just made sense. We even present at workshops together. I was not happy my first year as a principal until I met her.

The concept of mothering took on another role in how Avery interpreted policy. When asked about the relationship or tensions between her religio-spirituality and school policy, here is what Avery had to say:

> I'm trying to think about that. I don't see any tensions. I mean, I think most of the policies are just what they are. They don't vary that much from district to district. I am a Christian, but I am at work and so I don't think there has been a conflict. I am the principal and a lot of the procedures I make for my school, the district lets me do that. I think that what I like is that the district allows the principals to do what they think is best. I think that was actually one of the reasons I needed to get away from my assistant principalship because there were too many decisions that were being made that I had no control over and that I did not feel like were in the best interest of the child and I felt helpless to do anything. At all times, I ask myself, "Is it good for my students?" I try to make sure their needs are met. If they

need a coat, I get it. Shoes or food, I try to see what I can do. And that is what you have to do. I guess the reason that I feel that it isn't a conflict is because I do feel like I am in a position where I can make those decisions by myself. I can make the decisions. I feel like I can do the right things.

Avery believes that there was no conflict because of the level of autonomy she feels she gets from district leadership. Avery indicates a child-centered focus to her leadership, and it was clear that she believes that students' needs, whatever they may be, are an appropriate starting point for actions and decision making. Avery believes that recognizing these needs is a function of and due to her religio-spirituality,

> When you have a spiritual side, it makes you more in tune with others' needs. Some people just act like they are blind.

There has been a tradition of mothering in the African American community (Lincoln & Mamiya, 1990). The concept of othermothering (Collins, 2000) has gained some attention in the educational community through research about teaching (Beauboeuf-Lafontant, 1999, 2002, 2006). However, this concept has yet to be fully investigated in the context of leadership, with the exception of a few studies (Case, 1997; Irvine, 1999; Loder, 2005). Avery's story gives an excellent example.

The New Normal: Avery in Womanist Theology

The title of this section represents an idea taken directly from Avery's narrative. Several times during her narrative, Avery used the word *normal*. In describing how religio-spirituality informs her life and her work, she said:

> You get the normal drama in schools. As a principal, I break the rules here. Some may not call that normal. What is normal when there is nothing normal about the situation my kids live in? I have always kind of said you just can't do normal at a school like this because there is nothing normal about it for real. I had to practice what I preach because it's not normal for a principal to take a child home and to church and all of that but this isn't normal.

By her own account, Avery indicated that she did not have a normal life. Her own story concerning her emotional abuse and her mother's murder created what Avery described as an abnormal childhood. She identified with her students' abnormal childhoods, but indicated that the abnormalities are becoming too often the norm in certain communities and neighborhoods. Avery's goal is to create a "new normal" for her students, one that includes rising above the status quo of schooling and into one that is socially just for her students. The way that Avery works to ensure social justice for her students is through "mothering" activities.

The notion of mothering in the historical Black community has long transcended the boundaries of the biological, nuclear family. Fictive kinship (Stack, 1974) relationships have long been a part of the African American community. In many African American communities, having just the biological mother was not possible (Collins, 2000). "As a result, othermothers—women who assist bloodmothers by sharing mothering responsibilities—traditionally have been central to the institution of Black motherhood" (Collins, 2000). Communities were considered partners in the rearing of and caring for children and the concept of othermothering came to signify the community's responsibility. These kinship roles have emerged in other institutions such as school and church. The concept of mothering has been seen in churches and has been recognized by womanists as a vital part of the work of social justice (Mitchem, 2002; Riggs, 1994; Townes, 1993b). In her book *If It Wasn't for the Women*, Gilkes (2001) discusses the historical role that Black women have played in their churches and community. Work within the National Baptist Convention often centered on poor women and children and included "mothering" activities such as providing food and clothing, child care, and housing (Harley, 1982; Perkins, 1989). This work became foundational to the development of the nineteenth- and twentieth-century Women's Club Movement (Mitchem, 2002). These activities included biblical instruction, support and promotion of education, and individual and community needs fulfillment. Much like Avery's activities in school, these activities found their expression in places beyond the church and into daily society.

Avery's frequent stories highlight some of the activities she engages in as principal. However, Avery's stories communicate more about her belief concerning her roles as a religio-spiritual individual and as a principal and how these roles are related. From Avery's story, we see a blurring of the role of mothering in the home, the school, and the church. She sees it as her duty to take care of children no matter the setting. The womanist theological ideal mirrors the African proverb that states, "I am because we are." Avery discussed how one "should treat other kids as they would their own," and in her role as principal, the care for her own daughter overlaps with that of other students. She sees it as her Christian duty to do so. Although she indicated that she can not reach every child or every family, her ministerial mandate makes her acutely aware of the communality of the mothering process. "Work on African American principals suggests that motherhood and its associated values of nurturing, caretaking, and helping develop children are salient to how they understand and interpret their roles" (Loder, 2005, p. 304). For Avery, her mothering as a religio-spiritual act sheds light on the link between her religio-spiritual convictions and the leadership activities she employs as a principal.

African American women "construct religious identities from many sources such as grassroots organizations, familial values, mothering/nurturing, and community activism" (Mitchem, 2002, p. 54). The church is not only a place in which Avery helps others "find themselves," but where she found herself as well. The lack of religio-spiritual structure and self-definition that she experienced as a child was found in her involvement with church. When trying to determine how she conceptualized spirituality, Avery indicated that the church plays an important role in how she defines herself spiritually. She indicated that she became more focused spiritually and church provided a home for her. Through her own nurturing or mothering experiences in church, she began to involve herself in mothering others in the church through ministries and working with the youth. She found a way to name herself religio-spiritually through accompanying enactments in the church and the school. The radically subjective nature of Avery's principalship reveals her way of breaking down traditional meanings of leading in schools as managerial or dispassionate pursuits of policy. Her story displays a radical subjectivity not only in how she interprets policy, but also in some cases how she disregards policy in her actions. Avery has a preoccupation with addressing the perceived emotional, social, and spiritual needs of students, rather than simply academics.

The womanist agenda has always had an "embrace of the maternal" (Beauboeuf-Lafontant, 2002, p. 72). Avery's approach to leadership highlights historical understandings of the Black Church's relationship to other institutions and the community. Many of the ministries in Avery's church often center on providing economic, emotional, and spiritual assistance to communities, families, and individuals. Because of Avery's transcendence of religio-spirituality beyond the church walls, for her it is normal for these forms of mothering to extend to other sites such as schools and the larger community. Churchwomen are extremely active in "practicing their religious lives, yet at the same time…expand their concern for their moral development to their families, and ultimately take their concerns to the larger society through moral reform activities" (Townes, 1993b, pp. 81–82). Avery's overtly religio-spiritual enactments reflect a historical posture of the Black Church: education as mission and ministry. "If any one ministry could be identified as central…it would be education…. Black people defined education as a central task of the Christian mission" (Dodson & Gilkes, 1986, p. 84). For Avery and the Black Church, "educating children was part of their moral and social obligations" (Harley, 1982, p. 257).

Meditations

I am still stunned that Avery chose to share one of her most personal stories with me. After her admission that she had never shared the story of her abuse and her mother's murder with anyone, I wondered what was it about me or the research process that was liberating. Then I began to think about the notion of healing and catharsis. Is emancipation always linked to saying things out loud? Avery's seeming silence on the matter had actually found voice in her religio-spiritual acts. "Extended families, churches, and African American community organizations are important locations" (Collins, 2000, p. 101) where resistance can occur. Although these spaces can be perpetuators of oppressive practice, Avery experienced voice and found a way to express her religio-spirituality in a way that she believed was uplifting to the school and community in which she served.

"African Americans...have survived because of several central attributes: strong kinship bonds, strong achievement orientation, adaptability of family roles, strong religious orientation, and strong work orientation" (Hill, 2003, p. 170). Avery's narrative made visible these ideas. Womanist theology views as serious the rearticulation of "normal" androcentric, managerial notions of educational leadership. Mothering in religio-spirituality and educational leadership becomes an active framework for rearticulating constructions of leadership and the principalship.

TONI
MOURNING STORY

God don't like ugly. . . .You reap what you sow.
(Brown, 2000, p. 10)[5]

In her article, "Cultural Narratives Passed On", Holloway (1997) explored rituals of death in the African American community. This book also explored the intersectionality of race, class, and gender in the deaths and mourning of African Americans. Holloway said, "These are the stories of loss" (p. 654). As a modern-day mourning story, Toni's story centers on the painful event of the murder of her mother, and the impact of that event on her entire life and work. Theresa L. F. Brown (2000) in her book *God Don't Like Ugly* analyzes the ways that women's spiritual values are passed on by examining her own life and women's novels, poems, gospel music, and autobiographies. Brown discusses how life phrases often created meaning for an individual or family and served to frame their spirituality. The murder of Toni's mother and a subsequent life phrase defined her religio-spirituality. Toni's spiritual narrative was written as a poem with lines, words, and phrases taken from her narrative. These lines and phrases also serve as headings in this section. Toni's narrative is confessional in nature. The poem serves as a way of making the nar-

---

[5] T. L. F. Brown (2000). *God Don't Like Ugly*. Nashville, TN: Abingdon Press.

rative more accessible by capturing the dramatic nature of some of the feelings in her mourning story (Ely, Vinz, Downing, & Anzul, 1997).

> I Wear This Kind of Mask
>
> Violence, Tragedy
> Just trying to cover and shield myself
> Good girl, People pleaser, Bookworm, Wife, Mother
> Church
> Just trying to cover and shield myself
> Daily Bread
> Do the right thing,
> Cause I surely know,
> That if you ain't right,
> You reap what you sow.
> It's hard, it's hard, but what would He do?
> Impact lives, make a difference.
> Gotta do the right thing,
> Being in charge is hard.
> But I've said it before,
> That if you don't do the right thing,
> You reap what you sow.
> Trust me.
> I know.

Toni and I met during our time as doctoral students. She was always very quiet and somewhat reserved. I remember always thinking, "There is more there than meets the eye." Besides discussing our doctoral experiences, we talked about the principalship. Toni had become a principal almost two years after I left my principal position. We would often talk about our experiences as a new principal, but also those of being young, Black, female principals. We also discussed the similarities in our schools, which were both large magnet schools, and the challenges and rewards of being principals there. Soon these conversations turned toward faith as Toni often discussed the importance of her beliefs in managing her school. The initial interview took place during the summer months of the school year off-site.

Toni is thirty-eight years old and is in her eighteenth year in education. Prior to becoming a principal, she was an assistant principal, reading specialist, and elementary teacher. Her school is a science and foreign language magnet and serves students in kindergarten through eighth grade. Toni's school boasts some of the highest scores in the district according to state standardized test scores and rankings. According to Toni, her school serves students of "middle-class, educated families." The school population is almost equal in numbers of white students and students of color. Approximately 49 percent of Toni's students qualify for free or reduced lunch.

Violence, Tragedy

The two words above give a direct glimpse into Toni's personal life growing up and one that has continued to affect her as an adult. In the first few minutes of our conversation she broke into tears. I sat stunned thinking, "What is going on here? What are the odds?" As a researcher, there was something happening that I did not seem to be able to explain. For the second time that summer, another woman revealed to me that her father murdered her mother. Here I was with Toni, handing her a tissue as she cried and listening to a horrifying tale. Toni and another participant, Avery, knew each other, worked in the same district, and were both completing doctorate degrees together. During their seven-year friendship they had not shared their stories with each other or anyone else. Yet I was sitting there listening to another tale of domestic violence and murder.

> At the age of five my life changed. I remember my parents fighting all the time. "I'll just go ahead and say it: my father killed my mom in domestic violence. My mama had finally left him. She had actually moved back to her hometown and we lived in the projects for low income. He got so upset that she was leaving him that you know he couldn't take it. She came back to our old house to get her things. Why do women do that? That's why I say, material things, they don't matter, just leave them. So she came back with her niece and nephew and the truck to get her things. When she got there he told her, "You're not leaving me and you're not taking anything from me." And then BANG! He shot her. I wasn't home when my father killed my

mother. I was at my grandparents' home. He shot her six times. Had I witnessed it how would I be, I've wondered.

Shields

Understanding Toni's story becomes apparent when hearing how she described herself. In addition to describing herself as hiding behind a mask, Toni named all the different ways she defines herself, as she shields her secret and herself. After her mother was murdered, Toni went to live with her grandparents. Toni and her two brothers were split up when they went to live with relatives. One brother lived with Toni with her grandparents, and the other brother went to live with an aunt in another state. It was during this time that Toni began to enact certain roles that she still believes she retains today. Toni indicated that the family never really discussed what happened but that Toni did receive some therapy.

> One of my brothers did not have the same dad, so he went to live with my mom's sister out of state. My other brother and I ended up with my dad's parents, which is kind of crazy. Their son did this and then they got to raise me. But they were wonderful and things happened for a reason. And so, from age five until eighteen, I was raised by my father's parents.
>
> They did the best that they could with what they had. They were illiterate I guess you could say, because you know I'm not sure what grade they got to or even if they went to school because they were working on the farm in cotton and in all of that. My aunts and uncles were the ones who gave us a lot of support. My grandparents had to be in their fifties I guess when this happened; they took on their grandkids at fifty.
>
> My grandparents knew I was very sensitive to the topic of them talking about it so we never talked about it because they knew that would just upset me. They felt bad; they felt horrible that their son had done this. And of course his siblings, my uncles and aunts, you know, they felt bad. It was a touchy subject and we never really talked about it. I went to counseling, not very many sessions, but we went to counseling.

Although her grandparents were not educated, they stressed education for Toni. By Toni's account, education and books were a way to escape the pain of what had happened within her family. Even though these days were spent, by Toni's own admission, "wearing a mask" and feeling embarrassed, they serve as significant markers of future endeavors, as she discussed what motivated her into her current profession. Toni did not initially want to be an educator, but as a result of her ordeal, she always knew she "wanted to help people." Because of her family and her husband's family, and the importance they placed on education, Toni entered the education field.

> All during my childhood, even though they were not educated, they stressed education. I always had my face in a book, partly to escape. I was a big bookworm. I was always real obedient. When I look at my life now, as an adult, I still want to please everybody and don't want to make anyone upset, a lot of it stems from my childhood. I always studied hard and I got good grades. I was the only one who went to college. I couldn't wait to escape. But even with that I met my husband and eventually he saw something in me and encouraged me to go into teaching. He told me that I would be a good teacher. Maybe it is because I was a good student or maybe he knew that I could understand things my students may go through. I just remember being so embarrassed. I think I still am.

Reaping

There is a passage in the Bible in Galatians 6:7 (NLT) that reads, "Do not be deceived. God cannot be mocked. A man reaps what he sows." Reaping and sowing typically refer to harvesting and planting. However, in this passage, they refer to the concept of sowing the things of God and the fruits of the Spirit (love, joy, peace, patience, kindness, generosity, faithfulness, gentleness, and self-control) and that the results will be good. Moreover, if we sow sinful things, we will "reap destruction" (Galatians 6:8, NLT). When telling her story, Toni repeated this phrase more than once. The first time she used it was to describe the events surrounding the consequences that her father faced as a result of killing her mother.

> When my father killed my mother, of course he was incarcerated for maybe 2 years total. They considered it a crime of passion because he had no record.

Toni's father did not face a long prison sentence, but Toni believes that he "reaped" an unforeseen consequence for his deed. She believes that he and other people who do what Toni called "bad things" will be punished by God for those deeds. In the Black

Church, family, and community, individuals understand that God loves, "but will penalize…for behavior that is offensive, oppressive, deceitful, or injurious to others" (Brown, 2000, p. 89).

> My father remarried when he got out of jail. He had another family and I was thinking, "Nothing has happened to him and my momma's gone. I don't have this normal childhood, you know mother and daughter. But I said, "He's going to get his in due time, God is going to take care of him, just leave it alone." When he got out of prison, since he had a felony, he couldn't find a job so he worked for this logging company and made good money. Anyway, he had an accident where he was cutting a tree and it fell on him and it paralyzed him and so he was paralyzed. For eight years he lay there. I always wondered when he was going to come over to see us. I knew he had made good money with that logging company and I wondered if he would even give us some money. My grandparents didn't get very much money and I always wondered, "When is he going to get his? It's not fair." But, I always thought eventually he will get his, when you do something wrong eventually it comes around. It may not be when you want it and you may not even see it, but it does happen. That's one thing I've noticed. There have been times that I'll hear something about somebody who's done something. Just because your life had moved on, you just never know how they will get theirs—how they will end up being punished by God for what they have done.

While Toni believes that her father's accident, paralysis, and subsequent death were his "payback" for her mother's murder, she discussed that she and her family had to "reap for what her father had sown." The incident seemed to reap more tragedy in the lives of Toni and her siblings. They each dealt with addictions and strained relationships.

> I guess we have some addictions or things that we try to compensate. I eat, I guess a lot of times. One of my brothers did drugs. He drank and he did drugs. As a baby he had a heart murmur and so with the drugs over the years it enlarged his heart and had these effects. He was on all this medication but he eventually had a heart attack at thirty-three years old. That hurts me, because I'm like an only child now. My older brother was never around since he did not live with us after momma died. He really needs counseling. I tell my aunt who lives near him, my mom's sister, that he needs to go to counseling. He doesn't talk about anything. He is in the navy and is about to retire and he didn't even send me an invitation to his graduation. I used to think he just did that to me, but it's not only me. It's because

we didn't grow up in the same house and he really needs counseling. I mean, I can kind of mask mine as best I can, but he is very moody and mean to his step-kids and stuff.

Toni indicated that she shared her story with me because of a particular difficulty concerning her daughter. As a result of her upbringing by her grandparents and her own difficulty of coming to terms with her mother's death, Toni's relationship with one of her daughters is strained. Toni believes that her grandparents, her husband, and even the murder of her mother play a large role in Toni's religio-spirituality. Conversely, Toni also believes her mother's murder and her grandparents' influence created her emotional detachment.

> I have two children, a sixteen-year-old and an eight-year-old. My sixteen-year-old was talking to me the other night. Oh no, I am going to get emotional again. And I guess this is why I am even talking about my mom right now because this has been on my mind. My daughter and I are always clashing. I was afraid to tell her about momma and I didn't tell her. I think some cousins may have told her because a couple of months ago I had a conversation with her and tried to explain what happened and maybe this was the reason I acted…Well she doesn't think I am as close or as nurturing to her. She wrote me this long e-mail the other night and she said, "Mom, that should be even more reason because you didn't have your mother that you should be close to me." I don't know what it is, I don't know. My grandparents were not very loving and compassionate and they were just more functional and I'm wondering if that's why I am the way I am. Like you [referring to the researcher] seem so warm, so calm, and so godly. That is the reason I am doing this. There are not very many people that I would have thought to do this. I've always been in church; I mean we lived in church. We had to stay through Sunday School, regular service and be back for 5:00 and 6:00 services. I often wonder, I mean I often think had I been reared by my parents instead of my grandparents, would I have been in the church and I don't think so. Because I was reared by my grandparents and my husband had been reared by his grandparents, maybe that's why we've been married so long because we are from the same kind of values or whatever. Anyway, I don't know, I think it's because of my grandparents and I stayed in the church. I mean if you were going to go Monday through Friday to school then you were gonna get up every Sunday and you were going to church. We stayed in church.

Daily Bread

Although Toni discussed specifically the role of the church in her spirituality, she discussed the Bible as what she believes is the foundation for her religio-spirituality. At one point during our discussion, she pointed out that she "thought I might ask her some Bible verses." I told her that this was her story and she could tell it any way she wanted. She talked about studying the Word, but that she also reads a monthly devotional called *Daily Bread*. This devotional has a Bible passage focus for each day of the month with a story illustration or commentary accompanying it. Toni discussed that she has often consulted that devotional in her personal life, but also at work, to make decisions. For Toni, obeying God and the Bible means aligning her life with the Word. Even if she did not tell others that she was a Christian, she believes that how she lives will demonstrate her faith.

> I subscribe to that *Daily Bread* and so every day I'll read the short passage there and sometimes I just go in my office just to get away, to read something. I have always believed you have to feed your soul—get some Bread, so to speak. You have read God's Word. But I try to walk the talk; I really do, even though I haven't been in church for several Sundays. If you saw me, I think people would know I am a Christian; I tell people I'm a Christian.

As Toni's narrative points out, her family and her involvement with the church seem to be how Toni gained and now defines her ideas about spirituality. Although she did not define being a Christian as "going to church," she did place high importance on church attendance. Toni indicated feeling not as connected to her current church because of lack of attendance and involvement but also because of the size of the congregation.

> I was a member of our youth organization growing up. I was an usher, I was in the choir, everything. I mean when the doors swung open I was there, we had to be there. We couldn't just lay out and not go to church. I feel bad because a lot of times as an adult, it seems like it's harder to make myself go, I haven't been, I'll be honest, I probably haven't been to church probably in about two months. It is huge too. I was raised in a much smaller church. I just get consumed with so many things. I feel so bad because I was not raised like that. Even though I'm still a Christian and I'm spiritual, I still feel bad. Some people feel like you have to be in church or

then again, maybe I've been trying to justify it and say, "Of course you don't have to be in church."

Regarding school, Toni specifically discussed the legal issues of church and state. However, when there is a personal relationship with the students, Toni revealed that she discusses God with those students. In spite of her efforts to refrain from talking to "everybody," Toni did say that her religio-spirituality is something that is a deep part of who she perceives herself to be, and to do opposite of that is often difficult. Even though it is a subversive reality of her principalship, she believes her religio-spirituality compels her to do so.

> For my part, I know we are supposed to have this separation of church and state. Many times when I am talking with a student or having a conversation with a student, especially if it is about discipline, I ask them, especially if they go to Union Chapel as a lot of them do, "Now what do you think Pastor would think about this?" I do. And sometimes I have to catch myself and think, "Oh my gosh, I hope they don't go and tell anybody." Because it has been instilled in me, I mean, Christianity, spirituality, it's always been religion and it's been instilled in me and I can't do anything other than when I have an opportunity.

In going further in the conversation and discussing her religio-spirituality and school, Toni specifically talked about how her devotion to students at school overrides her ability work with students at church. She told me that even though she desires to "do right by" her students, that it is difficult. Toni believes, as she does with other areas of her life, that her personal well-being and blessing from God are directly connected to how she treats her students.

> I don't want to have anything to do with the youth at church, because I work with kids all the time. I feel horrible. I got asked about Vacation Bible School and I said no, not me. You think they would act better in church and they don't. I just don't have the energy to do it here and there too. Every morning, I say a prayer. I do try to always treat them, and everybody really, the way I want to be treated because I really believe you reap what you sow. So everything with school, with my job as an administrator, I try to do the right thing. Even though sometimes I get upset and part of me says, "I'm just going to be mean," I still try to stay focused and grounded. God can't bless me if I am mean.

What does it mean for Toni to do the right thing in school with her students? Even though she expressed that it was hard, what does the difficulty entail? Toni discussed her school situation and specifically talked about her religio-spirituality as a source of support while managing what she thinks are unfair school practices. Two of these problematic areas for Toni are the district support of magnet schools and discipline policy. According to Toni, the principalship enables her to have more impact in the lives of students. In comparison to the other participants' schools, over 55 percent of Toni's students are middle class and the families are well educated. The school has about 60 percent students of color. Toni's school is a magnet school and according to her, she is supposed to recruit students from an affluent area of her city to attract "more white students." Toni's religio-spirituality somehow gives her the strength to handle issues concerning the magnet school. Some schools in Toni's district are considered difficult because of low achievement or high "at-risk" students. Toni believes her higher-achieving school with more affluent families has its own set of difficulties.

> I am supposed to attract those kids, white and others, but most of those kids, the white kids, are choosing to stay in their neighborhood schools because they are nice facilities, high test scores already, good programs and so, its like you are trying to turn cartwheels trying to get them to come. And it's hard. I mean if I wasn't praying I couldn't do it. I don't feel like I have a lot of control over those things but I do feel like I have some control over the opportunity to have an impact on more kids.

Toni believes that the way she handles herself in school situations is one of the ways that individuals could identify her as a Christian. In particular, Toni discussed the discipline policies. Toni indicated that her practices are not the norm when compared to normal practice toward student discipline. Toni believes that any time her behavior in school deviates from the status quo, this is evidence to others of her faith.

> I guess I always err on the side of the child. I mean I am always with the kids. People say I'm a little too easy, and I don't know. We are expected to throw the book at them. Even when I was in another district, I never wanted to throw the book at kids. I think a lot of times kids make mistakes. For instance, the district is supposed to have automatic expulsion for certain of-

fenses. My goal is never to put kids out of school. That isn't the right thing to do. I think when you do the opposite of what is expected, people can tell.

In keeping with her understanding of the Bible and other religio-spiritual anecdotes, Toni summed up her religio-spiritual life in this way:

> I've got to be about the kids, I've got to be, you know, and that may or may not be different from somebody who doesn't consider themselves spiritual. You know a couple of years ago when the phrase "What would Jesus do?" was going around? I bought one of those bracelets with WWJD on it. That's in every decision I make, I try to make the best decisions and make sure, you know, that I'm doing the right thing. I am always thinking about what Jesus would do and that is what I try to do.

Suffering Servant

Tseng and Hsu (1991) discuss rituals of family importance and their relationship to values and beliefs. These values and beliefs are often transferred through family rituals that remain with individuals long after they have left and have transitioned from that unit. In the case of Toni, her grandparents had a large influence in shaping her religio-spirituality. Familial influence as articulated by Evans (1996) says that "ways of thinking, feeling, and behaving shape one's approach to problems and one's perspective on the world and begins early in childhood in the framework of the family and are firmly established long before one becomes an administrator (p. 197). Toni's family placed a primacy on rituals such as church involvement being religio-spirituality and this notion was retained well into Toni's adulthood.

While family is significant to Toni's spirituality, the idea of personal struggle is as equally important. Womanist theologians Jacquelyn Grant (1989) and Dolores Williams (2001) discuss the idea of suffering and wilderness experiences as a part of the African American experience and the response of religio-spirituality to this process. In *White Women's Christ, Black Women's Jesus*, Grant (1989) discusses the idea of sadness and sorrow in Black women's lives. Sadness and shame are often real responses to lives of raced and gendered realities of suffering and wilderness such as "the imprisonment of Black women in poverty, low wages, and domestic violence…and continued social invisibility." Shange (1977) has said, "Sadness and sorrow (the pains and the sufferings) are perpetually a part of the African American woman's reality" (p. 43). These experiences are not only situations borne historically from being Black, but also other intersecting realities. In other words, these wilderness experiences are not only "raced," but gendered and classed as well.

Yoder's (1998) work on spirituality discusses the impact of familial difficulties and painful personal circumstances in cultivating religious belief and spirituality. The murder of Toni's mother set the tone for receiving and perceiving religio-spirituality in Toni's life. Her mother's murder was a catalyst that caused Toni to create a spiritual worldview, yet the murder also currently influences how Toni grapples with issues of faith. African Americans take biblical parables and metaphors and often apply them to their lives (Cannon, 1988; Hopkins, 2005; Williams, 2001). This is seen in how Toni appropriated the concept of reaping and sowing to her life and her work as a principal. Faith in God serves as a coping mechanism for her, and also as an imperative for how she lives her life and conducts herself at school.

"Suffering is any mental or emotional, spiritual or physical force that disrupts lives" (Mitchem, 2002, p. 108). Womanist theology, by beginning with Black women's suffering, reconfigures doctrinal themes related to salvation, including sin, community, and responsibility (Mitchem, 2002, p. 109). When African American women have reexamined their lives following pain, a response has often been greater dedication to the life of the community, to networking, to working for others. Toni's story becomes a paradox in how she lives out the notions of community, religio-spirituality, and social justice as a principal. Religio-spirituality in the other narratives represented in this research seems to promote a greater sense of accountability to the community and the students whom the principals serve.

In much of the womanist literature, there is often the valiant narrative that emerges from suffering. The response to oppression is often seen in a somehow renewed commitment to communal concerns and the serving of others. In research concerning Black women in educational leadership, the response to injustice in schools is often a renewed commitment to justice and community enactments such as servant leadership and othermothering (Alston & Jones, 2002; Benham, 2005; Case, 1997; Loder, 2005; Lomotey, 1989). In Toni's case, these concepts are particularly burdensome to her and ones that caused her to admit that she "did not want to be in this position for very long" or have another principalship. She went on to discuss another principal who had left the principalship after three years and Toni indicated that she understands the inclination to do that.

Womanist theology always seeks to make what I call "communal connections." While there is a strong position for individual self-love, there is an undergirding of community that assumes a "natural" propensity toward "group good" (Floyd-Thomas, 2006a). Every study I reviewed in the literature and womanist theological works has the predominance of communality. Toni stands in some contrast to the other participants in this research and to other literature in this area. Rather than affirm a taken-for-granted communal connection, Toni's story highlights a burden of communalism and uplift. Toni indicated being a Black woman and a Christian somehow requires her to "do the right thing." She feels a responsibility toward all of her students, but a particular expectation for the students of color.

> I feel sometimes that I should be doing more, especially for the Black kids. But I just can't. I feel sorry for some of these kids and really want to help them, but I am burned out. I guess I feel like God understands.

This role expectation is difficult for Toni. She discussed how hard it is for her to actually to meet the obligations that she believes her religio-spirituality requires of her in schools and even sometimes in her personal life. Toni's religio-spiritual requirement to be conscious of what she "sows and reaps" is more of a personal requisite rather than a communal commitment. There is no mistaking the toll that a thirty-year-old event has had on the lives of Toni and her family. By Toni's admission, she needs therapy. This lack of healing from her mother's death coupled with her religio-spiritual sense of duty creates a gap among the management of her own life and her duty and regard for others. Although Toni declared all the "good" things about her life, she indicated the hardship of being a principal and engaging in how she wants in the rest of her life to proceed as well.

> I have had a lot of good things in my life. I graduated from college. I've done everything I want to do. I'm finishing my doctorate, sure. I've always,

always enjoyed education and learning and I always thirst for knowledge. But I had a tragic childhood. Sometimes I think I should join maybe, a domestic violence support group or whatever because I'm thirty-eight years old and people think, "She's fine. Look what she is doing and what she has achieved." But it's hard, it's still hard. Being a principal is hard and apparently being everything else is hard too. I guess I am not fine.

Womanism does privilege the tenet of self-love. A part of this self-love is an exposure of violence of any kind and finding healing. Responses to pain and suffering highlight women's agency, their ability to create their own good (Mitchem, 2002). However, the idea of this good cannot only be couched in the womanist understanding of community, service, and the concerns of others. Toni's story highlights that this understanding of agency may stand in direct opposition to the care of others and the "communal responsibilities of faith" (Mitchem, 2002, p. 109). Toni's story reminded me of a passage I read by bell hooks (2005). She writes:

> Many Black women are brokenhearted. They walk around in daily life carrying around so much hurt, feeling wasted, yet pretending in every area of their life that everything is under control. It hurts to pretend. It hurts to live with lies. The time has come to attend to that hurt. (p. 19)

When one attends to the hurt, she truly engages in agency and self-love.

Meditations

Toni left me truly wondering what to do as a researcher. While talking with Toni, her pain was almost palpable and left me thinking about this other layer of the research process. All at once, I felt like a counselor and felt a need to do something. At some point I decided that being committed to my particular standpoint as a researcher or our relationship did not force me to be objective. However, I decided that sometimes the researcher must just be present. Many of my research questions seemed unimportant and a review of transcripts found me absent in many places. Her story felt confessional in nature, and it was important just to hear it.

Toni's story also made me think more deeply about the concept of agency. A part of the process of naming and agency means that I choose for myself who I want to be and what I want to do. Yet it seemed that these womanist theological tenets always led back to community or at least it was advocated as if they should. Toni's own struggles seem to block her ability to communally engage in the work of religio-spirituality. At one point while listening to her story, I wrote a note: "Would it be wrong religio-spiritually for Toni simply to heal and not try and save the world and simply to save herself?" This seemed to be a tension for Toni as well as she struggled in the long journey after her mother's murder. Toni's story left me with one overall thought and one I will continue to ponder: To share communal experience with others does not ensure the enactment of it.

PATTIE
PSALM

What shall we leave behind for the next generation?
(Woodard, 1997, p. 100)[6]

Pattie's narrative is centered on Psalms. Pattie identified Psalms as her favorite book of the Bible, and often referred to Bible verses in her narrative as a way of expressing herself. Pattie's husband is an associate pastor at a Baptist church. While not involved in preaching herself, Pattie is heavily involved in ministry at her church and serves on several church boards. Sentences from Pattie's interviews form the lines of the poem here, and contain her favorite Bible verse at the end. Contemporary theologian Marsha Woodard served as an inspiration for this narrative. Woodard's sermons were psalmic in nature and contained frequent Bible verses or personal poetry as stand-ins or parables for essential ideas she wanted to discuss.

> No matter what happens to me,
> What can man do to me?
> It is well as far as I can see.
> Ain't nothing wrong with me.
> Honey, it is well with my soul.

---

[6]M. Woodward. (1997). "No Greater Legacy." In M. Y. Riggs (Ed.), *Can I Get a Witness? Prophetic Religious Voice of African American Women: An Anthology.* Maryknoll, NY: Orbis Books.

> My slanderers hound me constantly, and many are boldly attacking me. But when I am afraid, I put my trust in You. O God, I praise Your word. I trust in God, so why should I be afraid? What can mere mortals do to me? They are always twisting what I say; they spend their days plotting ways to harm me. They come together to spy on me—watching my every step, eager to kill me. Don't let them get away with their wickedness. You keep track of my sorrows. On the very day I call to You for help, my enemies will retreat. (Psalm 56:2–9, NLT)

Pattie and I have been friends for five years. Of the four participants, I maintain the closest relationship with Pattie. Data from Pattie consist of interview transcripts and notes from frequent conversations between the two of us. It was often difficult because of our close relationship to get much information from her. It was expected that I knew her mind on many things. I found myself having to stick to the interview script much more rigidly than I did with the other participants to get the information I needed.

Interview data with Pattie took a total of four hours. However, this does not include all of the informal and anecdotal information I gathered and recorded in notebooks after one of our many professional and personal discussions. Formal interviews took place at her home. Other discussions and follow-up interviews took place on the phone or via e-mail. Pattie's primary school is attended by students in pre-kindergarten to second grade and by all students of color. This school was in another year of successive identification by the state's Department of Education as "low-performing." This school is located in an area of town characterized by low human and fiscal capital, few capital improvements, and a majority of students who qualify for free and reduced lunch. The school has also been designated as a Title I school. The school currently receives funding from Reading First as allocated by the U.S. Department of Education for low-performing schools to improve reading instruction and achievement.

Pattie's district is undergoing what she would term re-segregation practices. Students are assigned to schools by zones of the city. It was viewed that certain students were assigned to Pattie's school based upon the neighborhoods in which they live. Some of these neighborhoods are characterized as high-poverty and have large numbers of people of color. Pattie's school has also been subject to high teacher turnover rates. In fact, during the time of our interviews, Pattie was trying to staff several teaching positions that were yet to be filled after months of searching.

"Don't Mess with God's Children"

The Black experience was foundational to Pattie's story. During the initial visit to Pattie's home, I saw a book on her fireplace mantel. The book was about Blacks in the Bible. Upon closer examination of her den, I noticed several books about African American history and theology. Pattie reminded me that her husband is a pastor and also a history teacher. When I pointed out and asked about the books, Pattie discussed them with me.

> We have a lot of books about our Black folks. Got to learn about my people. It is important for me to teach my boys about their heritage and their spiritual heritage. You know my husband is always reading something about history. But I also think that helps him as a pastor too. He can speak to folk about what something means to us. I like to know about my history also. Some folks act like they don't wanna talk about slavery or things like that, but it is a part of Black folk experience. No need to be scared of it.

For Pattie, there is a strong link between the African American experience and religio-spirituality. This is rooted in a certain aspect of her church experience. However, this church life is rooted in her experience with her family and the community. For instance, Pattie was not present during slavery or the civil rights movement; however, ideas about historical episodes such as these were passed down through her family, church, school, and community. Smith (1982) proposes that often values are passed down to children in the form of 1) action or obligation—what morally ought to be done; 2) character and virtue—commendable or reprehensible personal qualities; and 3) goals and ends—what makes life good or bad (pp. 60–61). "Often the Black church, Black family, and Black community exist in a mutually supportive relationship" (Brown, 2000, p. 46) and transmit these values. Pattie grew up in a city that was home to some of the major civil rights incidents in history, and these events strongly impacted what her family, her school, her church, and her community emphasized while she was growing up. Black Christians often share a "preoccupation with...how to account for the justice of God in light of the persistence of suffering and inequalities" (Brown, 2000, p. 46).

> You know where I grew up. Martin Luther King marched up and down my streets. My family often talked about the bombings, and marches and rallies and stuff, all the violence. This is what I grew up hearing about. When we went to church, we talked about this stuff. Our community was really close too. So we were always discussing these things with my mama and daddy's friends and other people in the community. I guess I learned at a real early age the things that were not right. My family didn't shield us from stuff like slavery. We talked about it. So I am really being interested in Black history and learning about my heritage.

Pattie associated many of her beliefs about God and her religio-spirituality with justice and freedom from oppression. Her story often highlights religio-spirituality not only as a coping mechanism, but also as a motivation to contest certain conditions. Pattie believes God is in close relationship to people and the circumstances of discrimination and oppression.

> Ya know, I see stuff every day. Somebody don't like somebody because they're poor, or another color, or whatever. And God don't like none of this stuff. He ain't happy with this junk—how badly we treat one another. And that's what I keep telling people, "Folks better stop messin' with God's children. Don't mess with God's children." And people don't get it. How you gonna mess with what you didn't make? God made people and I think when we mess around with them, we mess around with Him. And you are messin' up real bad if they are Christians! But that's just the thing. We shouldn't be judging people anyway, but we don't know who we are judging when we are doing things to people. That's why it is important to do right by everybody, but also to do something about bad stuff when we see it. I don't stand by when someone is doing something wrong to another person. I say something. To serve God is to take care of other people.

When asked to elaborate on what she meant by "doing right by everybody" or "doing something about bad stuff," Pattie turned her attention to her work at school.

> I mean, I don't stand by and watch things happen that are wrong. Since we are talking about school, I guess I will talk about that. Every year, my school ends up on some list in need of improvement. I mean that not all about my

kids being incompetent. But I do agree that for too long my kids have not gotten the teaching that they deserve.

Pattie has a strong commitment to student achievement in her school and sees this as one of the ways she can achieve justice for her students. Pattie indicated that she believes "the deck is stacked against" her students in terms of student achievement. However, rather than seeing her students' families' social and economic deficiencies as a cause of low achievement, Pattie viewed them as an outcome of what she sees as racist practices.

> A lot of what my students have to go through is about race. I am not saying they don't have family problems; that's true. But when you look at it, a lot of it comes down to race. Racism is what keeps neighborhoods the way they are. My kids come from some of the poorest neighborhoods with little business. Then they come to school, and there is racism here. Some of my teachers, I know they don't like my little Black kids. The school board doesn't care about them. They would much rather give the white schools all the attention in the world rather than my kids. So it is hard. It is hard as a principal to deal with some of this stuff.

One way that Pattie counters racist practices is through her religio-spirituality. Dealing with racism has been a historical focus of the Black Church experience (Lincoln & Mamiya, 1990). Pattie told me that her church has often had a focus on dealing with racism and coping with and eradicating racist practices. Patti talked about the social, material, political inequities in a way that the other participants did not. She and her husband are well read in African American history, culture, and theology. Pattie told me that her husband often has outspoken views on the treatment of Blacks in history and in contemporary society. However, these kinds of discussions also find their way into the church and into their home.

For Pattie and her husband, church and their religio-spirituality provide ways to recognize and contest racist practices. Pattie emphasized her belief in a theology that highlights God's relationship to Blacks and His rejection and a reckoning of oppression.

> My husband and I always talk about how racist stuff is. Racism is not of God. But I think it is also important for our folk to know that they don't exist just so they can be mistreated, ya know? They have more value than that.

> We weren't made to be slaves and we weren't made for the stuff we go through now. Sometimes I see stuff happening or doing racist stuff and I say to myself, "Just wait. They gonna get theirs." That's why I tell people to just wait.

Her religio-spirituality and her ideas about God often move her to a very pointed fight for social justice for her students. Pattie discussed making sure that social agencies are very involved with her school in assisting with students' material and emotional needs. For instance, Pattie has a "direct hotline" to the city Department of Social Services. She mentioned that she has sought outside help in connecting students with agencies to get resources such as clothes, food, medication, and glasses. However, Patti talked the most about student achievement and particularly in the form of trying to raise test scores. Even though "the test isn't everything," Pattie believes she has had to "play by the rules we have."

> I think that what I am doing in my school is my Christian duty. I would be doing these kids less than a service if I did not do my best to make sure they had the best education possible. Look, I know these tests are biased. And it is a vicious cycle. But I also know that a test score somehow gives you opportunity around here. Shoot, a test score gives a school credibility. I want the scores for my students and my school because, face it, there are benefits. I want them to have benefits. If they go to high school, they will get the best teachers and the best programs if they have the scores. If they have that then they can go to college and have some good lives. The scores don't mean anything to me, but they mean something to me because they mean something to this society. These are the rules we have right now. I play by the rules we have until something better happens.

Even though Pattie acknowledged the importance of standardized tests, she also recognized the restrictive nature of these tests. Pattie has worked to increase what she views as rigor in teaching and to improve teacher practice through professional development. Although working to raise test scores is a huge part of what she does in school, Pattie talked about the ways she tries to achieve this goal. She writes grants for extra materials, but also works really hard to distribute federal monies she receives wisely. She also tries to make sure that she holds special meetings in which she reviews articles and books concerning working with kids of poverty. She makes sure that teachers receive professional development, not only to improve teaching practice but also to develop dispositions that she believes are beneficial for her students.

> I do believe that we have to prepare kids for the test. But I believe good teaching does that, not "prepping." I make sure that my teachers are well aware of the type of teaching that I expect. We don't lower expectations here. I was observing a teacher the other day and she was not teaching during the reading time. She had students working on worksheets. I was so mad. She needed to be teaching! I want them to teach. But I also want them to be aware of these kids' home life. I tell every teacher that I hire that we have poor kids here with a lot of needs. Our students need us to care about them in ways that some schools may not have to. And they need us to make sure we are doing our best teaching for them. My kids do not have one year to have a bad teacher. That is why I stress professional development. If my teachers want to do anything to improve their teaching or their understanding of our kids, I do it 'cause that only benefits the kids.

> My school is a Title I school. So I get money for that. And we get extra money from the state to improve reading and math. People like to act like we are getting so much. But it is a real challenge to allocate that money right. I have to make sure that I am spending it on the things that matter. For instance, I am not gonna spend it on some test-taking preparation program, which I can. But what I may spend it on is getting an extra teacher so classes aren't so crowded. Or I may spend it on an afterschool tutoring program. But you know what I mostly spend it on is my teachers, so they can be better teachers of my babies.

Pattie discussed teacher development as one of the ways to provide opportunity to her students; however, she also believes in providing students with experiences that they would not otherwise receive. These other experiences for students include field trips, school assemblies, and afterschool activities.

> Some of my kids would never get to do some things if they were not through the school. We do a lot of small field trips but we take the older kids to places they have never been. One year we took them to Atlanta. One year we took them to Chattanooga. This year we went to the beach. They were so fascinated with the beach. It was good because I got different groups to fund us so the kids would not have to pay. I also try to make sure that we have programs at school that introduce them to an activity or something that they may not get anywhere else. For instance, we had a magic

group come in. Where else would they see that? I also wrote a grant to provide music lessons for students who want it. Some of my kids are doing violin.

Pattie believes that it is her obligation as a Christian to enact the principalship in the ways that she does. However, Pattie also believes that she has a special responsibility to her students because they are Black.

> God has charged me to do my best wherever I am in whatever I am doing. That is first and foremost. I owe it to these kids to do my best. This may be wrong, but I especially feel like I have to do this because they are Black kids.

Whom Shall I Fear?

Often in the Black family and the Black Church, "core beliefs were located in Scripture, a constant struggle for freedom for all persons…The principles of justice, centrality of the Bible, and social activism are inherent" (Brown, 2000, p. 45). The Bible is often seen as the standard for living and the source of hope. These functions of the Bible are seen in Pattie's life. Black Christians often identify with certain passages and apply them to their lives (Brown, 2000). One of Pattie's favorite Bible passages is taken from Psalms 56:2–9 (NLT):

> My slanderers hound me constantly, and many are boldly attacking me. But when I am afraid, I put my trust in You. O God, I praise Your word. I trust in God, so why should I be afraid? What can mere mortals do to me? They are always twisting what I say; they spend their days plotting ways to harm me. They come together to spy on me—watching my every step, eager to kill me. Don't let them get away with their wickedness. You keep track of my sorrows. On the very day I call to You for help, my enemies will retreat.

When Pattie was growing up, her family often had devotions and memorized and discussed Bible verses. It is no wonder that Pattie discussed the importance of the Word to her life and her work. Her husband and her two sons have maintained this tradition. Although this verse was one that she "meditates upon" to help her understand the plight of the larger Black community, it is also one that Pattie uses to understand life events that happen to her. According to Pattie, she has experienced racism in her current school district. The city in which her school is located has been historically characterized by great racial division. The school district in which she works has had several of its Black administrators file complaints against the school board and district administration. Many times Pattie has felt as though her students have been targets of racism, and that she has been as well. In many conversations, Pattie talked about how her religio-spirituality helps her cope and remain in what she has described as a racially charged city and school district.

> It is hard to come to work every day knowing that I will have to work ten times as hard as everyone else. I sit in meetings with other principals and watch how the white principals are treated differently. They are often praised districtwide for any little thing they do. I know I am doing a good job and taking care of my kids and my school and I know other Black principals who are doing the same thing. Yet, they don't say nothin' about our schools or our kids. I mean, it is always a climate where Black folk in the district are scared that something is going to happen to them. The slightest little mistake and you are gone. But ya know, I go back to the Psalms. People better recognize who my daddy is. God is my daddy and he owns and runs everything. I ain't scared of these folks. I come to work and do my job and trust that God has it all under control. "The earth is the Lord's and the fullness thereof."

Bible reading is a big part of Pattie's religio-spirituality. She discussed her memorization of scripture because she often thinks of Bible passages to apply to her life and situations at work. Pattie keeps her Bible on her desk and also keeps one in her car. She talked about "speaking the Word" in certain situations in her personal and professional life.

> I believe the Word is alive and well and there is power in speaking to a situation with the truth of the Word. My sister has been battling cancer. And we all have just been speaking the Word over her. We pray and recite Bible verses that speak health into her instead of death. I often speak into situations that threaten me. I always say to myself, "Do not be afraid." So when I feel like I am being discriminated against or being plotted against, I remember that. Again, I remember who my daddy is.

"The educative and ego-building role of the Bible is critical" (Brown, 2000, p. 47). Pattie "learned who she is" in the Bible. Because of what the Bible says about her, Pattie has been able to learn to resist labels constructed for her as a person and as a principal. The Bible also affirms the value and worth of others for Pattie and serves as motivation for her behavior in her personal life and in school.

> I learned what the Bible says about me is true, not what the world says about me. I mean I know how some people may see me. I am hard. But I am hard because I want what is best for the students. I make people treat me and them like they should be treated. I am precious to God and so are they. So when people only see them as poor Black kids, I see them as jewels. When people see me as the crazy principal, I know that it is not true. When people look at me and see all the stuff they call Black folk, I know I am more than that. What they say about me is not true of me. That is what determines what I do in my life and at school.

Children of God: Pattie in Womanist Theology

In my discussions with Pattie, she indicated that the church has great influence in her life. Pattie holds several positions in her church: deaconess, children's choir leader, matron, and Sunday School teacher. Historically, these were among the positions in churches in which women could serve. In the Black Church, the period between 1880 and 1920 was seen as the "women's era" (Higginbotham, 2003). During this time, women contested racism, poverty, and illiteracy, often through services to the community through the church. The church also served as a platform for political activism. "Through the efforts of women, the Black church built schools, provided clothes and food to poor people, established old folks homes and orphanages, and made available a host of needed social welfare services" (Higginbotham, 2003, p. 188). Often in the Baptist Church, women were duty-bound to be conveyers not only of culture, but also of religion, education, and hard work to the Black community (Higginbotham, 2003). Indeed many contemporary Baptist churches retain these same ideals as they once did historically.

It is clear that Pattie sees herself as a part of the same historical mission. Black women have historically addressed multiple personal and societal oppressions through versions of spirituality (Dillard, Abdur-Rashid, & Tyson, 2000). For Pattie, addressing these oppressions occurs through her actions in school as defined by her spirituality. Dillard et al. (2000) define the intersection of spirituality and education as "education with a purpose, liberatory work" (p. 1). To understand her liberatory work, it was important to examine how she views God and how she views herself. Pattie understands God as being in particular relationship with people of color. For Pattie, God is particularly committed to justice and love, the poor and oppressed, of which Blacks have all been and still are (Mitchem, 2002).

Pattie constantly referred to herself as a "child of God" and others as "children of God." Familial connections are often seen in religio-spiritual belief systems and in churches. Concepts of church and family are inextricably linked through role definition and function ("God the Creator is the universal parent. The pastor or spouse or older members of the congregation are often called father or mother. Jesus, God's Son, is called the elder brother. The congregation members are often called brothers and sisters" (Brown, 2000, p. 28). Having her identity rooted in being God's child, Pattie somehow finds moral authority and agency to enact the principalship in the ways that she does. In the Black Church there was often an "adoptionist" mentality (Brown, 2000, p. 28). Individuals in the church were seen as family members. However, those outside the church were also seen as familial because of their creation by God and potential to join the family. Respect was given to the entire human race because everyone had the potential to become a part of the family (Brown, 2000). Communal care was to be exhibited to everyone. Brown echoes this sentiment by stating,

> Every person created by God is a member, an equal member, of God's family. There are no stepchildren.... God is no respecter of persons...regardless of race, creed, color, gender, denomination, age, income, neighborhood, sexual proclivity, intelligence, or residence.... One cannot ignore the needs of others. (p. 115)

Being a child of God afforded individuals an expectation of being treated as "a child of a king." Being treated as a child of God builds self-esteem by recognizing one's strengths regardless of what someone else says about them. External entities tell Blacks that they are less than others, while internal ones tell them they are God's children.... Children and adults are reminded that they came from a rich heritage and possess unlimited possibilities because they are children of God. (Brown, 2000, p. 56).

For Pattie, recognizing others as children of God determines her leadership practice and the activities in which she engages in the principalship. Pattie has a desire to truly change her community through education and what she does in schools. "Classrooms can be places where educators attempt to reduce knowledge.... In our antiquated educational system, teaching has been reduced and cheapened into a privatized delivery of facts. Classrooms are often places of violence" (Floyd-Thomas, 2006a, p. 135). It is this kind of classroom that Pattie seeks to eliminate. Education is seen as an emancipatory act and the classroom and the school as sites to contest the status quo of society.

"Speaking the Word" has a strong link to the womanist theological construct of naming. Naming is one's ability to define something, to speak her own truth (Floyd-Thomas, 2006a). Grant (1989) states that Black women use the Bible as religious validation to follow their own truth. Black women apply passages of the Bible to the situations they face and to contest multiple oppressions (Brown, 2000). Inherent in the womanist idea is one that "conjures new possibilities" (Floyd-Thomas, 2006b, p. 129). The conjuring of these possibilities leads women to follow their own agenda rather than one set out for them by any dominant social group (Brown, 2000; Floyd-Thomas, 2006a). By speaking and naming, Pattie engages in a "spirituality of resistance" (Floyd-Thomas, 2006a) to transcend intersecting oppressions.

Meditations

As Pattie and I were talking on the phone one night discussing the news, one of the things she talked about was what we were leaving behind for the next generation of children. As I looked back over the transcripts and notes of our discussions, I remember thinking that this could serve as a motto for what she does in her school and in her life. As someone who knows her personally, I knew that this idea defines what she does in her church, community, school, and life. She often speaks about improving conditions in the world so that the next generation of individuals would "have something."

> Girl, I look at some of the things that are happening in the world and I know we are to blame. We are not doing right by kids. We are not leaving

them anything better if we keep this up. What is gonna be left when we get through? I know the Bible tells us things will not get better until Jesus comes back. But until then I guess we gotta at least try. We gotta at least try to make it better for people. That is all I wanna do. Even with my own boys, you raise 'em right and give 'em to God, but you try to make things better for them. I see these kids at school and I know I gotta at least try so they will have something long after they leave my school. I try to love 'em, make sure they are learning, get 'em some things they need, but ultimately I give 'em to God too.

Unlike the other principals, Pattie does not consider school a place to discuss religio-spirituality. Religio-spiritual musings, meditations, and prayer take place in private. Broader themes of respect, honesty, care take the place of more specific religio-spiritual actions. Although her Christian faith explicitly informs her actions in school, these acts are often cloaked in these more general out-workings of faith.

This chapter has highlighted each woman's spiritual narrative. These narratives have illuminated some of the ways that these principals perceive religio-spirituality and the workings of that in their lives and profession. The womanist theological tenet love of spirit is pervasive in their stories. Their narratives firmly establish the intersection of religio-spirituality and schooling and frame much of their decision making in schools. However, this intersectionality is seen in how they also address issues of race, class, and gender as they live their lives and enact the principalship. The next chapter presents a cross-narrative analysis and emphasizes the research questions and the themes embedded in all of the participants' narratives.

Chapter 4

Exegesis

> *Readers can learn something from believers even without becoming converted.*
>
> (Moody, 2003, p. xi)

"*Exegesis* is described as an explanation of interpretation of texts, especially religious ones" (Cannon, 1988). Pastors or teachers in the church are considered as exegetes, or ones who interpret and help make sense of the Bible as it relates to matters of theology and the lives of people. Although I claim no pastoral responsibility with this work, the participants have left me the challenge of interpreting and presenting their texts. Chapter Four represents the efforts at interpretation of the spiritual narratives presented in the previous chapter. For these reasons I have called this chapter "Exegesis." The analysis in Chapter Four explores each spiritual historian's spiritual narrative and themes peculiar to each. This chapter also explores the women's personal lives in more detail and the way that religio-spirituality impacts their lives outside of the workplace. However, the big assumption in this book is that their professions as part of their lives are also influenced greatly by this religio-spirituality. This chapter discusses the communal nature of their narratives through cross-narrative analysis and conceptualizes the broader themes in their narratives as they relate to the role of religio-spirituality of Black female principals, particularly as principal.

Cross-Talk: Religio-Spirituality and Cross-Narrative Analysis

"Cross"-Talk discusses the use of religio-spirituality in the lives of the women and their reliance on a relationship with God and the "Cross" of Christ in their lives as Christians. This section addresses how religio-spirituality is conceptualized. "Principle/als" focuses its discussion specifically on the principalship and what is "going on" when religio-spirituality impacts the school and the principalship.

While completing this cross-narrative analysis, these questions and their analyses are consolidated into the major ideas inherent in them and serve as the heading for these sections.

One of the research questions explores the role of social justice as it relates to religio-spirituality and the principalship. One of the main assertions this chapter makes in cross-narrative analysis is that social justice is the major thread that weaves through the participants' lives. Social justice has many different definitions and is framed around several "issues (e.g., race, diversity, marginalization, gender, spirituality), including those formidable issues of age, ability, and sexual orientation" (Dantley & Tillman, 2006, p. 17). Social justice is framed by educational leadership theorists to correct social, political, economic, and educational inequities (Tillman, 2002). Each section in this chapter explores the ways that social justice, religio-spirituality, and the principalship intersect. Womanist theology provides a frame to view ways that educators integrate religio-spirituality in the form of personal faith and how they "use" and conceptualize that faith to interrogate marginality, promote social justice, and initiate their form of social activism in schools.

As the educational leadership literature moves toward a social justice framework, administrative practices become more of a focal point in analyzing how administrators engage in the process of social justice. For these women religio-spirituality is not neutral in matters of social justice and leadership in schools. Indeed, social justice and the spiritual often collide and are the same thing. To be religio-spiritual *is* to be socially just. "Historically, many African Americans have felt strongly that...theology is central to...justice" (Siddle Walker & Snarey, 2004, p. 4) and vice versa. For the women in this study, religio-spirituality is justice and often when talking about one, they are talking about the other. This research examines what Black female principals with a religious worldview believe, and it indeed translates as social justice for the students in their schools. Romo and Roseman (2005) have said that social justice is an outcome and a process. This research shows how the process of social justice is articulated as religio-spirituality and how social justice is achieved or worked toward as an outcome through expression of certain acts in schools.

Across the narratives, four conceptualizations emerged as they relate to the participants' meanings of religio-spirituality. Religio-spirituality is identified as *church/denominational identity, conversion, wilderness and warfare,* and *culture*. The section after that discusses conceptualizations of the intersection between religio-spirituality and the principalship.

Religio-Spirituality

Religio-Spirituality as Church/Denominational Identity

This books grapples with how these Black female principals conceptualize spirituality and how it impacts their daily lives. In their narratives and subsequent analyses, all of these women indicated that their spirituality is the most important feature of their lives. Particularly, this spirituality is rooted in their Christian faith and their church denominations and church bodies. Although their total religio-spiritual sphere includes many different peripherals, the foundation is based upon their religious belief and that of connection to church. These women's identities are first and foremost Christian, but this Christian belief is also tied to what they received from their churches.

All of these narratives share a common strand, a connection to the Baptist Church. One unexpected idea from these narratives is the issue of identity. I do not seek to specifically examine religious identity and/or plan to conduct a far-reaching probe of the Baptist Church. The spiritual historians are not asked about their denominational affiliation when discussing their spirituality. However, all of these women locate their spirituality in institutionalized religion, particularly the Baptist Church. For these woman, church membership plays a big role in how they view themselves. Inasmuch as they view themselves as Black, female, and even at times principal, they identify as Baptist.

At times it may be hard to track what it actually means to be spiritual, religious, or even Christian. Their particular faith tradition "presupposes that 'Baptist' is a distinct and meaningful identity feature as a subset of 'Protestant', which itself is a distinct and meaningful identity feature of as a subset of 'Christian'" (Nelson-Brown, 2006, p. 181). The Baptist denomination holds many tenets. While each woman did not state specifically the Articles, they expressed certain beliefs about religio-spirituality that are congruent with the Articles of the NBC:

1. There is a triune God as represented by God the Father, Jesus the Son, and the Holy Spirit.
2. The Bible is inerrant and factual and is the Word of God.
3. God directly intervenes in individuals' lives, acts on their behalf, and gives them His power.
4. Human beings are sinful and need to appropriate Jesus' death on the cross to atone for their sins. He is the only Way of salvation, to make one holy and able to live the Christian life.
5. Christians should profess their faith to the church body and be baptized by water immersion.
6. Prayer is a way of communicating directly with God.
7. Attending church on Sunday was vital to observing the Sabbath.
8. There are righteous and wicked people.
9. God takes care of the righteous and the righteous have the hope of heaven.
10. Christians are to tell others about Jesus.

Although there are no essential qualities to being Baptist, they all have a strong identification with the denomination.

Although the members of the Baptist denomination believe the ten views above, what does being Christian or Baptist entail? The women's Baptist worldview is one that had been "passed on" to them by significant members of their families or friends or by participation in Baptist activities:

> We were in church every Sunday with my grandparents. You also participated in youth group and you did Sunday School. (Toni)

> My family was involved in church. Daddy was a deacon. Mom worked in the church. (Bobbie)

> We love our church. I grew up in church. My husband was an associate pastor at our other church. I am a deaconess. You gotta stay close to your church. (Pattie)

The participants talked about their church attendance and faith as a choice, and they drew from their own interpretations about the Bible and what it means to live that faith. However, their Christian identity is introduced by and is so rooted in family and community that it begs the question of whether they truly make these choices of faith for themselves. One participant even expressed guilt over not attending church: "I feel guilty when I don't go to church. I mean, I wasn't raised like that" (Toni). Although not as wanted, each of the women's narratives yields strong "enculturated social inheritance" (Nelson-Brown, 2006, p. 187) of their faith and their upbringing, and how they raise their own children and even how they gather others to the faith. Inasmuch as religio-spirituality is personal, it is also communal, social, and a place to connect with others.

> It's just nice to be in a place where it matters if you don't show up. If you haven't been to church in Sundays it's not like she's not holy. It's like I know who Avery is and hey, I haven't seen her. Do we need to do something or call? (Avery)

> Personal salvation is important, but you have to be in a church family. (Bobbie)

The participants indicated that "doing" faith or doing certain acts is important to their Christian identity. The participants did not specifically name the Articles, the history of the Baptist denomination, or all of the doctrine associated with it; however, the ten core beliefs expressed above complete their view of what is means to be Baptist and Christian. They did not express that one has to be Baptist or be a Christian or spiritual. However, maintaining ties to the church congregation represents the beginning of their religio-spiritual identity and the maintenance of it. Each woman identified church attendance, engaging in church activities, service in the church and the community, and "witnessing" as important acts to a Christian. Studying the Bible, prayer, and lifestyle and professional choices aligned with the Bible are important to living out their faith. All of these acts are most fully lived out in community with others and able to be passed on in church:

> The church where I am now, I love. I visited the church with a friend of mine and I just enjoyed it. I came back several times and I just loved the closeness, it truly felt like a church family. I'm actively involved in several different ministries and my daughter is secretary of her youth group, she ushers, she is a liturgist. On any given Sunday, I am up speaking to my church about my school since they adopted the school. (Avery)

> We changed our church membership. We believe we can better serve God here. (Pattie)

> I feel like something is missing because I am not plugged into activities in church. (Toni)

Each woman has her own initial conversion story in the Baptist denomination and current participation, but the denomination is not completely constitutive of whether each identifies as Christian. Even so, the participants do agree that there exist different interpretations of the rituals and customs of the Christian/Baptist belief system. For instance, Toni and Avery discussed their views on church attendance and rules for conversion and church membership,

> Even though I'm still a Christian and I'm spiritual, some people feel like you have to be in church. (Toni)

> Sometimes I wake up on Sunday and my daughter and I sleep in. I think this is okay. (Avery)

> I joined the church when I was nine years old but I believed even before then, it was just, you know how those old traditions are, that you have to confess and they have you out there seeking God for a week or two, praying. I had to go through the ritual. There were always church people saying, don't you get up there on that bench until you know for sure. They'd have me out there praying all day in a room by myself, yah know doing revival, and I was thinking, "I already believe. What else am I supposed to do?" (Bobbie)

In spite of a strong church/denominational identity, each woman indicated a need to be comfortable and happy with the particular congregation in which she is involved. Bobbie left the denomination but retains a Baptist religious identity and has returned to a Baptist church. Avery is now Presbyterian, because it is more important to her to be a part of a congregation that feels like a family. Pattie is still a Baptist but recently changed congregations since she and her husband no longer felt comfortable with the direction of the previous congregation. Toni is still in a Baptist congregation, although it is much larger than her previous congregation.

Religio-Spirituality as Conversion

Conversion has been defined as a "saving change from sinner to saint" (Bassard, 1999, p. 23). "What this means is that those who become Christians become new persons. They are not the same anymore, for the old life is gone. A new life has begun!" (2 Corinthians 5:17, NLT). Conversion involves turning: a turn away from sin and a turn to God (Bassard, 1999). When this happens, one is "saved" from hell and saved from the evils and troubles of this world (Hayes, 2006). Conversion also involves adopting a new worldview, humans' place in it, and how one should live. Each woman's narrative involves a moment when she believes these events happened for her. In relation to conversion, salvation is said not to be just a moment in which salvation is bestowed, but rather a daily process of being saved and made new by the Holy Spirit's work in us (Yancey, 1999).

It is interesting that the participants did not spend much time discussing their initial conversion experience. Bobbie discussed it in two or three paragraphs' worth of words. Pattie, Avery, and Toni discussed it in only a few sentences. Each referred to initial conversion very briefly as "joining the church," "accepting Christ," and "getting saved"; however, I note they did not go any further in explaining that experience. It is significant that all of the participants' conversion experiences occupy only a fraction of their responses. When asked about the experience directly, each participant did not stay "on topic." These conversion experiences often segued into larger global life experiences with religio-spirituality. For instance, Pattie simply said she "got saved" when she was a child and immediately began discussing her life after that. Toni talked about "joining the church" and getting baptized, and then discussed her past and present church attendance. Avery spoke of going to church with her mother when she was younger while her father stayed home, and then moved to describing her conversion experience. What is clear is that each participant has multiple and varying ways of viewing the initial conversion experience and what conversion means for her. The initial conversion experience does not present itself as the most poignant aspect of spirituality; instead, it is the life after the conversion experience that is the most important. The conversion experience is bound by temporality and represents a fixed point in time. The new life they experience is a result of the initial conversion experience, but the life experiences change and evolve over time.

This evolvement is indicative of the historians' religio-spiritual experiences. Although they all had an initial conversion experience, each one of them indicated that her ideas about spirituality are constantly changing. Although they retain belief in the same basic precepts of their faith, there is a *situational* and *interpretive* nature to what they believe. These basic precepts may vary in their application and the degree of application. They all indicated different phases in their lives in which their interpretations of things changed. For instance, Bobbie changed her views about what she had always believed about worship and emotionalism over time. Even though she did not grow up with this style of worship, there came a point in her life in which she needed it and thus it was interpreted as "okay." Bobbie also discussed women preaching as an idea that changed over time after she realized the unique contributions of women in her church. Toni referred to a time when she would have been involved in "every activity in church" when she was younger and prior to her becoming a principal. However, since she views her school as a weekly mission field and because she works with kids all day, it is okay to refuse to teach Sunday School or Vacation Bible School. Avery realized it is okay to be a Christian even if she is not Baptist and that church "is about getting what you need where you need it and being a part of a family. If a congregation cannot provide certain things, it is okay to leave a denomination or church body." This idea was echoed by Pattie, who left a Baptist congregation for another because she did not agree with how some people were living the Christian life.

Avery, Bobbie, Pattie, and Toni all discussed varying influences upon their changing faith. In addition to situations determining their interpretation of how they live out the words of the Bible and their Christian beliefs, they also discussed the impact of people and other ideas of spirituality. The participants also had some things to say about the role of the various stages of their lives and the bearing of that on religio-spirituality,

> I know differently now. I know what I have to do and what not to do. It is not the same as it was when I was little. (Toni)
>
> My life has taught me so much about who God is. (Avery)
>
> You have to figure things out for yourself. The older you get, the more you learn about this life and the Christian life. (Pattie)
>
> The older I get, I recognize how more deeply involved I am in my spirituality. I am at a different level. Earlier in my life, I knew it was the right thing to do. My faith has always been a part of my life and not just an isolated part. It has always been all I have ever known to do. I went to church. I believed in Jesus. I did know Him, but I knew nothing about advancing. (Bobbie)

The women discussed watching television programming on the Christian networks such as Trinity Broadcasting Network (TBN), Black Entertainment Television (BET), and other major networks. They also discussed reading other spiritual books by authors such as T. D. Jakes. Each of the women discussed involvement with civic organizations, sororities, parachurch groups, and professional and cultural organizations. This religio-spirituality as conversion/change has to do not only with an initial tie to religio-spirituality, but also with a sustaining link and a continual evolving of it.

For these women, religio-spirituality is not a static thing but one that changes. However, religio-spirituality is still supported by a certain foundation. That foundation is not just the triune God, but His outer workings as well. The women consider themselves co-laborers with Him, as they are His workers and His vessels. In their view, it is their responsibility to share this life of conversion or testify to others.

This is not simply a call to a one-time conversion, but one that continues for the new converts and results in continual evolvement and change.

Religio-Spirituality as Wilderness and Warfare

This research discusses the concept of warfare permeating each woman's story. This warfare takes the form of fighting "evil" in this world. Belief regarding this evil includes "powers and principalities" of the devil; but social injustice is also considered a part of the story of evil. Each narrative contains battle metaphors that speak of fighting the fight. However, another concept I interpret as *wilderness*. Wilderness, as described by Williams (2001), denotes oppressed moments in life that one endures before being liberated from these moments. Each woman spoke of many different times of discrimination and times of facing tremendous adversity. Any person or system that serves to impede life progress or success is seen as evil and a part of the wilderness process. This wilderness has a direct relationship with the role of religio-spirituality in their lives. Moreover, these wilderness experiences are seen as directly correlated to being religious or spiritual:

> When you are Black and female, you are gonna go through trials; but even more so because you are a believer. The devil don't want us to have nuthin'. Jesus went through trials too and look at Him. I am a child of God so I know I will be all right. (Pattie)
>
> White people are gonna take care of each other, that's a fact. It's all just so evil. But I serve a greater God. He allows these things for my good. My spirituality is taken to another level. (Bobbie)
>
> Losing my mother was one of the worst things that could have ever happened to me. I know that I am still not over it. But it has made me who I am. It has given me faith. (Toni)
>
> What was meant for evil has turned out for my good. No weapon formed against me will prosper. I am more than a conqueror. I know that. (Avery)

As their comments suggest, the wilderness is both a sacred and harsh place. It is sacred because this adversity is interpreted as a part of being in the world as Christians: "In fact anyone who wants to live a godly life in Christ Jesus will be persecuted" (2 Timothy 3:12, New International Version). As with history, suffering and persecution are considered par for the course for the Christian, and African American peoples appropriate this view to explain some of the suffering they have endured in life. For these Black female principals, because their religio-spirituality shapes the whole of their lives, every hardship becomes a way of suffering for God's sake. Suffering is not only a way of identifying with Christ's pain, but also His overcoming. "Now if we are children, we are heirs—heirs of God and co-heirs with Christ, if indeed we share in His sufferings in order that we may also share in His glory" (Romans 8:17, NIV). For these women, wilderness is not only a place where these women meet God. Wilderness often explains the wider world of society as a hostile place. For these women, being Black, female, or a Christian makes wilderness as a metaphor for their lives and adversities that they will be freed from "someday."

Religio-Spirituality as Culture

For the women represented in this book, religio-spirituality is also *religio-cultural*. Each of the women made reference to faith as familial and community centered, but also entrenched in race and culture. This is particularly evident in the intersection of religio-spirituality with discussions of the civil rights movement, incidences of racism and sexism, and other forms of oppression. These things are particularly important to African American people. As equally important is the African American culture. For the women, there is the idea of exposing unjust practices and fighting against them. The idea of exposure and fighting certain life narratives that society creates for African American women are what White (2001) calls "Black counterdiscourses." White (2001) states that these counterdiscourses

> expose the ways that race, gender, sexuality, and class categories intertwine and transform each other. Categories such as race and gender are created to help the world make sense to us. These categories do not exist "out there" in the world. Rather, they are analytical categories that are always structured hierarchically and that have real consequences for real people. (p. 15)

As stated earlier, all of the participants have a strong connection to their churches. In fact, the Black Church is one of the "organizational and expressive cores of the Black culture and community" (Dodson & Gilkes, 1986, p. 82). Church is very vital to how each woman views religio-spirituality, yet it is also important in how they see themselves culturally. Just as their religio-spirituality is a mixture of influences, their identities are just as complex. There is an inseparability of their womanhood as it relates to race and religio-spirituality. Indeed, when talking, these women did not separate their Black experience from a larger Black Christian experience. The women made parallels to their own struggles with those of Black people both historically and currently. For instance, Avery and Bobbie discussed in detail their experiences with the murders of their mothers due to domestic violence. While discussing these events, Avery talked about the prevalence of domestic violence in the Black community and the silence of the Black community on this issue. Pattie and her husband consider themselves students of African American history and often reference it during conversations. By being involved in the church they now attend, Pattie believes they are closer to "doing what God wants them to do." They believe strongly that a part of God's will for them involves them specifically ministering to the Black community. Bobbie frequently referred to the civil rights movement and sees her life and work as a continuation of this struggle. All of the women discussed specific instances of racism that they encountered and that of family, friends, and their students. They indicated an obligation to fight racism on behalf of themselves, their communities, and workplaces, and for Black people as a whole.

In reiterating the importance of church to these women, their narratives highlight a need to unify their identities. Each talked about a multiplicity of roles and identities that gave insight into how they view themselves. Their roles include being Black women, principals, mothers, Christians, daughters, church members, friends, wives, employees, among others. However, the one unifying identity is that of being Christian and a Black woman, in that order. When asked as a follow-up how they view themselves, they used phrases such as "believer," "child of God," "Christian," and "saved." When pressed further, the participants talked about their being Black and women and those two terms were often repeated as one characterization instead of two. Their religio-spirituality provides holism for their lives and how they view and portray themselves. Being Black in turn became a unifier for some of the understandings that they hold of their religio-spirituality. On more than one occasion, their religio-spiritual view of themselves was linked to their Blackness and their predominately Black churches. Although each of the women indicated feeling race very acutely, they also repeatedly spoke of their religio-spirituality as a holistic frame of reference for their identities.

It is important to recognize that as the literature review suggests, spirituality is complex in nature. The term that is used in this research is *religio-spirituality* to describe the intermingling nature of the spirituality and religion for the participants. Spirituality is spoken of in religious terms and forms the basis for it. However, it is important to note the various and varying terms used by the narrators interchangeably with religio-spirituality. These words include *faith*, *belief*, and *personal relationship with God*. Some of these women see religio-spirituality as private in some ways but not "hidden." For each woman it is a distinct and very real part of her life and found its way significantly into her work.

Principal/les

Part of this research specifically explores the import of religio-spirituality in the lives of principals and its impact on decision making in schools. This work also concerns issues of social justice or what these principals perceive as justice in schools and how that justice is carried out. The themes were compacted to include educational beliefs and philosophy as they relate to the women's roles as principals. Other themes examine organizational tensions and administrative application and practices. These themes and subthemes highlight religio-spirituality for the individuals as it relates to schools.

Worldview: Educational Philosophy

The first theme was conceptualized in their educational philosophy as *worldview*. Worldview is a widely used term in Christian thought to indicate core knowledges and sets of religious beliefs that outline how an individual thinks and makes meaning of his existence and life choices. This word is used here to describe how the women in this study understand their purpose in education and leadership. Somewhere at the core of this research was the question, "Why do principals do what they do and how do they think about it?" One thing was clear: Their religio-spirituality is made up of their educational philosophy. Their educational worldview or philosophy carries the themes of *mission, pastoral care,* and *ransom*.

The participants had various reasons for choosing their careers. For Bobbie, there were many possible career choices she considered before becoming influenced by a woman in her community. For Pattie, it was something she had always wanted to do, an almost innate desire to teach. For Toni, it was an extension of the comfort that school had always provided her after the painful death of her mother. Even though many in her family were hospital employees, Toni decided upon a career in education after encouragement by her husband. Avery had several other careers and was eventually "steered by God" into her current position. While religio-spirituality was not primary in their choices to become educators, once they became educators, it impacted how they saw their work and the activities in which they engaged.

Mission

It is often rare to find people who use the same metaphor to describe a particular phenomenon. However, when asked how they view their principalship, each woman used the word *mission* or the phrase *mission field*.

> School is a mission field. (Avery)

> I felt like I had a mission and I was on a mission. (Bobbie)

> This ain't just school. It's a mission. (Pattie)

> I'm supposed to be doing this. It's a mission. (Toni)

The idea of mission transcends beyond just the personal and extends to the community, church, and their professions just as it did with historically Black women in education.

> The missionary zeal with which Black women approached the problem of social change and racial uplift had a revitalizing impact on the Black community. The women's race consciousness united contending segments of the Black community into new organizations.... If any one ministry could be identified as central to the Black sacred cosmos of the twentieth century, it would be education.... Evangelism was a taken-for-granted aspect of church life.... However, Black people also defined education of the oppressed and the oppressors as central tasks of Christian mission. (Dodson & Gilkes, 1986, p. 84)

These same ideas represented above highlight the participants' own narratives of spirit.

What exactly is their mission? When asked, the participants found it hard to give specifics. What is clear, is an overall need to make things better for the students that they serve. Their mission is closely tied to their idea of social justice. Although social justice has become an important topic of exploration in education, one often wonders, "What does social justice look like?" For this section in particular, "What are the beliefs of a philosophical mission of social justice for these women?" Although these women did not all necessarily call social justice by name until specifically asked, many of their beliefs about schooling and the principalship extend to what they believe are fairness, equality, and equity.

> Social justice is making sure my kids have everything that everyone else has. Sometimes that may mean giving my kids more than you give other people who already have. It may not be fair but life hasn't been fair to my kids. (Avery)

> I want what is fair. The people on the other side of town have everything. (Bobbie)

> Every child deserves the best that we can give them. (Toni)

> I understand that we can't do everything for children but I am tired of seeing white folks be the only one with a chance. (Pattie)

This idea of social justice also did not correlate to "following the rules" either. As one participant put it, "Sometimes the rules have to be broken to achieve social justice" (Bobbie). Another put it this way:

"I don't always do what is considered normal. There is nothing normal about the kids I serve." (Avery)

Although their discussion of social justice is not exhaustive, the historians spoke of many different aspects of schooling. The women believe that schooling should not only extend opportunities for material realities for students, but also provide for the material realities that students may not have. The majority of students at all the principals' schools were considered impoverished based upon free and reduced lunch percentages.

I want my students to have everything that everyone else has. The school can't do everything but it can do something. School is a ministry within itself. (Avery)

I am always on the side of the kid. They should have opportunities. (Toni)

Some of my kids don't have shoes. I need to be worried about that just like everything else. (Pattie)

I was always fighting to get things in school that the kids did not have at home. Like computers. None of my kids had these at home. I fought for a lab at school. My school needed it more than the rich school they were trying to give it to. (Bobbie)

The participants value providing students with other experiences besides the "basics" of schooling. Closing the achievement gap among their students and rejecting a deficit model of schooling are among their beliefs. Bobbie and Pattie are principals of low-performing schools that are considered "school improvement" schools by the state. Avery's school had been in "school improvement" and at the time of the interview, her school had just been released from this distinction. Toni's school is a magnet school with a higher number of achieving students than the other schools represented in this research. However, Toni mentioned that her school's scores had increased due to her intense focus on achievement.

My kids may never be top achievers by somebody else's scale. And I do believe that education is key. But without that exposure to a different life they are not going to understand it. These kids are trying to survive. It's like you

> want so badly for them to somehow see that there is something else out there outside of these walls and what they see every day out there. (Avery)

> These kids are smart. I am tired of people worrying about what the kids don't have and think about what they bring to the table. They can't help who their parents are. (Pattie)

> When I stopped focusing so much on achievement at my school, our test scores increased by 19 percent. The purpose of school is not just about scores. I realized that. (Toni)

There also was an intense belief in a two-way community support system in performing their mission in schools.

> I tried to become a part of the life that they lived. I even stopped going to my beautician and I got a beautician on the west side, and I still go there now. I don't think I will ever leave her because back then in that beauty parlor, the kids came back through there, the parents come through there, they got to see me, they got to know me, they go to talk to me and that they go to see I'm just like ya'll. (Bobbie)

> A lot of my students in my school are a part of my community and even attend my church. (Toni)

> You've got to know your community to serve it. (Pattie)

> I understand this community and they trust me. I couldn't do what I do if the community wasn't behind me. Not every parent agrees with me, but for the most part they do. (Avery)

Prominent in their philosophies is also the idea of a responsibility to the mission of calling others to spirituality, even in their capacities as principals and educators. In some cases this involves openly proselytizing or at least portraying certain principles that they feel are spiritual.

> I felt like I did a lot of good. I think the way I carried myself and the way I handled situations and then my relationships with like parents and teachers and kids, I think my spirituality was relayed that way. (Bobbie)

> I often remind them in school of how what they are doing would not please God or the pastor. (Toni)

> I just honestly feel like without bringing God into the picture there is not a whole lot I can do because its not about ABC's and 123's. (Avery)

> I don't tell students about Jesus. That is a sure way to get fired. But I believe you have to be Christian in what you do and how you conduct your school and deal with people. (Pattie)

Undergirding each woman's philosophy is the idea of racism. Eradicating racial injustice is interwoven into each narrative. When asked what they believe is the biggest problem they have to overcome, they cited perceived inequities rooted in race. When discussing issues affecting schooling such as test scores, poverty or wealth, community tensions, or student households, race or racism as a theme overlapped with these issues. It is also clear from the participants' responses that the ideas of race and class issues are entwined with one another in the idea for social justice. Although the participants saw some of these inequities in schools as rooted in other sociocultural issues, they also saw them as spiritual issues that needed to be overcome.

> My belief is that all of this stuff is rooted in the devil. Besides, God still runs this. This world I mean. At the end of day, I don't take this stuff home with me because He is still the one in control. I have to do my part with that. (Pattie)

> Prayer is the thing. You can't fight something as big as this with flesh and blood. You are in a spiritual battle for these kids. (Bobbie)

> I take some of my students home with me. I take care of them. That is the Christian thing to do. I know that this is a part of educating them. This thing is spiritual. (Avery)

> Sometimes I am just plain tired. I deal with issues all week. But I keep coming back to my faith. (Toni)

For these women, it is clear that their religio-spirituality is what informs their ideas about educational and leadership philosophies and that these form a mission of social justice. From each narrative, it is clear that social justice and spirituality form a significant overlap.

Pastoral Care

The historians indicated a belief in the inherent worth of each of the students. This belief in the inherent worth of students has been associated with educational notions of care (Gilligan, 1982; Noddings, 1984). "Care means liberating others from their state of need and actively promoting their welfare" (Siddle Walker & Snarey, 2004, p. 4). Pastoral theology has been called a "practical" (Burck & Hunter, 1990, p. 867) theology. The ordinary, practical everyday spiritual lives make up this research. However, a theme of this research clearly asserts that religio-spirituality overlaps the school setting. While traditional ethics of care in schools present a dichotomy between care and spirituality, the kind of caring enacted by the spiritual historians does not. For this reason, I have termed their caring *pastoral care*. Pastoral care differs from the traditional theories of care in that it is concerned with spiritual development in the concept of caring for the whole child.

Much like that of a pastor or spiritual guide seen in churches, these women believe not only in the academic well-being of their students, but also in the holistic care of mind, body, and spirit. The care these principals engage in seeks to address interlocking systems of material realities, community realities, and spiritual realities.

> It was a good thing that I was there, you know, for the children, because they needed someone who was compassionate and who cared about them. That is what I kept hearing from the community. They know I am Christian and when all is said and done, they know I care for these children and I try to model Christ for them. (Bobbie)

> At the end of the day there is not a person in this building or outside this building who can say I don't care about these kids. You can say whatever you want but at the end of the day there is not a person here who could question my passion and my desire to help these kids. (Toni)

> Some of these parents don't take care of these babies. When they are here, they are my babies. And I gotta make sure they have what they need. They need some Jesus too and I do the best I can without getting fired. (Pattie)

> I've got kids whose parents are on drugs. Ninety-eight percent of them live in poverty. Some are under that care of DHR because they are neglected. I honestly don't believe we can do it without God. (Avery)

The principals take on a lot of responsibility for this care in schools. It is clear from their narratives that they want to call others to this same sort of spiritual mission. However, throughout their interviews, none of the principals mentioned other individuals in the school setting that could attend to the religio-spiritual aspect of schooling. It is clear that their idea of mission is their calling first. They believe that they are the overseers of this particular facet of their schools. This seems to mimic the hierarchy of the traditional church organization. There is little "delegation" in this area, and it is clear that they view this as a peculiar duty of theirs as principals.

> Some teachers would tell me that they didn't have time. I realize teachers are busy. But I guess that is why you have the principal there. There has got to be somebody who is going to take an interest in them and really care. (Bobbie)

> This is what I am supposed to be doing. I have to answer to God about how I treat these babies. (Pattie)

> I can't say that I don't get tired. But it is my responsibility. (Toni)

> Even though I had all these jobs, I always wanted to be in education. As a principal, I can help more students and make more of a difference. I can do what I am supposed to do. (Avery)

The participants see themselves as a part of "God's active care for the disposed" (Murphy, 2000, p. 137). In each of their narratives, there is a belief that they are an extension of God's care for their students. God is seen as actively involved in the affairs of the school and the lives of its students. It is this relationship or lack of it that the spiritual historians believe would have the greatest impact upon the lives of students. It is this relationship that the women seek to introduce or nurture in the lives of their students.

Ransom

The Christian notion of ransom has been described by Williams: "Jesus' death on the cross…paid…for the sins of humankind" (Williams, 2000, p. 162). "To ransom," from this same perspective, is seen as rescuing, saving, and lifting out of a particular circumstance (Williams,

2000). The idea of ransom takes on new meaning when examining the principals and their philosophies and ideas about the principalship. The participants see school, religio-spirituality, and education itself as a means for ransoming students from their circumstances.

> With this community and with my kids, I feel like I have to save them. (Avery)

> Child, I have to tell ya. I wish what we were doing in school just had to do with school. I'm trying to give these kids some kind of life. (Pattie)

> Maybe just maybe, I can show these kids that they can make it. They can get out of the situation they are in. (Bobbie)

The participants feel a responsibility to ransom based on their duty they believe they owed to God. As one of the participants put it, "What am I going to do when God asks me what I did for these kids?" (Pattie). The service to their students is service to God. The women believe their role as principals and the role of schools can be to provide a chance for academic, professional, economic, social, and indeed spiritual success. These women see themselves as direct agents of change in these areas.

The concept of ransom takes on another meaning as well. The Christian idea of ransom also highlights the sacrifice that Jesus made on behalf of mankind (Williams, 2001). These principals all indicated a willingness and responsibility for their students at great sacrifice to themselves. Although they all indicated that they do not want to lose their jobs, they all discussed that it is more important to do whatever it takes to help their students.

> I have been written up and reprimanded. But I am not worried about that. (Bobbie)

> I don't let these folks worry me. And I don't take this mess home with me. If they wanna fire me, fire me. I'm here for the kids. I am not here for them. (Pattie)

> My administration is supportive. They let the principals run their schools. But I have no problem doing what I need to do for the kids. A job's a job and God put me here for a reason. (Avery)

> I try to do what I know Jesus would want me to do. Sometimes that means doing things that may not be popular. But I have to do what it right. (Toni)

This belief in advocacy on behalf of their students mimics the ideas of racial uplift and reciprocity. The Black Women's Club Movement in the nineteenth century introduced the concept of racial uplift through social reform activities in response to repressions, such as lynching and legalized segregation, of their day (Johnson, 2000). This concept has been repeated in womanism (Beauboeuf-Lafontant, 2002). Womanist theology and African American perspectives of care and justice ((Floyd-Thomas, 2006b; Snarey & Siddle Walker, 2004) apply uplift to social justice in schools. Reciprocity is also an element in the fight for social justice. Reciprocity is concerned with womanist theological alliances in the womanist theology project (Floyd-Thomas, 2006b). In other words, communality is extended to others outside of self and the core group. This term contains in it a reciprocal commitment to uplift oneself and others who are bound by unjust practices and institutions through communality and spirituality. The women in this study mimic these processes on behalf of their students.

Thematic conceptualization yielded the ideas of mission, pastoral care, and ransom as it relates to the educational philosophies of the principals. Each section containing these headings reflects intersection in these areas as they relate to educational philosophy. However, these philosophies closely resemble those contained in the context of social justice. Mission, pastoral care, and ransom intersect in their theological literature, and this is echoed in the spiritual narratives in this research. Each concept framed the other and formed an important understanding for how these women view the philosophy of their principalships. These narratives show this same belief of social correction in their philosophies.

In examining their ideas about their philosophies, the principals' beliefs signaled a more directive leadership model. This is a departure from studies concerning spirituality, Black female principals, and social justice by highlighting a more collaborative, transformational approach to leadership (Bloom & Erlandson, 2003; Meux, 2002; Sanders-Lawson, 2001; Sanders-Lawson, Smith-Campbell, & Benham, 2006). The principals clearly see themselves as the heads of their schools, and it is their responsibility to carry out the vision. They believe the vision and mission to have been given by God. Although there was discussion of a need for allies in the process, there seemed to be little evidence of co-participation in this process. Their idea of social justice clearly extends to the students first (and in some cases solely). The students are clearly meant to be the recipients of this justice. In attending to the transcripts of their interviews, the omissions in their stories shed some light. They rarely mentioned teachers, school staff, parents, or district personnel as either co-laborers or beneficiaries of social justice. The participants indicated a belief in relationships and believe that establishing and maintaining relationships are important. However, in discussing their schools, the principals had little to say about shared leadership or collaboration. There was such an individual purpose and mission in their principalships, that this may have undermined their efforts at building relationships and collaboration.

These leadership philosophies also placed emphasis on the students who "have it bad" (Pattie). All these schools have the majority or at least a majority percentage of students who would be considered at-risk, living in poverty, and suffering other dire circumstances. These students are clearly the priority of the principals.

Stumbling Blocks: Organizational Issues

For a definition of an oft-used term in theology, one can find several in the Bible. Romans 11:9 says, "May their table become a snare and trap, a stumbling block." Romans 14:13 says, "Make up your mind not to put a stumbling block or obstacle in your brother's way." The First Epistle to the Corinthians 8:9 says, "Be careful that the exercise of your freedom does not become a stumbling block for the weak." From these verses one can infer that stumbling blocks are not just physical and material obstacles or obstructions, but can apply to other institutional and social oppressions as well. A strand of the research examines the tensions or stumbling blocks among religio-spirituality and the principalship.

One of the greatest challenges among educational leaders who possess religio-spiritual convictions is how to remain true to those convictions in schools (Shields, 2005). These convictions are often met with external resistance in various forms by other stakeholders in the schooling process. There is also internal conflict that inevitably occurs with the leaders. There can often be an incongruence and a disconnect among their personal identities and how these identities are able to be lived out in the school.

Hierarchy and District Concerns

One such stumbling block is the hierarchical nature of schools. Like many schools, the ones in which these principals work follow the distinct pattern of top-down leadership decision making and processes. This has an impact upon what is enacted in schools. For instance, Toni and Avery discussed being able to "live out their faith" in their schools due to the district leadership. This leadership does not necessarily sanction or even know of what they do in their schools. However, for Toni and Avery, it is the freedom they feel as principals to "run their own schools" (Avery). The district leadership has a hands-off approach, which allows each principal free reign in her school. For Toni and Avery, this translates as a freedom to set their own procedures and frameworks in their schools and even to violate district policy. For instance, when asked if the policy allowed for them to openly discuss God with their students, they both indicated that it did not. In fact, they both indicated that if their discussions about God were to come under scrutiny, they believe they would be supported by their mostly female, Black district administration.

> If there was an issue that was brought before the district regarding this, I feel like I would be supported. They know that I care about my kids and I am a good principal. If I needed to be defended to the School Board or whatever, I think I would be. (Avery)

> We have to do something with these kids. Besides, there are many women in leadership in the district. Plus the superintendent understands some of the challenges we are facing. She knows there has to be something else. (Toni)

In stark contrast is the situation in the district in which Pattie and Bobbie work. Their district has mostly female district leadership, including a female superintendent. However, this leadership contingent is white. This seems to be significant for Pattie and Bobbie in how they believe they can lead. As each woman indicated in her narrative, a strong undercurrent of racism divides the city in which the school district is housed. This city was the site of a major civil rights conflict in the 1960s, and the city had been deeply divided. Bobbie and Patti indicated that this district had a long-standing practice of not hiring Black administrators. In fact, until the mid-1990s there had been only two Black district-level administrators and three Black local principals in a district that had become 60 percent Black in the late 1980s. There were no Black school board members until the district converted to an elected school board in the late 1990s. Bobbie and Pattie believe that Black principals are often unfairly targeted and that any behavior that steps outside of policy would be grounds for reprimand or dismissal. Pattie and Bobbie also indicated that this history in the city and the district is a part of this problem. Among the women, it is clear that Bobbie and Pattie consider their justice-seeking behaviors more of a risk than do Toni and Avery.

All of the participants discussed the hierarchy in schools. Avery and Toni indicated a more lenient view of their administration, and Bobbie and Pattie indicated a more "micro-managing" (Pattie) environment. Nonetheless, the impact of their religio-spirituality is still determined by what they perceive as a "top-down" organizational climate in their districts. Bobbie and Pattie said on more than one occasion that they do not think that most of their leaders or other principals have the same religio-spiritual values that they have. Avery and Toni differed, indicating several people they know who they believe are Christians, but they do not think that these people necessarily have the same goals that they have. All of the participants indicated that their respective leadership does not seem to have a child-focused agenda in the manner that they do. In their district, Bobbie and Pattie said this was even more salient because of the number of new principals coming into the district. They believe that the new principals are more focused on following policy and the views of district personnel and are being recruited and inducted to be less concerned with matters of justice for students. Avery and Toni also believe that new principals have a more technical focus of the principalship, but seem to view this as a necessity.

All these new principals are being brought in by the superintendent and school board. They are puppets and will not stand up to them. (Bobbie)

They are bringing in who they want as principals—people that won't ruffle any feathers. (Pattie)

I understand. It can be hard for a new principal. You are just trying to worry about how to make sure that everything runs smoothly. (Toni)

Yeah. New principals are just trying to figure out how to keep everything afloat. I understand trying to keep your job in the process. (Avery)

School board politics, management style and religio-spirituality of the district administration, and new principals' focus all impact what each principal thinks she could accomplish in her school. The women vary in how they view the hierarchy in the district. However, it is clear that the organizational hierarchy impacts the realization of their religio-spirituality in the workplace.

No Child Left Behind Act

The No Child Left Behind Act (NCLB) of 2001 brought about widespread changes in the educational community. Some of the major items of the act include requirements for highly qualified teachers (HQT) and adequate yearly progress (AYP) by each child and each school in state-mandated assessments in reading and math. NCLB also requires a scientifically based program for math and science. The educational act also provides extra funds for teachers, teacher coaches, programs, and materials in each of these subjects. Along with NCLB's authorization, widespread critique accompanied it at as well. For these women, some of the mandates in NCLB create stumbling blocks to their religio-spiritual mandate toward social justice. The women indicated that because there is such an emphasis on test scores and accountability, this often makes it difficult to focus on what they see as the real issues with their students. Issues with home and other problems needing attention are often ignored in favor of simply making sure that students "achieve" or make an acceptable score on the test. All of the principals indicated that students need more than just academic skills to succeed. However, they all indicated feeling "stretched thin" in trying to meet these academic needs and what they believe are real needs of their students.

> I want my kids to have the best. I want them to succeed but with all I have to do with curriculum...sometimes I get burned out trying to help them with everything else. (Toni)

> While I am here, I will do all I can to help them with the test. But I have to tell you, it's not my main thing. (Avery)

> My school will always be at the bottom based on how the state assesses us. So I'm tired of worrying about the test. I got other things to do. (Pattie)

> I'm trying to promote excellence. But I am trying to promote excellence in every way. (Bobbie)

Funding was also discussed. Most funds in both the districts are funneled toward academic concerns, and the principals believe that much more needs to be provided for them to advance their justice agenda. Bobbie and Pattie indicated that monies that are received independently are also directed by the district and they are told how to spend the money. Although there is more autonomy in Avery and Toni's district, they did indicate that monies are examined at the district level to make sure that they are being used "appropriately." All of the principals indicated a belief in high achievement and considered it a spiritual obligation. However, these principals contend that increased centralization and federal and state mandates are not the way to do it.

> How much more money can we throw at the test? Don't they know that there are other problems with these kids going on? (Pattie)

> My school has improved greatly. But it is just not in the way that they want. So they keep telling me how to spend my money and things are not improving as much as they could if I could do what I needed to do. (Bobbie)

In both districts, the participants indicated there is some professional development, but not much for principals or they do not have time to attend. The professional development is also not the type they believe principals or staff need. When professional development is required, it is mostly geared toward reaching and maintaining high student achievement through testing or schoolwide discipline concerns. Pattie said:

> We really need some help at my school just learning how to cope with some of the issues that students bring with them. My teachers don't know how to treat these students. We are in professional development every five minutes to help increase scores. But what about knowing what to do when these kids come to school with emotional problems? The counselor can only do so much. The folks at the central office are no better. They need some training themselves.

Each principal was careful to point out that there *are* some good aspects about NCLB. When asked, they all agreed that there is increased funding for materials and programs that they had not normally received. However, as Pattie put it, this increased money also means "new adoptions and programs every few years until something does the magic." They all are advocates for accountability. In spite of this, the accountability does not seem to focus on the things that they considered were bigger issues with their students. Pattie was concerned with how NCLB provided for at-risk students, but the at-risk interpretation is very narrow for the state. An "at-risk" characterization includes poverty based on free and reduced lunch and low achievement, which is defined as the lowest four stanines on the state achievement test. She defined how this southeastern state defines at-risk:

> Poverty plus low achievement equals at-risk. This is how they look at at-risk with poverty as a factor but all the money goes toward is getting more "school stuff." What if I needed money to get a social worker or an extra counselor? Sure Title I money can pay for that, but I just don't understand you having poverty as a factor but no funding to do something about it. They need something else too. (Pattie)

Government initiatives such as NCLB place a burden on district and school administrators to be intensely concerned with test scores. This is a stumbling block to religio-spirituality since the principals view caring for needs other than academic ones so crucial to performing their school mission.

The Spiritual vs. the Secular

This section examines the organizational barriers and tensions to religio-spirituality expression in schools. However, an underlying issue is what the participants perceive as a difference in the religio-spiritual commitments of others. Their spiritual commitments are at odds with what they view as the secular concerns of the others. As stated earlier, the principals see their position as their mission of faith. When asked about co-laborers with them, the principalship is perceived as a solitary mission. Select individuals outside of the school, such as church members or parachurch organizations, are seen as allies to this mission. However, there was little discussion of other individuals inside the school, such as teachers and staff, being committed to the same concerns as they are. Overall, the school is seen as a secular place and a part of the wilderness experience that they have to endure. The principals seem to view others as "outsiders" to the religio-spiritual process and the principalship. Leadership styles seem to be authoritative.

Differences in belief among stakeholders also play a part for the principals. For instance, Toni and Avery feel that community members and parents of students do not mind if they speak to their students about God. There is a general perception that because their neighborhoods have mostly African American families, there is an acceptance of openness of faith. This makes it easier to put programs and activities in place that allow them to live out their faith. Avery discussed a mural project going on in her school. When visiting her school for an interview, I viewed the mural. It had likenesses of Martin Luther King, sports figures, musical notes, scripture, books, drawings of boys and girls, and street signs, among other images. When asked why the school chose the images they did, Avery indicated that "these were all things that were important in that community, to the cultural heritage of individuals in the community, and to the students. It is important that they see those things." African American history and spirituality is considered an integral part of the culture of the community and the school. Avery also discussed the "adoption" of her school by her church. Toni discussed that many of her students attend the church she attends, and so this makes it easier to do what she wants to do. This was not a proclamation that everyone in the community is Christian, and Toni and Avery indicated that they know this is not the case. However, when asked why she feels the freedom to talk to her students about God, she indicated that many of them attend her church. But also, Toni indicated that

> Black people are spiritual. I grew up always hearing about God because I think there is just something there in the Black community.

Bobbie and Pattie indicated that their schools attempt to partner with different churches in the community for support in the form of tutoring, resources, and mentoring. The district administration allows these partnerships. Bobbie and Pattie do not believe that all the families of the students are necessarily spiritual; yet they do not believe families would object because of the standing that the ministers and churches hold in the community. In the case of Bobbie and Pattie, there remains some suspicion surrounding religio-spirituality. In the case of Bobbie, the district "kept an eye" on her in this area after she was accused of proselytizing. Although she indicated that this was a district ploy to "get dirt on her" to remove her from her position, its effects were felt in the community as well. In Pattie's and Bobbie's cases, churches are a large part of both of their communities in which their schools are housed. Because of this, there is some suspicion among stakeholders with regard to which churches the principals are most closely aligned.

In spite of all of this, Bobbie and Pattie indicated that what they think is the bigger concern is the lack of religio-spirituality of the school board and district administrators. When individuals display opposition to the vision for the school that Bobbie and Pattie hold, then these individuals are not believed to be Christian or religio-spiritual:

> How can they want the same things we want in our schools? These people aren't Christian. Just look at what they do at the central office. How can you not care about kids and be a Christian? (Pattie)

> I don't know. Some of these people just aren't saved and that sort of explains why they do what they do. You can say you are saved all day long but if you don't live it, then…When they favor certain schools over others, if

they treat my kids like they are less than these others, that ain't right. (Bobbie)

Actions by the school administration are not considered child-focused or particularly ethical. According to Bobbie, politics and career advancement are seen as more important.

> Everybody seems to be on a power trip or trying to go to the next level. Actually doing what is best for kids is not the strongest priority. That's not ethical. They are too busy doing favors for each other to do what they should do. (Bobbie)

Demographics and lack of religio-spirituality of the administration seem to be stumbling blocks to religio-spirituality in schools. Legal and policy issues and increasing societal secularism are also seen as barriers to religio-spirituality and social justice in schools. Schools are seen as managerial and technocratic rather than concerned with the whole child.

> When I was growing up things were a lot different. There was a concern for kids. And the community took responsibility. Leaders were responsible for children and not all this other stuff. (Bobbie)

> Principals now have to be concerned with so many other things. It has even changed since I first became an administrator. The test is all folks think about. They publish your scores in the paper and principals are judged on that. They are judged on how much money they bring in or the test or whatever. We aren't judged on whether we are helping kids and doing what is right. (Pattie)

> The world is a lot different now. Society is a lot different now. God isn't that important to some people. (Avery)

> I know I don't go to church every Sunday, but it seems like folks don't even care about that. (Toni)

A lack of role models for new principals is also an obstacle. With a principal's and district administration's concern with what the participants see as secular concerns, they noted an inevitability of what they consider injustice in schools spreading. Although each of the participants has found mentoring and support for themselves, they have not always found it in schools. Trust among them and other administrators and district personnel is a factor.

> I do not really have a mentor. I have people that I can ask questions, but no one really gets it. I think so and some people say well who, and that's why I call Avery and I talk to her and get ideas but it's not the same because she and her mentor have a relationship. I feel like I am the third wheel. (Toni)

> I created my own mentorship with another principal, she and I have partnered our elementary schools and we do our leadership training together; we did a retreat together and we just took a cruise together, both schools. We bounce ideas off of each other and we partner a teacher at each school with a teacher at the other school. I was not happy my first year, until I did meet her. (Avery)

> Child, please! Mentor?! I just do my own thing. I can't trust anybody in this district. I talk to my husband. I talk to my friends. And my friends don't have nothing to do with this district. (Pattie)

For Bobbie, it is even harder to have support or mentorship when she has more experience than most administrators in her district. She also believes it is harder because her conflicts with the school board on behalf of her students. Veteran principals do not support her and new principals have been "briefed" about her.

> The new people all think I am crazy because of my situations with the district. I am seen as the loud mouth. (Bobbie)

No notion of separation of church and state keeps them from their mission. Not one participant indicated the legal ramifications of professing her religio-spirituality. Each actually indicated a willingness to take the risk in that regard. However, the level to which they can live out their missions of social justice is the bigger concern. The tension lies in the acts that they consider expressions of their religio-spirituality or truly living the whole of their lives religio-spiritually. Their challenge lies in maintaining integrity, authenticity, and true power and the ability to do what they feel they want to do. There is a desire to be "true" to themselves as Christians, which they believe impacts every part of their lives. In spite of this, the principals' narratives highlight a perceived difference in who they are publically and privately. They maintain the core of who they are, but the difference lies in the expression of their personal and professional character.

> I think I am the same *person* in and out of school. I am just not able to express myself in the same ways. I have to be a lot harder than I would be outside of school. (Bobbie)

> I try to live the way I should live all the time. But I don't let myself get too close to people in school. There is a "principal" way to act and then there is me. (Toni)

At times the women stand at cross-purposes with their district and community in matters of religio-spirituality. However, leadership style and religio-spirituality of those who are "in charge" impacts the degree to which the agenda of the local school can be promoted. Levels of political agendas and the culture of the community impact the free expression of religio-spirituality but also the principals' ideas about social justice. These things are seen to directly threaten the autonomy of the principalship and the autonomy to be fully themselves as Christians. There is no direct mandate by either school board to suppress or promote their religio-spirituality. Yet the general climates in the districts are seen as promoting a religio-spiritual neutrality.

Works: Educational Practice as Social Justice

The Bible states, "Faith without works is dead.... Faith is made complete by actions" (James 2:17, 22). *Works* as they have been posited in Christian spirituality are good deeds, acts of righteousness, or acts that accompany "living out" the profession of faith that an individual has made. Quite simply, belief does not exist in a vacuum without evidence of that belief. It has been discussed how the participants conceptualize their religio-spirituality and how they conceptualize social justice. Moreover, a part of this research asks, "What are some of the works they perform that accompany their religio-spirituality?"

Social justice in schools continues to be a challenge to understand because there is not one particular meaning. Rizvi (1998) has written,

> Social justice is embedded within discourses that are historically constituted and that are sites of conflicting and divergent political endeavors. Thus, so-

cial justice does not refer to a single set of primary goods, conceivable across all moral and material domains. (p. 47)

Morwenna Griffiths (1998) stated that social justice is achieved through the "right distribution of benefits" (p. 4). In the realm of educational leadership, social justice has been highly contested because of an incoherent body of research regarding it. "Theory building in social justice has been scant.... Without a common language, theory development is difficult at best and unlikely in the worst case" (Merchant & Shoho, 2006, p. 108). Before social justice can become coherent, all narratives and understandings concerning it have to be considered. Besides a wealth of information concerning African American women's history, African American understandings have not been widely considered in social justice in schools. African American women's history may add to the understanding of social justice and contribute to a more full-bodied view and help enlarge the scope of social justice in schools. "Without listening to those who have come before, who will confront future, reconfigured injustices?" (Collins, 1998, p. 75).

"Traditionally, a belief in social justice worked closely with the theology of Black Christian churches" (Cannon, 1988, p. 27). Because of this, Black women have been able to have a broad understanding of social justice and one that includes the intersection of religion, spirituality, and ethics (Higginbotham, 1993). "Spirituality, especially that organized through and sanctioned by Black Christian churches, provides one important way that many African American women are moved to the struggle for justice" (Collins, 1998, p. 244). In many cases, African Americans appropriated moral authority by indeed claiming that Jesus was compelled toward social justice and therefore so should they be.

Of social justice, Collins (1998) stated:

> Emphasis on search for justice...sheds light on the difference between doctrine and faith.... Doctrines constitute fixed and timeless systems of beliefs to be followed blindly. In contrast, faith constitutes a *process* whereby individuals and groups use ethical framework grounded in deeply felt beliefs to construct meaningful everyday lives.... How Bible stories are used illustrates this process: Everyone knows and shares the same story. However, the changing collectivity constructing the stories—new interpretations, lis-

teners, tellers, and the context itself—changes the meaning of the story with each retelling.... Whereas doctrines become discredited, faith persists. (p. 200)

The above quotation has implications for social justice in schools. First, it makes explicit that it is not a useful process to reduce faith as merely a doctrinal, theological concern and one that does not have relevance to the social justice and education process. Second, it legitimates social justice as not merely an outcome but a process that is constantly being interpreted and articulated in a way that is consistent with core beliefs. Third, these core beliefs are not just a reproduction of doctrine in schools, but also a deeply felt ethic of care that can move one toward just acts in schools. African American social justice was couched in collectivity, personal and community advocacy, moral authority, care, and spirituality. "Spirituality comprised articles of faith that provide a conceptual framework for living everyday life" (Collins, 1998, p. 245); and part of that everyday life was the commitment to social justice in all areas of life.

W.E.A.P.O.N.S

Each participant believes that her religio-spirituality exerts influence in her prinicipalship. Battle metaphor fills each of their narratives. "Weapons" is used as an mnemonic to describe the administrative practices of the principals: **w**ord, wisdom, and witness; **e**thic of religio-spirituality; **a**rmor and activism; **p**rayer and perseverance; **o**ntology and epistemology; **n**aming; and **s**piritual fruit. How do people perceive the principalship and, more important, who do they perceive as performing the principalship and in what acts do they engage? The idea of metaphor in this instance is important. The Bible is filled with battle and warfare metaphor. As seen in different parts of the spiritual narratives of the participants, a great part of their lives is correlated to the spiritual battle they see as occurring in their lives. The whole of life is considered a part of the battle, including their principalships. These principals consider themselves as co-warriors with the triune God to fulfill a calling.

The significance of the spiritual historians' religio-spirituality is one that does not portray itself in current educational leadership literature concerning spirituality. In much of the literature, spirituality is often not linked with religion. Spirituality is seen as a benign, self-actualizing process, or a theoretical, exoticized orientation. There is a paucity of research in educational leadership that links spirituality with religion and that addresses it as a process that invites participation in activism, protest, and alternative enactments of the principalship. Womanist theology offers a scaffold for work that links ordinary, everyday acts of justice, religion, and spirituality in the principalship.

Word, Wisdom, and Witness. The Bible plays a part in decision making. "It is not unusual for African Americans to use the Bible as rock-like foundation and as major sources for validating life experiences" (Grant, 1989, p. 39). Each woman indicated that she is committed to frequent Bible reading and often refers to the Bible for wisdom in making decisions. Bobbie indicated that if she is having difficulty making a decision about something, then she often "go[es] to the Word to see what it says."

> Real wisdom lies in the Word. I don't look to the world to tell me what I should do. I keep my Bible in my office, too, on my desk. (Bobbie)

As seen in Pattie's narrative, the Bible is an important part of her life. Her family often completes devotion and prayer time together. She often memorizes favorite Bible verses to help her with decisions in and out of school. Of this process, Pattie said:

> I love the Psalms and Proverbs. Ya know, the Bible says to "bind the Word around your neck." I try to do that. When I am making decisions, God will bring things to mind from His Word that helps me understand what I should do.

Toni discussed keeping her Bible on her desk at school. She indicated that she tries to allow the "scriptures" to guide what she needs to do. She even indicated that she wanted the scriptures to guide her even as I conducted our initial interview.

> I subscribe to that *Daily Bread* and so every day I'll read the short passage there and sometimes I just go in my office just to get away, to read something. I have the Bible open on my desk. Some people may think that I am pretending. But I really do try to walk the walk. On the way over here, I

even tried to think of some scriptures since I thought you may ask me about the scriptures.

Avery discussed the Bible and sermons that she reflects upon to guide her in her work. Avery reflected on one instance in which she used a Bible story from a sermon to make a particular point to her faculty:

> At my school, I sometimes refer, in my Monday morning memo, to one of the sermons at church. The sermon was about God letting us into heaven and how He makes the quick judgment and asks, "Are you a sheep or a goat?" I told them I was referring to the sermon and I quoted the scripture and everything as it relates to our kids. My point was either we are here for the kids or we are not. I wanted the teachers to see that either your goal is to do the very best that you can to educate and prepare these children for life or you are not. You know, are you a sheep or a goat?

Each participant indicated that wisdom is an important part of making decisions in schools. When asked what wisdom was, they all had different views. However, what they all seemed to agree upon is the idea of situational leadership (Hersey & Blanchard, 2007) in matters of decision making. Stringent, inflexible policy demands are not considered appropriate for the participants; their personal beliefs determine how they handle policy.

> I don't think there is one clear-cut way that is right all the time. It takes some wisdom and you have to look at each situation. I know what my kids need. I mean, sometimes with discipline, you just gotta follow the policy. But sometimes situations are different. Sometimes mitigating circumstances may have something to do with that child actin' up. Ya know and then all this stuff with curriculum policy. I can't stand that. What I really can't stand is when I feel like the Board uses policy to hurt these kids. And I really don't like it when some of my teachers try to use it against a kid they don't like or to try to prove a point to a parent. (Pattie)

> Most of the policies just are what they are. I keep in mind that I'm a Christian. I always err on the side of the child. I mean I am always with the kids. People say I'm a little too easy, and I don't know. I had a discipline situation where some kids brought beer to school. My assistant wanted to throw the book at them. This was my issue in my other district because I never wanted to throw the book at kids. The policy always seems to give them the most severe punishment. I think it really depends on the principal. I really didn't

want these kids expelled. I don't want them to have to go through that. So they were put on superintendent's probation for the first semester. So if the policy was too harsh, I'm not going to go with that. I'm here to help kids. I'm not here to crucify kids. The goal should never be to put them out of school. (Avery)

Well I try to follow board policies because I knew that was a quick way to get fired. I tried to follow things like the code of conduct but I would think about the situation. As far as number of days, sometimes some people would give five suspension days for anything and I wouldn't do that. It had to be something really bad for that. Otherwise, I'd send home for a day, or maybe give two to three days in school suspension, depending on the intensity or the severity of the behaviors. (Bobbie)

Witnessing involves modeling for others examples of what they believe are religio-spiritual behavior. Interpersonal and organizational relations are determined by their religio-spirituality. For Bobbie, fairness and honesty are two hallmarks of how she handles relationships and runs her organization. She also expects her teachers to do this as well.

I'm going to be fair with you and I'm going to be honest. People know I'm always up front. They can count on me to do those kinds of things and they know that as far as treating them fairly that I am going to do that. I'm going to do that no matter what and I don't play favorites. With the kids, I tell the kids up front, I don't play favorites because everybody is important to me. My parents and my teachers know these things about me. And this is what I expect from my teachers.

Toni indicated that she often goes "above and beyond" academics for the students in her school. She works hard on behalf of her students and this one of the ideals she wants her teachers to understand and model.

Teachers are kidding themselves when they think that they are just going to be able to go into their classrooms and just teach. And there is so much more to teaching than teaching.

Pattie indicated high expectations as one of the defining characteristics of her school and one she believes is essential to the success of her students. Student excellence is a part of what she views as her mission in schools.

> My students know I expect the best from them. I don't play that. And I expect the best from my teachers too. They better get in there and teach my babies. No half-steppin'. Whenever I am dealing with anybody, I am constantly thinkin' whether that is the best they can do. If I have a teacher issue, I am measuring that against whether they are doing the best they can do. With parents, I am thinking, "Are they getting that?" I know God expects my best. I expect the best from people I deal with too.

Ethic of Religio-Spirituality. It has been discussed how ethics of care and justice and even how religio-spirituality in schools actually translate into a commitment to social justice in the lives of the spiritual historians. In educational leadership, leaders are now facing increasing ethical and moral decisions. Foster (1986) explained, "Each administrative decision carries with it a restructuring of human life: that is why administration at its heart is the resolution of moral dilemmas" (p. 33). Morality and ethics are indeed not seen as separate, just as religion and spirituality are not seen as separate from ethics and morality (Shields, 2005). In educational leadership, a multiple ethical paradigm (Shapiro & Stefkovich, 2005) has been proposed, one that includes an ethic of justice, ethic of care, ethic of critique, and ethic of the profession. According to the model of Shapiro and Stefkovich(OK?) (2005) and the writers they draw upon, each of the ethical paradigms is defined as follows:

> *Ethic of justice* is part of the liberal democratic tradition that concerns itself with laws, rights, and policies and a faith in those. (Delgado, 1995)
>
> *Ethic of care* addresses the needs of individuals and challenges the often patriarchal ethic of justice. (Gilligan, 1982; Noddings, 1984)
>
> *Ethic of critique* is critical of the ethic of justice and challenges issues of race, class, gender, and other areas of difference. (Freire, 1996; Giroux, 1991)
>
> *Ethic of the profession* is concerned with ethics of the community, the personal and professional codes of the educational leader, and the professional codes of professional organizations. (Shapiro & Stefkovich, 2005)

The ethic of justice "has profoundly affected...education and educational leadership" (Shapiro & Gross, 2008, p. 21). In addition, many ethical and moral models in schools "lack color" (Siddle Walker & Snarey, 2004, p. 15) or the perspectives of people of color. White, androcentric approaches to ethics and decision making in schools have dominated educational leadership activities. For this reason, a multiple approach to ethics is beneficial. However, as revealed in this research, there are many different facets to an ethical model. Womanist theology and this research reveal a cultural, theological construct to the ethical debate and highlight how a person's ethics are applied to personal and professional lives.

The women in this study exhibit what I call an ethic of religio-spirituality that is closely aligned with womanist theological tenets. Womanist theology has provided a frame for analyzing how these principals define spirituality, educational philosophies, organizational concerns, and personal practice. Womanist theology has pioneered the notion of theo-ethics, or the ethics grounded in theology and spirituality. In theo-ethics and in educational leadership, there has been a link among commitment to social justice and equity (Capper & Keyes, 1999). Womanist theology clearly uses a multiple ethical perspective as well, but also carries a cultural, communal, and historical relevance needed as alternative ways for viewing ethical and social justice practice in schools.

The participants discussed the ethical and moral nature of their practices in schools. However, this ethical and moral practice is embedded in their religio-spirituality. Pattie put it this way:

> I look at some people and I think that they have no morals or ethics. God values integrity. I try to live my life with some integrity. I try to run my school with integrity.

The next sections highlight more of the ways the principals view principal practice and social justice and the ways both are considered and performed.

Armor and Activism. One of the themes that keeps emerging from their narratives is protection. Closely related to this is the theological construct of armor. The phrase "putting on the armor of God" is taken from Ephesians 6:14. The principals often viewed the institution of schools and the principalship as a harsh place. Their individual schools were also viewed as harsh environments and ones in which they have to guard themselves. Parents, district and state administration, teachers, and community members are sometimes seen as individuals from whom to guard themselves.

> I just try to protect myself. Not everyone means you any good. And that is a hard lesson to learn but you have to do it. Not everyone means well or means you well. (Pattie)

> You have to be on guard. Ya know, the Lord tells us the same thing. There are definitely wolves out there. They have their own agendas. It felt like I had to guard myself from everyone, parents, teachers, folks at central office. (Bobbie)

> I mean, you definitely cannot trust everyone. That's why I am at least grateful for my mentor. This job is hard and you won't make it if you don't have someone to talk to. But you gotta limit that number. (Avery)

Because schools are viewed as such harsh environments, even maintaining religio-spirituality or engaging in acts of social justice is seen as subversive. Pattie viewed district administration with suspicion and does not consider them ethical or having a conscience:

> Sometimes you feel like you have to pretend like you don't have a conscience to get some stuff done.

Through their religio-spirituality, these women believe that God protects them in hardships that they encounter.

Recognizing the often-detrimental effects of school policies on the lives and educational opportunities of children, the principals engage in acts of creative insubordination to undermine these detrimental effects and to ensure the well-being of their students. As seen in some of the discussions above, these acts often come in the form of "tweaking" certain policies or procedures. Among the examples of creative insubordination, principals cited interpreting retention policies, curriculum mandates, and suspension policies in ways that provide opportunities for children to succeed:

> I don't always do what I am supposed to. I mean, there are ways around some of the things the Board tells us to do. I can remember when we were

told to use a certain reading program that I did not agree with. We bought the program and we used some of it. But my teachers used what we knew worked for our kids, especially the struggling ones. (Pattie)

One thing about my district is that we don't have people in our faces every five minutes. I mean, it's not like people are coming over to my school all the time. Nobody checks to see if I am doing something. So I pretend we did. I sleep fine with that. (Avery)

I had people checking on my school all the time. I felt like I was being watched all the time. So I mostly did what I was asked to do. I was asked to keep up with every grade each child had in an entire middle school and record how many were failing and all of that—just a whole bunch of stuff that other principals didn't have to do. They were trying to find something on me. But you know what? While I was doing that, I was also in my teachers' faces making sure they were grading fairly and actually teaching the kids something. I also did not allow teachers to retain students without my approval, even though the policy says that if you are failing two or more classes, you can be retained. They had to have evidence all year that shows why this was the case. (Bobbie)

These seemingly individual actions can be interpreted within the broader context of the life histories of African American female principals who are oriented toward the world in ways that are specifically tied to their faith. The African American female principals depicted in this book employ alternative practices considered by the womanist literature as "transgressive" (hooks, 1995) and "subversive" (Foster & Haywood, 1995). These women operate through a womanist theological perspective in achieving socially just outcomes for the students in their schools.

African American history is rife with examples of women, accountability, and activism in education. Indeed, "Black education developed within a context of political and economic oppression" (Johnson, 2000, p. 27). "Black women often feel accountable to...the Black community's children" (Collins, 1991, p. 129). Because of this accountability, activism on behalf of students occurred. Activism has been described as "strategies of everyday resistance that have largely consisted of trying to create spheres of influence, authority, and power within institutions" (Collins, 1991, p. 154). These acts culminated into an everyday advocacy for their students. The principals seek to gain agency for themselves as principals through creative insubordination. Some of their self-descriptions are closely aligned with the notions of "tempered radicals" (Meyerson & Scully, 1995) in their district and in their schools. While recognizing the needs of their students and the limitations of the policies dictated by local, state, and national policies, these principals act to counteract the effects of these policies without violating "the letter of the law." Bobbie directly challenged the board policy and was demoted because of it. Through community support, protests, boycotts, and a lawsuit, she has established herself as someone who is a radical figure in the district. However, the other participants' activism has been less open and direct. Their behavior aligns with Collins (1991), who stated that sometimes activism "does not directly challenge oppressive structures because direct confrontation is neither preferred nor possible" (p. 141). Fear of retaliation and a lack of belief in the need to be openly confrontational or political has led to their "silence."

> I don't have to say anything necessarily to get something done. I simply do what I do. I actually get more done by not getting in someone's face every five minutes. That just puts you on the radar. You don't say anything, you can't get accused of anything. I accomplish plenty by doing what I do. (Pattie)

> I quietly go about my business and do what I think I need to do. That's enough. I suppose if I needed to say something, I would. But so far I am doing a lot of good. (Avery)

> I guess I am afraid to be too vocal about things. I mean, I don't wanna make anybody mad. That's just who I am. But I still feel like I can do what's right. (Toni)

Prayer and Perseverance. As noted in each woman's narrative, prayer is an essential part of their personal lives. However, prayer plays a critical part in their leadership activities as well. Prayer for these women is a part their rituals before the decision-making process, but also serves a reflective process at the "end." They often cited being in prayer daily about their schools or before major decisions or particularly difficult ones.

> Anyway, every morning as I'm coming to work I say a prayer, "God help me to make good decisions and do what's best for these kids. (Toni)

> Sometimes my pastor will come and pray with me in my office. Sometimes it is just for the school in general but also when things are going on. (Bobbie)

> I pray all day long. You can't do this job without it. There is too much to do. I pray for wisdom all the time. (Pattie)

The principals also discussed praying when potential harm could come to them as principals.

> I have been praying many things. There was racial discrimination since the minute I stepped foot in this system. Well, you face so much. Things that were done to you unfairly, you always got the bad end of every deal. You just had to pray, God help me. I had to pray about it a lot, what was going on and what I wanted the Lord to do, to help me with. To change people's hearts and minds about things, not just bad things against them but to change their heart and give them a different way of thinking about it and to deliver me from it, deliver me from that place and help me find somewhere else to go. (Bobbie)

> I always say, "These folks better not mess with me 'cause I am God's child. They don't know who they are messin' with. Even what people may mean for harm, He can take and turn it right around. (Pattie)

The participants do not just pray in times of difficulty. There are also moments when they pray after some success or positive moment.

> When my school's scores went up, I just thanked God for it. (Toni)

> Like at graduation, I looked at these babies and think to myself, "Lord just be with them." They have their whole lives ahead of them. (Pattie)

> I just pray for them all the time. I pray when something good happens and I pray when bad things happen. (Avery)

Just as there is a situatedness to their decision making and religio-spirituality, certain circumstances require certain types of prayers. Bobbie said:

> Some situations call for drastic measures—when you feel like there really is an attack from the devil. There and times when I would have to anoint myself with oil and anoint my office.

Each of the participants discussed the difficulties with the principalship. While all of them have gained satisfaction from doing what they feel "called" to do, the majority of their stories dealt with the hardships of the principalship. Prayer is a way to overcome the hardships of the principalship. For Pattie and Bobbie, they remain in their positions and can cope because of the strength they get from their religio-spirituality.

> I could have left a long time ago. It is because of God that I can make it. He is the reason I stay. (Bobbie)

> I will stay until He tells me to do something else. He never promised us this life would not be hard. I knew this job was deep when I took it. So did He. If He saw fit to give me the position, then He thinks I can handle it. He doesn't give us more than we can handle. (Pattie)

Bobbie and Pattie seem to be bound by their sense of accountability to God to remain in their positions. They have found strength in the moral authority of the mission they believe they have been given. Toni and Avery also have found strength in this same way, but indicated more an agency in their mission. Although they do view their jobs as callings, they do not want to remain in the principalship.

> I don't wanna do this the rest of my life. I don't understand these people that stay here forever. I have more of an opportunity to have an impact on more kids, you know, and so as an administrator, it has been more power and influence even though I don't want to stay in this position very long because it is no fun. (Toni)

> I agree with that. It's not something I want to do for too much longer and I don't ever want another principalship. The only way I can see myself doing this again is if I've moved out of state and just had to have a job. But as long as I'm around here, I mean, if I'm going to be a principal, I'll just stay where I am. I don't ever see myself having another principalship. I'll never say never, though I don't see it happening. (Avery)

Prayer is a large part of their personal and professional lives. They believe that prayer has the power to truly effect change by moving God to act in their lives and in their schools. This has caused the principals to make decisions and persevere for as long as they hold their leadership positions.

Ontology and Epistemology. The participants' narratives and this research have given primacy to Black women's religio-spiritual experience in matters of educational leadership. The women discussed hold true to this concept. Rather than relying wholly upon policy, administrators, or dictates by stakeholders to inform their decision making, the participants looked to how they define themselves and their own experience and knowledge to guide their actions. Brumet (2000) states, "Spiritualities are systems of explanation…. Spirituality undergirds a system of knowledge and tells people how to draw conclusions and truths from certain experiences" (p. 123). Undeniably, the participants' interpretations of situations and decisions in school are drawn from their religio-spiritual beliefs. The whole of their identity as Christians and Black women locates itself in their principal practices.

Educational leadership research has allowed only partial exploration of the relationship between spirituality and education and has ignored certain epistemological and ontological frames such as religion and faith. Shields (2005) states:

> One of the reasons why religio-spirituality presents epistemological challenges…is that it is inseparable from ontological positions. In other words, how we come to know is embedded in who we are and how we choose to live our lives. (p. 9)

In other words, one cannot separate who one is from what one knows. In the same way, the participants cannot separate their identity, knowledges, and experiences from their practice in schools. These ideas can be best described by Pattie:

> I am a Christian. It is who I am. I have no choice but to have my faith show up in school. To me it is the same as being Black and a woman. Can't do nothin' 'bout that either.

Each woman has a way of applying her own specialized way of knowing the decision-making process. For them, an interchange happens in the synapse between problem to solution, idea to decision. Prayer and communing with God, consultation of the Bible or other religious resources, reflection upon past experiences, and application of their religio-spiritual views influence the outcome or practice.

Womanist theology values all ways of knowing, but also ways of being, and particularly those of religio-spiritual African American women, in every sphere of life. Womanist theology also values a broad spectrum of knowledge (historical, theological, spiritual, professional, personal, collective, and individual, to name a few). No matter from where the knowledge emerges, what matters is the way it "works" and impacts the individual life. However, the collective struggle of Black female principals to work toward social justice is deeply embedded in a set of cultural practices and lived experiences that privilege the epistemic and ontological claims of spirituality as a guiding force. What they know and how they know *and* who they are or perceive themselves to be inform their practice.

Naming. The participants frequently engage in behavior that is not considered normal or traditional leadership behavior. They have the ability to name and rename what traditional notions of leadership behavior are by the practice in which they engage. For instance, leadership behavior de-legitimizes religio-spiritual practice by an overemphasis on technocratic, managerial and policy-driven skills (Shields, 2005). These principals' beliefs and actions take religion and spirituality from the margins. They do not couch spirituality as solely a secularized spiritual endeavor to make it more acceptable. The participants name spirituality as religion and make clear the ways that it informs their practice through working for social justice. By identifying and naming their educational practice with religio-spirituality, the performance of the principalship becomes de-normed. Their narratives highlight how their lives and practice name, confrontationally or non-confrontationally, acts of injustice in schools and some ways in which they attempt to "do justly" (Micah 6:8) in schools and society.

And I feel a need to be there because not many people have the courage or the guts or whatever you want to say, to speak up or stand up for what is right. (Bobbie)

I don't have to do it often but I will say what I need to say if it is not right. A lot of times, I just do what I want to do, ya know, the direct opposite of what central office says to do. But sometimes you have to let people know what they are doing wrong. (Pattie)

The women's narratives noticeably reveal that practicing their religio-spirituality does not mean "that one disregards the organizational context in which they [are] embedded" (Starratt, 2005c, p. 70). Womanism theology takes the unique positionality, experience, and practice of African American religio-spiritual women and critically applies them to "normal" institutional practice. This theoretical perspective considers the experiences of Black women as normal, and not as a derivation or variation (Beauboeuf-Lafontant, 2002).

Indeed, most leadership theories affirm the primacy of bureaucracy) and are often considered as the grand narratives of the field. In addition, aspiring leaders and principals are socialized to certain behaviors considered as authentic leadership and atypical behaviors are "dismissed as...deviant or deficient" (Marshall, 1996, p. 275). Current administrative licensure agencies have reduced school administration and leadership to a set of value-free knowledges, dispositions, and performances that mirror current masculine leadership practice.

The practices of educational leadership often have very little to do with either education or leadership.. As the principals indicated, for them the principalship and its activities are about more than education or simply leading and "running" a school. These women's narratives highlight an alternative narrative to educational leadership practice and one that emphasizes care, social justice, activism, and deep spirituality.

Spiritual Fruit. The participants constantly discussed being compelled by God toward right behavior in the principalship. While the list varies, their leadership behaviors are ones of partnering with God as their leader, and they in turn provide leadership to the school. Much of their discussion centered on their principal practice as social justice, but they also want certain outcomes. They want their leadership behaviors to "bear fruit."

> I want to bear fruit. How hard I work should bear fruit. God tells us that we will be known by the fruit we bear. I mean if I am running around barking at people all the time, that won't bear fruit. I might "fruit" my way on outta here! But the things I work toward should help, not hurt. (Bobbie)

Spiritual fruit serves as a representation of some of the specific ways that the spiritual historians have attempted to achieve social justice in their schools. Creating a just environment for their students is rooted in their religio-spiritual mission to provide equitable and successful fruit for their students. In the narrative, this fruit is highlighted in (a) improvement and maintenance of the physical plant, (b) securing and distributing resources, and (c) increasing student achievement.

Improvement and maintenance of the physical plant. The school environment is particularly important to all of the principals. As one participant said, "I want my students to be happy while they are at school. This should be a haven for them" (Avery). Much of this environmental change comes in the form of beautifying the school or fighting for structural improvements. Avery hired an artist to create a mural in part to promote the culture of the school by the depictions of it. Yet she also indicated that she did it to make the school "pretty and happy." Avery discussed the age of the school buildings and one incident in which she had to fight for improvement.

> My school is pretty old. Was built in 1955. You have to let the water run because the brown rust stuff comes out first for a while. When you go to the bathroom, you think, "Why is the water in the toilet that color?" I was thinking it's just school water, but it is more than that. I realized it was the pipes and I needed to do something about it. Overall I think the schools in my district are very well maintained. I mean 1955, that's a pretty significant age and they have done a decent job. But the water, we had to do something about that.

Toni described her building and her support of becoming involved politically to gain capital improvements or get a new school.

> My school was built in the 1940s. It is not, I mean we are supposed to get a new school. This is why we need this sales tax.

Bobbie's school is very old, and there was much debate in the district about what to do with the school. Options for her school included rebuilding, moving to an existing facility, or making improvements to the existing structure. Bobbie was in favor of rebuilding the school to make matters equitable for her students since they were placing new schools in other parts of town. Bobbie fought by repeatedly making her position known in school board meetings. She also solicited community support in this endeavor.

> I got tired of them doing things on other parts of town. I wrote letters, got my teachers to write letters, parents to write letters. I got the community leaders involved too. We would go to the school board and let them know that we wanted a new school too. My kids are no less than anyone else. (Bobbie)

Pattie's school had been redesigned more recently with significant upgrades to the outer structure and the addition of classrooms. However, Pattie maintains strict procedures with teachers to make sure their rooms and displays are child-centered and aesthetically pleasing. Pattie's school also partnered with a local university to create a school garden to add to the overall aesthetic of the school.

> I go into teachers' rooms to check bulletin boards and stuff. I look at how neat they keep their rooms and I check hall displays. If it's one thing I can't stand it's going in someone's room and it looks bad. My kids can't learn in that mess.... Children should have a nice place to come to. We have our little garden and they love it. It makes things look nice.

All of the principals discussed making sure that the school staff and janitorial staff maintains an orderly, organized, and clean building overall.

Securing and distributing resources. All of the principals discussed school funding inequities. In addition, they discussed the issue of poverty for some of their students. School resources in each district are often scarce or inequitable. The principals discussed raising school funds for school activities and materials through soliciting donations or extracurricular fundraisers,

> I work with the churches a lot to get things for my school. Sometimes they make donations. Sometimes we will have a dance or something and charge a dollar. We hold fundraisers and sell things like cookie dough. (Bobbie)

> We ask for donations and fundraisers. I don't like doing it, but we need things. Sometimes I just pay for things from my own pocket. (Avery)

The principals also discussed distributing the funding that they do receive appropriately. Pattie said that appropriate distribution of funds within the school is necessary to achieve social justice goals:

> We could always use more money, but I try to use what I do have the right way. Some schools don't use these funds right. Some principals don't know how to say no to certain things or certain grade levels to make sure needs are being met. You gotta make sure you are directing funds to the things that truly need improving.

Appropriate distribution of funds and resources at the district level is also considered important. Bobbie discussed fighting for equity in distributing these funds and resources:

> Other schools in the district have families with money. There are schools that have money just sitting in a general fund that is all donations. I need books or computers, why not give that to my school that doesn't have families who pump extra money in the school. I remember an issue with my school and computers. Other schools had computer labs that the school itself had funded. Then the district decided to furnish computer labs. Why would you give that other school computers when they already had new ones? Just because you wanted things to be equal? I told the central office that my kids needed more computer labs.

The principals also discussed attempting to find resources for their students and their families that are not necessarily academically related. These resources come in many forms and from various agencies.

> When I know that a child doesn't have something or the family has a need, I contact the ministers. Sometimes kids don't have coats or the family doesn't have food. (Bobbie)

> My church has kind of adopted my school. I can usually count on them if there is a need. (Avery)

> One thing you have to do is establish a good relationship with the community agencies we have around here. Everyone should have at least one contact in Child Services and places like that. (Pattie)

Grant writing is another way to secure resources. Pattie wrote a grant in which she received funding for extended-day activities. These activities include art and music lessons, tutoring, and field trips.

The principals also discussed trying to increase parent participation as a resource. Parents are resources for services such as tutoring, mentoring, and classroom assistance. The principals actively solicit parents for field trips, PTA involvement, and volunteering. Parent volunteers are used all over the school, and not just in their children's classrooms. Parents assist in beautifying the school environment with yardwork, painting, and school cleanup projects.

All of the schools are classified as Title I schools, which provides these schools with a parent involvement coordinator. This coordinator solicits assistance from families and also serves as a resource to students and their families. The principals and counselors often put families who need resources in touch with appropriate agencies.

Increasing student achievement. The participants consider achievement a part of their religio-spiritual obligation. All of the principals pointed out that one of their biggest priorities is to raise their students' test scores. They all are aware of the realities that accompany state and federally mandated achievement tests. For schools failing to meet AYP, these achievement tests can result in increased oversight and bureaucratization in their schools. For individual students, the results can be retention, labeling, tracking, and increased external pressure to "pass" the test. In most instances, the goal is not so much to make sure their students pass the test, but to make sure their students are learning and gaining the knowledges and skills they need to succeed beyond their time at school. Avery spoke about this:

> I don't care about the test per se. I care about whether my kids are learning. If they are learning, then the test will show that. That is why I want to im-

prove test scores. They do tell us whether students are learning in the classroom.

The principals have different ways of making sure their students are successful academically. All of the principals discussed making sure that at-risk and struggling students receive appropriate intervention. NCLB requires that students receive intervention in reading and math; however, the local school principal has to enforce that. These principals indicated that not all principals make sure this happens, but it is important to them. Intervention comes in the form of remedial classes, tutoring, working with specialists, and extra assistance from classroom teachers. Providing intervention also comes in the form of securing materials and programs for their students.

> I always did walk-throughs to make sure that teachers were teaching. I check all grades and I sign every report card. I also make sure that those that need help are getting it. (Bobbie)

> I don't always have a lot of time, but I try to write grants or get my teachers to write grants.... I review test data all the time and make sure our intervention classes are working well. I don't let them pull students from the classroom anymore. Students have to get intervention in class. (Pattie)

> I make sure that struggling students are getting extra help. It's hard because the teachers have a lot on them but we try to make sure everyone is being served. (Avery)

It is worth noting that test scores are not the only aspect of achievement for the students. Test scores are only a measure of whether their students are experiencing success in various areas. The principals indicated wanting to make sure they create various learning opportunities for their students, and they all work hard to fund field trips and have assemblies at their schools. The principals also want the students to experience success in their home lives. By securing resources for students and their families, the principals believe they are also helping them experience success.

This section highlighted a few of the actions that the spiritual historians enact in achieving social justice that is part of the spiritual fruit of their lives. When asked what they hoped to accomplish, the participants gave various responses.

In the end, I hope they see God in how I live my life. I want to please God, do what I am supposed to do. Live how I am supposed to live. (Bobbie)

I want my kids successful. I want them to have a fair shot in life. This life is hard, but maybe I can give them something that can help them overcome that. (Avery)

I don't know. Some days I wonder what I am doing here. I am doing the best I can, the best I know. (Toni)

They all discussed the principalship and the work of social justice as an ongoing process. They all expected outcomes for themselves and for their students. By engaging in acts that they believed promoted the cause of social justice for students, they believed they would bear much fruit.

Meditations

It is difficult to separate social justice from the idea of religio-spirituality (Ross, 2002). Although they did not have one particular definition of religio-spirituality in the narratives, the principals engage in the work of social justice and equate it with religio-spirituality. Ultimately their goal is to emulate Christ whose work is considered the work of justice (Mitchem, 2002). The work of religio-spirituality is one grounded in a particular worldview and one that is also met with obstacles within and outside of the school. These obstacles and the struggle of leading religio-spiritually becomes one in which there is redemption in the struggle. Wilderness becomes a space in which change may occur on behalf of students.

Religio-spirituality became a nexus of inspiration, motivation, and meaning-making (Dantley, 2003) in the lives of the principals. Religio-spirituality has established and stimulated their sense of equity and composed their notions of calling, mission, and purpose. Indeed, religio-spirituality has *narrated* their lives personally and professionally. Although the principals indicated the difficulty of the principalship, their religio-spirituality is not just one to which they turn in times of stress. The principals participate in those areas of administration that are harmonious with their religio-spiritual views and in some ways reject what they view as incongruent with their faith. The principals exhibit creative insubordination (Jones & Licata, 1995) in the interpretation of policy to promote social justice through articulating womanist theological principles. Their religio-spiritual belief system impacts pedagogy, practice, social justice, and leadership in schools. Their lives are a pursuit in living authentically, unifying their identities, making congruent their personal and professional character, and bringing all they know to bear upon their lives.

While there is no one way to enact or define social justice, womanist theology demands no one definition. Womanist theology inspects and critiques the multiple ways justice is lived in the ordinary lives of women. These women's narratives bring to the forefront how religio-spirituality acts as social justice in schools. In their cases, it is simply "righting wrongs."

The next chapter explores the uniqueness of womanist theology in the research on religion, spirituality, and educational leadership. It proposes new theorizing in these areas with womanist theology as a frame for doing research and leading for social justice. The chapter also looks at the limitations of the study, ponders future research, and offers concluding thoughts.

Chapter 5

Spirit-led: The Dialogic of Womanist Theology and Educational Leadership

A good way to understand people is to study their religion, for religion is addressed to that most sacred schedule of values around which the expression and the meaning of life tends to coalesce.

(Lincoln & Mamiya, 1990, p. xi)

When one is said to be guided by God, she is said to be led by the Spirit (Houchins, 1988). The women discussed in this book led with their spirituality and were led by their spirituality. They clearly exhibited that leadership and religio-spirituality intersected in a way that significantly impacted the ways they thought about and enacted the principalship. When I initially began thinking about conducting this research, I kept thinking, "Can religion and spirituality have anything to offer in educational leadership and vice versa?" Can the religio-spiritual process have anything to offer to the literature in a way that sheds more light on the process of leadership? This research has taken spirituality from more of a vague concept and offered insights into the ways that religion frames spirituality for some individuals. Rather than over-reminding that spirituality in educational leadership is not always identical to religion (Starratt, 2005c), this research tends to the ways in which it is. The womanist theological tenets of reciprocity and critical engagement espouse the idea of seemingly competing ideas being in communication with one another. The separation of church and state has presented an often-artificial dichotomy among religion, spirituality, and schooling. This research examined ways in which seemingly disparate ideas occupy the same space in schooling and in leadership.

This idea extends to my idea of the goal of this research. Testimony has often been defined as telling what God has done in one's life (Ross, 2006). In Chapter Four, "Testimony," the spiritual narratives highlight the import of religio-spirituality in each principal's life and how it impacts the principalship. This was done through examining educational philosophy, organizational issues and tensions, and educational practice. However, womanist theologians discuss the concept of testimony as a reflexive process grounded in dialogue with other perspectives. "Instead of keeping worlds alien to one another…worlds [are] in conversation with one another" (Floyd-Thomas, 2006b, p. 63). The field of educational leadership and the religio-spiritual experience have important ideas to teach each other. There stands on one side the taken-for-granted notions of the world of educational leadership. On the other are two perspectives that have been silenced in educational leadership narrative. The perspective of the Black woman and that of the religio-spiritual individual are added to the literature as "serious" (Walker, 1983) considerations for the principalship in practice, policy, and theory.

Warnick (2004) suggests that education must engage religious and spiritual thought or it risks remaining outside the field and thus outside the scope of understanding or examination. Lack of engagement carries with it the burden of alienating those to whom religious thought matters. "A large number of people look to their religion for meaning and guidance and education is not exempt" (Warnick, 2004). In an effort to provide space in education for work that explores religion and spirituality, Warnick (2004) offered the idea of "interpreting religion and its influences on contemporary life" (p. 346). "Any inquiry such as this asks what a religious or spiritual tradition *means*, or *what its import is*" (author emphasis)(Warnick, 2004, p. 347) for the individual; it does not attempt to answer whether the religious tradition is true nor does it attempt to find agreement. These ideas scaffolded my thinking surrounding discussion of religio-spirituality in schools instead of solely in the area of theology. This research did not seek to examine the truthfulness of any of the participants' claims, but to understand the participants' meanings of them.

Principals' values and beliefs influence their vision of the school as well as their behaviors (Greenfield, 1991; Hallinger, Bickman, & Davis, 1990; Krug, Scott, & Ahadi, 1990). Greenfield (1991) states that the principal's belief system is important to understand because it colors practically everything the principal does on a daily basis (p. 6). Krug et al. (1990) concluded that the principal's interpretation of that belief and the leadership activity is of primary importance. For me, womanist theology became a unique framework for understanding these beliefs. "Womanism in theory and action are not distinct and separable parts, they are often synonymous" (Borum, 2006, p. 347). A womanist theological approach and spiritual narratives can provide the field of educational research a way to understand the lens of religio-spirituality and the field of educational leadership. It gave a unique way of examining oft-taboo subjects in education (religion and spirituality) while engaging the diverse voices of educational leadership narratives, particularly those of African American females. The perspectives of these women were un-silenced, given access in schools, and understood as ways of "creating coherence, attaching meaning, caring, wrestling with new questions, resisting, contesting inequities, and propounding change" (McLaughlin & Tierney, 1993, p. 238).

Synthesis and Implications of Findings

In the case of this research, the personal meaning of religio-spirituality was defined. For these women, religio-spirituality was one that was personally defined by each principal, albeit it one that had been grounded in the Baptist denominational tradition. Each woman's faith was a mixture of spiritualities and one that was conversional, situated in wilderness and warfare, and one deeply rooted in culture. However, the notion of interlock and intersection (Crenshaw, 1991; Martin, 1998) was seen in their religio-spirituality and in their positions as principals. Religio-spirituality served as an intersection and sense-maker for all of their self-proclaimed identities. However, religio-spirituality also served as a means to contest hegemonic tendencies located in these identities by staking their claim as Black women to the principalship and working on behalf of students through social justice. Their ordinary theologies name not only the interlocking and complementary nature of these identities, but also the intersecting realities these women faced in their lives and in their work.

Gender-Racing

Gender roles and expectations did have an impact on the moral, ethical, social, and psychological development of the participants. There was a distinctive worldview of these women. "In a racist and sexist society the concept of a Black woman empowered by God is doubly radical" (Tate, 1992, p. 152). Because of this unique way in which the women's stories and their principalships were experienced, I offer that their religio-spirituality is *gender-raced.* Being Black and being a woman was central to the unique ways in which they experienced their religio-spirituality and their various life roles and identities.

School highlighted some of the ways that they perceived gender and race as coloring their experience. A specific question of this research dealt with the tensions among schooling and religio-spirituality. In their district, Bobbie and Pattie perceived an overlap in how they were viewed as Black women and as religio-spiritual individuals. For instance, Bobbie was viewed as a possible proselytizer or practicing witchcraft by some individuals at the school and at the district office. Bobbie believed this was in large part due to her being Black and a woman. She stated several times that this incident and other issues surrounding her principalship would not have happened to her were she not a Black woman. Similarly, Pattie indicated how she did not discuss her religion at school. She did not want to give anyone any ammunition to fire her, since the district administrators "don't want Black women at the top anyway." For Bobbie and Pattie, religio-spirituality seemed to result in a more visibility in their principalships and an increased loss of voice as principals. Each of them discussed being excluded from certain conversations and district decisions. Bobbie discussed the fact that when the district did not want to give her money for something, personnel would remind her that she "had all those churches in her neighborhood and she could ask them." Religio-spirituality was regarded as a particular of the African American community in which her school was located. Yet, her own personal faith was seen as exotic or emotional, and she was known as the "holy roller." Avery and Bobbie were different in that they openly proselytized to students, but attributed this to their largely African American communities and the large number of female administrators in their district. When asked what they meant, they specifically talked about the superintendent and other district administrators as being more "understanding." They also indicated that they believed that their actual placement at their schools was possibly because they were Black women and religio-spiritual. Of this, Avery said:

> Our schools are hard. I think our superintendent weighed where to put us. She knows our schools. It takes a special person to be at our type of schools.

It was difficult to ascertain to what extent these claims were fact, but each of the women seemed to indicate that they experienced their religio-spirituality in schools in a gendered and raced way. The intersection of race, gender, and religio-spirituality impacted their principalship. It is interesting that at school, the women seemed to enact less traditional roles than they did outside of school. Each of the women's narratives indicated more traditional beliefs about their roles in their families and in their churches. They all in some way showed their agreement with roles in churches and the male hierarchy of their churches' leadership. In their families, three of the women indicated a belief in the notion of the male as the head of the household. (As a divorced woman, however, Avery did not comment on this issue.) In contrast, they embodied different ideas concerning authority and roles in schools. They all clearly indicated the belief in their own headship at school.

Each principal indicated some challenges to her authority in schools. However, each woman attributed it either to being a Black woman, or to a lack of shared vision in some way with other stakeholders. The participants discussed having to make decisions that they felt were best in spite of other stakeholders. The participants also discussed the intent of their religio-spirituality, regardless of the value system that others may possess. In some instances, there also was an assumption on the part of the principals that their values were shared by others. Although the principals acknowledged that not all parents were religio-spiritual, they assumed the parents would have no objection to their value system. A consideration could be that some of these challenges to authority were a by-product of a lack of shared or communicated values, and not solely an objection to the principals' gender or race. By considering their mission as an individual endeavor, the principals quite conceivably were excluding the voices of their stakeholders. Each principal was so firmly rooted in her belief system and her mission that it could be construed as monolithic and exclusionary. A central question becomes, "What happens to those associated with the school who are not religio-spiritual?"

Women's leadership has become a focus of research and scholarly practice. Even so, there is a long way to go in engaging African American and religio-spiritual perspectives in the dialogue. This research does not attempt to offer a formula to become a religio-spiritual leader nor does it attempt to generalize what it means to be a Black female leader. There is a danger in essentializing notions of feminist leadership (Court, 2005). In fact, an unexpected outcome of this research indicated a disconnect between their metaphors and the traditional ones often applied in Black female leadership. Metaphors such as "othermothers" and "servant leaders" have appeared in research concerning African American teaching, leading, and spirituality (Alston, 2005; Beauboeuf-Lafontant, 1999, 2002; Case, 1997; Foster, L., 2005; Foster, M., 1993; Keyes, Hanley-Maxwell, & Capper, 1995; Loder, 2005). However, the women in this study highlighted the "burden" of these metaphors and their ensuing roles and required enactments. "Burden" became a new metaphor for and highlighted these often-assumed roles of the Black female principal. These women eschewed these gendered and raced norms of what it means to be the Black female principal. These gendered and raced norms are too simplistic. This research highlights that there are no fixed norms of leadership and certainly none for the Black female or religio-spiritual leader.

Through the theoretical framework, this research attempted to explore religio-spirituality as a way to name a new narrative of educational leadership—one that names Black religio-spiritual women's experiences to recognize, create, and explain that which is meaningful for them in the principalship. Although these principals experienced their religio-spirituality as gender-raced, this is not an attempt to arrive at another framework or "prescriptive, normative ethic" for the woman in leadership (Cannon, 1988, p. 5). Too often, research concerning women in educational leadership has been one that is uncomfortable with the ambiguity and situational nature of the principalship. In an effort to give voice to the female perspective, it is one that has become narrow in its focus of women's ways of leading. This research is not simply to promote these women as "brave social activists (as literary historians do) or exemplary nurturing Christians (as Womanist theo-ethicists do)" (Moody, 2003, p. 166). When a Black woman leader declares herself religio-spiritual or grounded in her own way of knowing, there is a danger of a reduction to the sentimental, overly subjective, emotional, and "feminine." Moreover, often in the field of educational leadership, religio-spirituality becomes gendered and raced as an overly applied notion of care or another construct of the urban school.

Religio-Spirituality and Social Justice

Although social justice has become a priority of educational leadership, discussions are often colorblind, gendered, liberal, and separate from the religious (Siddle Walker & Snarey, 2004; Thompson, 2000). Although a white, androcentric form of justice has profoundly affected education and educational leadership, care has been cited as immensely important in schools (Shapiro & Gross, 2008). Rather than simply promoting the addition of a religio-spiritual perspective, womanist theology may provide a bridge from African American perspectives to cross-cultural ones to further advance the increasing social justice agenda in schools. This research offers the perspective of four Black female religio-spiritual principals. However, "in speaking of the Black experience, one can still talk to the human condition" (Angelou, as cited in Blakeney & Blakeney, 2004, p. 147). The idea of pastoral care presented in this research opens a new door between care and justice, and removes it from one that is gendered and raced. One perspective of social justice is not valued over another in school. The notion of pastoral care takes traditional notions of care that have claimed a universalistic, white, middle-class approach. This is one that I believe is formulaic and impersonal and applies a universality to the needs of individuals and groups. Traditional notions of care do not allow for the many ways in which care is enacted or the various motivations for it. This research highlights a form of care that is motivated by religio-spiritual ideas, yet one that can be applied broadly whether it is motivated by relgio-spirituality or not. The women in this study applied care and responded based on individual needs, situations, and contexts. Their form of care carried a familial and communal response that takes responsibility for the care and individuals in ways that traditional notions of care do not. For instance, Noddings (1984) espouses care in such a way as to posit that the application of care will ensure results. Unlike established notions of care, the pastoral care these principals engaged in sought to address interlocking systems of material realities, community realities, and spiritual realities.

This research does not argue that Black female religio-spiritual principals have a monopoly or uncontested truth about religio-spirituality, social justice, or leadership in schools. In womanist theology there is a value in the ethic of critique. The critically engaged individual may be obliged to ask, "What about stakeholders in schools who hold competing values? Must one be religio-spiritual to further a social justice agenda?" These are valid questions. However, an outcome of this research is to add another conceptual tool in understanding and bringing coherence to the realm of social justice and the educational leadership process. "No single voice is ever adequate, so a plurality of tongues is essential" (Blakeney & Blakeney, 2004). As with critical engagement and reciprocity, other concepts are welcome and through dialogue, all concepts can be critiqued and examined. The bigger danger is in silencing any voice in this process. "A consistent flaw in our leadership practices over time has been their failure to deal with social justice issues" (English, 2008, p. 1) on *any* level, no matter the perspective.

"Social justice is more than simply a political movement or policy statement" (R. Mitchell, personal communication, April 16, 2008). It is not a new concept, and it is a commitment forged in the entire nature of the individual. In *Educating School Leaders for Social Justice*, Cambron-McCabe and McCarthy (2005) discuss the themes of social justice as equity, values, justice, and care. Even so, there is no exploration of the origin of these ideas and no mention of religion or spirituality. As seen in my research, core commitments inform the idea of social justice rather than a policy framework for social justice. These core commitments include religion and spirituality. These values must be discussed to free them from the misunderstandings we have about them.

Some of the principals discussed openly proselytizing; and even those who did still indicated a strong inclination toward communicating their religio-spirituality and helping others realize this same religio-spirituality. However, the principals who did discuss religion openly with their students specified that they did so in relationship to that particular community and with individual students. Even so, the religio-spiritual principal would do well to complete careful self-examination and possibly exercise caution. Research surrounding religion and spirituality has been completed in urban settings and as a taken-for-granted assumption of culture or womanhood. Critical engagement is silenced or subdued by applying those labels to religion and spirituality and failing to address or highlight the tensions among stakeholders. Current research has failed to examine how to deal with those whose beliefs do not align with those of the majority.

The principals in this research indicated a strong commitment to the individuality of their mission. This could cause them to exclude the voices of other stakeholders in goal-setting, vision-making, and attainment. These principals indicated a desire to transform their schools for the better. However, a part of transformation is an emphasis on collaboration. The challenge to this transformation process may be in realizing that leadership is not done by just one person, but it is a process that brings together a community of stakeholders around a vision.

To simply interrogate these women's narratives as religion gone awry or crossing the line of church and state is to diminish the narrative. "A dogged refusal to acknowledge the good whatsoever in religion" (Nash, 1999, p. 2) is to deny the "powerful and beneficial role that...faith often plays in the lives of believers" (Nash, 1999, p.3). Having a dialogic interaction of religion and spirituality and schools does more than debate knowledge claims or truthfulness. In support of this idea, I cite Nash (1999) who said:

> The genius in all religions...resides in their power to help us discover and create meaning...I ask the questions...Does it work? Does it tell a convinc-

ing story, move people, provide a sense of purpose, foster community, inspire moral action, and explain the unknown? (p. 6)

The intent of this research is not to give a rationale or promote the idea that principals who engage in certain religious behaviors are merely about social justice or are harmless. There are real questions about how needs are identified and the correct response to them discovered. For example, the women in this study all had a religio-spiritual response to what they perceived as the needs of their schools and of their students. While identifying needs is a part of the principalship, such an individualistic approach to their leadership is problematic. How valid is the needs assessment without the input and support of other stakeholders in this process? Such a highly private approach to leadership in such a public organization can undermine the work of social justice, derail the very outcomes these principals were trying to achieve, and fail to be dialogic with others and their ideas.

In spite of these issues, I would offer that for real dialogue about social justice, ethics, or morality in schools to occur, there must be an effort to explore religion and spirituality's contributions in the educational leadership literature. Through dialogue, individuals can learn to "articulate, clarify, and deepen the underlying…beliefs that drive their practices" (Nash, 1999, p. 6). In addition, dialogue can shine the light on, unpack, and critique all sides of commitments that influence schools. However, a position cannot be critiqued until it is examined and understood (Comstock, 2004). A failure to dialogue around these issues is to keep all sides misunderstood and secret, both issues that we know impact social justice and schooling in general.

Beyond Standards: Principal Preparation, Practice, and Research

The Interstate School Leaders Licensure Consortium (ISLLC) Standards are the national standards for educational leadership. The standards were recently revised and are now renamed the Educational Leadership Policy (ELP) Standards: ILLSC 2008. These standards exist to provide a foundation on which to base principal practice and preparation (Young, 2008). Each standard begins with the phrase, "An educational leader promotes success of every student by

..." and is aligned to current research concerning effective leadership. What is heartening is that the notion of effective leadership and success has been broadened to include the practice of democracy, social justice, diversity, and equity. Regardless of the frames that inform them, these ELP standards create a demand for increased understanding of the practices that accompany these standards.

The University Council of Educational Administration (UCEA) is a network of 92 doctoral degree-granting institutions in educational leadership that is dedicated to providing research and professional development to build on the success of schoolchildren by addressing the challenges affecting school leaders. This premier organization and its leadership have begun to recognize that the role of educational leaders is not as narrowly defined as it once was . UCEA has partnered with ILSSC to promote quality standards for educational leaders, yet there is a focus by UCEA to build preparation programs that move beyond a narrow list of standards. According to UCEA, part of moving beyond involves "expanding intellectual, conceptual and research boundaries in the…field and exploring…values, social justice, ethics, and diversity" (Jacobson, 2008, p. 4) Principal preparation programs are being redesigned to meet the challenges of various schools, leadership settings, and district needs and concerns. These programs are also being redesigned to explore social justice, ethics, and diversity of principals and other stakeholders. In this same way, principal practice is evolving beyond the traditional scope of how leadership has been defined, enactments of leadership, and the way this practice is evaluated. What have been considered appropriate, quality, or effective leadership and other "best practices" are being reexamined.

A part of this moving beyond the standards is reexamining the types of research that have been used to inform the field of educational leadership. Quantitative studies made up the "lion's share" of research in educational leadership, yet this trend is seeing a reversal (English, 2008). New forms of research, methods, and texts are being promoted to gain a more full-bodied understanding of the field and one that seeks to better understand the individuals engaging in educational leadership (English, 2008). Voices that have traditionally been silenced in educational leadership are given an opportunity for voice. The narrative research I have completed can add to these new understandings. According to the current president of UCEA, new forms of research should

1. Make use of a variety of individual points of view, perhaps borrowing an individual's angle of vision when it suits the purposes of the piece or the nature of the inquiry;
2. Engage in generalizations from narratives using critical comments;
3. Discover and describe multiple traits and facets of characters or cultures under study readily and plausibly without having to work things around to bring any single point of view within discovery range. (Brown, as cited in English, 2008, p. 2)

These new forms of research also include using uncommon theoretical orientations, marginalized perspectives, and unusual methods (English, 2008).

New research could lead to desired practice that assists the field in supporting principals in practice that moves beyond that which is policy and legally based to one that is critical, reflexive, and socially just. Certain research can assist administrators in coming to terms with "their own personal values and priorities as they engage in the activities required of principals" (Daresh, 2001, p. 95). In fact, Daresh promotes that principals should possess an educational platform that represents core nonnegotiable aspects of a principal's life. He suggests that these personal platforms define the principal's bottom line. Daresh goes on to remind us that one of the most important behaviors of principals was to be able to articulate one's personal beliefs and values. Principals not only need to "learn" the school, district, and community organization, but also need to establish and clarify their philosophies, beliefs, and vision for the school. Without the freedom to explore these ethical and philosophical commitments, principals are at a disadvantage to promote socially just policies, school practices, and frameworks that challenge inequities and create truly effective schools. Ideas presented in my research also suggest that district and state education administrators, researchers, and educational leadership organizations develop their own socially just and ethical frameworks beyond the scope of the present concerns of "ethical" behavior, which are often confined to legal rules and procedures. For example, licensing and accrediting bodies for educational leadership still have legal policy statements at the forefront of their codes of ethics. These bodies stand in direct conflict with the concerns of leadership unions, professional agencies, professors, and researchers in the area of social justice who favor developing the knowledge, character, and temperament of social justice (English, 2008). Until these licensing and accrediting organizations adopt more dispositional goals for ethics, they cannot provide leadership and autonomy to local school administrators to enact their own socially just agendas in school. This dilemma was seen in the spiritual narratives highlighted in this study. There was often a disconnect between principal requirements as dictated by policy and everyday practice in their schools.

Ordinary Theologies: Spiritual Narratives of Black Female Principals

Although womanist theology has been employed to analyze difficult intersecting concerns for years, its usefulness in educational research is still not obvious. Although the push for alternative research methods, narratives, and viewpoints for educational research has been promoted, the process is slow paced. The field of educational leadership has begun to seek deeper understandings of social justice, ethics, diversity, and equity and ways to create change in schools. However, I believe these changes cannot occur until we begin to examine personal value systems and their imports in the lives of educational leaders and their connection to certain matters of schooling. Traditional research in educational leadership has not used appropriate investigatory methods and frameworks.

> Research in educational leadership will generate useful knowledge to the degree that it captures and interprets the full complexity of educational leadership as a meaning-driven search for regularities in the antecedents and consequences of leadership practice. They could profitably also seek to understand the conditional nuances that characterize leadership at different times and places. (Riehl, 2007, p. 12)

This research adds to the body of scholarship that examines ways in which women "enact, think about and interpret leadership differently from traditional models" (Kezar, 2000, p. 723). Yet this research also examines the ways that religio-spirituality influences models of leadership in Black women's enactments of the principalship. "The spirituality that issues from Black women's lives is found in the...wisdom of African American women. This wisdom can be found in autobiographies, speeches, novels, poems, sermons, testimonies, songs, oral histories—in their lives" (Townes, 1995, p. 11). Like many writers before me, I wanted my research to tap into these lived, ordinary theologies. Like the theologies of these women in my research, womanist theologies are always ones that seek to delve deeper into the workings of theology as well as into social issues that are present in our society. In addition to unpacking these social issues, womanist theology also seeks to "push beyond what is the ordinary or the norm of Black life" (Townes, 1995, p. 11) and to forge "new normals." While this research is not exhaustive by any means, I have attempted to illuminate how womanist theology provided a frame for reading these principals' narratives and some of the concepts among religio-spirituality, schooling, and how they relate to society.

Womanist theology has been described as social witness (Townes, 1995). There is an emphasis on "a world crafted for on justice and love...rather than in a hierarchy of oppressions" (p. 10). It is spirituality that reduces the split between who one is at work and who one is at home. Spirituality

> is a way of living. It is a style of witness that seeks to cross the yawning chasm of hatreds and prejudices and oppressions...to self and to others. It holds together the community in a soulful relationship.... Womanist spirituality is the working out of what it means for each of us to seek compassion, justice, worship and devotion in our witness. (Townes, 1995, p. 11)

This social witness becomes important in understanding certain paths to social justice. Womanist theology has provided a useful framework for understanding how individuals think about religio-spirituality and the practice that develops in school: "God-talk and God-walk" (Mitchem, 2002, p. 124).

This research also highlights the importance of examining narratives and metaphor in the process of the principalship. Some questions this research leaves us with are the following: What metaphors do individuals use to describe the principalship? What metaphors do principals use to describe themselves and the process of enacting the principalship? "The basic theories and root metaphors of the field center on organization, whose assumptions include legitimacy, hierarchy, and self-interest" (Sergiovanni, 1994, p. 214). Blackmore (1999) underscores this fact by stating that "leadership is treated...as a set of generic competencies rather than holistically; the social and ethical...of leadership are leached out" (p. 5). Educational leadership has also been marked by increased corporatization. However, it is interesting to note that while corporations have embraced efforts to explore concepts such as the role of religion and spirituality in boosting work performance and worker retention (Mitroff & Denton, 1999; Mohamed, Hassan, & Wisnieski, 2001), the education community has not. The metaphors created by participants do not denote these same assumptions. Their metaphors show these Black women as transgressing certain masculine *and* feminine ideas of leadership and religio-spirituality. They resist androcentric ideals of the principalship by being intensely student-focused, resisting hierarchical expectations, and employing an educational worldview of care and social justice. These women contest any universal Black feminine ideal of care and servanthood by focusing on having a situational response to social justice, one that is tied to specific actions in schools. Metaphors are telling concerning meaning-making and enactments of the principalship such as educational philosophy, organizational theory, and educational practice. Educational leadership is more than a set of objective competencies one "puts on"; it also is an inner process of ideas, values, and beliefs that "comes out."

Through this research, a deeper understanding of the dilemma of attracting and retaining female principals, especially Black females, emerges. Research in educational leadership has focused on the overwhelming duties of the principalship. However, as this research has pointed out, the tension lies not in what the principals are asked to *do* but in who they are asked to *be* in the principalship. The issue becomes one of a divergence of performance and identity. Principal preparation and professional development often involve becoming proficient in the skills of leadership, but little attention is given to personal development. The metaphors of the research reveal a strong emphasis upon a personal mission. It could be that assisting principals in understanding how their value systems impact their leading and effective practicing of the values can offer ways for principals to see themselves in leadership and remain there.

In recent years, research on women in educational leadership "has brought a growing awareness of the role and influence of women in the organization and control of American schools" (Campbell, Cunningham, Nystrand, & Usdan, 1990, p. 367). However, this awareness in schools has been confined largely to issues of equality, which many individuals attempt to argue that society has achieved. There remains certain either/or stances concerning spirituality and social justice. Furthermore, this research on women, leadership, spirituality, and social justice has been located in a European, white, accepted form of wisdom (Snarey & Siddle Walker, 2004). For instance, Shapiro and Gross (2008) point out that models of leadership and ethics are still largely located in the legal system. This white, accepted form of wisdom fails to recognize the interrelatedness of certain standpoints. There is little room for child-centeredness and/or community (Shapiro & Gross, 2008). Womanist theology provides a framework to examine African American experience and provides a reconceptualization of spirituality, leadership, and how they define the thoughts and practice of the principalship (Beauboeuf-Lafontant, 2006).

Womanist theology is about freedom from the status quo, being free and freeing others, empowering one and others, and resisting oppressions. Womanist theology provides a way to examine these freedoms in light of beliefs in achieving justice and the overcoming of human conditions (Snarey & Siddle Walker, 2004; Williams & Williams-Morris, 2002). Womanist theology helps to deconstruct white, male, technocratic, and normed epistemologies, descriptors, and articulations of leadership.

> If we are alerted to the work being done by the...discourses we are invoking, we can then more effectively reflect on and change limiting and disempowering discursive practices, such as those that have marginalized women in the field of educational leadership. (Court, 2005, p. 16)

In Swedish schools, Johansson (2005) conducted extensive research on job descriptions to determine what principals needed to know when they first entered the field. The most important criterion that emerged was "good pedagogical experience." However, over a span of ten years, Johansson observed that the changing nature of schools called for a change from traditionally held notions of leadership. A greater demand for alternative leadership skills and understandings became apparent. Johansson's research found that traditional leadership models that relied heavily upon technocratic skills were not wholly appropriate to address issues such as poverty. I would argue that the same holds true for schooling in the United States. In my research, the principals addressed issues of poverty, racism, and student achievement. These women exhibited the idea that leadership was not simply a "value-free practice or set of generic competencies that were readily transferable into any domain of activity" (Blackmore, 1999, p. 1). These principals enacted leadership as communal, situational, cultural, and religio-spiritual.

Womanists "embody a womanhood much at odds with the compliance" expected from female leaders (Beauboeuf-Lafontant, 2006). Sometimes principals have to locate themselves in rule-breaking behavior to achieve their goals in schools. My research highlighted the ways that these principals engaged in creative insubordination (Lomotey, 1989) to live out their religio-spirituality and to achieve social justice in schools. Policy and procedures in their schools were often at odds with their justice agenda. Schools often practice systemic "shutting out" of certain types of groups and cultures, and the "rules" of schooling are forged in the mainstream of society. For the principals in this research, leading meant acting in opposition to the norms of schooling. This came in the form of "tweaking" certain policies and practices to fit contextually and situationally in a frame of ethics, care, and justice. One author notes that womanism "is not about being nice...or not upsetting people. Instead it represents...womanhood encompassing outrageous, audacious, courageous, and inquisitive behavior...It's about being someone to reckon with" (Thompson, 1998, p. 530).

"Pluralism and complexity are inherent in moral conversations and the moral life" (Snarey & Siddle Walker, 2004, p. 6). Pluralism and complexity dominate schools as well. Womanist theology offers ideas concerning educational leadership and offers a way of broadening the dialogue for schools in promoting social justice. African American female principals can forge a creative tension in schools (Snarey & Siddle Walker, 2004). Creative tension was achieved by the principals in this study as they enacted their work as more than a managerial enterprise. In Hebrew a word exists that literally means "work as worship." *Avodah* indicates little separation between religion, spirituality, and work. In the case of these principals, work was seen as an extension of living out religio-spirituality. In creating dialogue, a demand for space is needed. There has to be space to discuss the overlap of those in religio-spirituality and principals must have "safe" spaces to explore these appropriate connections to these meanings in schools. Any platform developed without this safe space runs a risk of becoming an institutionalized platform, one that continues to ignore true leadership development and cultural contributions from principals. The overly bureaucratic nature of schooling makes this difficult for principals. Principal preparation, induction, and mentoring programs still represent a chasm between what is expected from leaders and what leadership behaviors schools allow to be nurtured, fostered, and created.

Principals make decisions through certain lenses that the individual brings to the job (Daresh, 2001). Most decisions made by principals are matters of personal choice, and motives and reasons behind them are often implicit and deeply embedded in the individual's frame of reference. Religion and spirituality have long been connected to women and their work. Additional research in this area can make these frames of reference clearer to the outside observer. Theorizing concerning Black women, religio-spirituality, and their work and having spiritually grounded methods and methodologies that explore these intersections can help.

Confessions and Prophesies: Limitations and Future Research

This research does not reveal all about religio-spirituality. In some ways, I ended up with more questions than I "answered." This study was limited to the spiritual narratives of four Black female principals in two districts in one southeastern state. Each woman was located in a Judeo-Christian religion and in a Baptist denomination. While this research focused on the saliency of religio-spirituality African American females, one should keep in mind that religion or spirituality is not limited to any one group nor is a particular religion or spirituality limited to any one group. Moreover, the women in this study highlight the fact that religion and spirituality can often be insular and unaccommodating. Each principal had an isolated way of thinking that is at odds with reciprocity. Further studies with other belief systems and groups should be explored. Leaders from diverse cultures and spiritual bodies can add to the literature in this area. The principals' narratives in this research focused on the unique context of their schools and situations with their students. However, this was juxtaposed against the particular context of community. Would these principals react the same way in other schools and other communities and with different district leadership? Adding this facet to this research and others like it should be explored. This work shed light on the participants' current leadership positions and how they function in those positions. However, another strand to be more fruitfully explored is the role that religio-spirituality had upon their socialization into the roles of educators and educational leaders.

Additional research that uses alternative research texts and narratives can yield a fuller body of work and one that adds traditionally marginalized and silenced voices to educational leadership research:

> The development and critical analysis of personal histories with those who have been silenced and denied access in schools in particular and in society as a whole represent ways of creating coherence, attaching meaning, caring, wrestling with new questions, resisting, contesting inequities, and propounding change. They permit new perspectives on how we view our life circumstances. They connect us to organizational life and to the world at large and allow for the critical examination of these interpenetrations. In so doing, we understand in fundamentally new ways ourselves and other who have been traditionally denied, marginalized, and kept quiet. (McLaughlin, 1993, p. 238)

In particular, the alternative research texts provided here are my interpretations of their narrative interviews. Although the participants "approved" these interpretations, creative narratives written in their own hand would have been better. This is a project that I would like to pursue. Other research in this vein could illuminate even further how individuals position themselves in story and how they think about their lives.

There is no right way to engage in leadership and we must be skeptical of formulaic models of leadership (Hughes, 1999) and research that reifies these models. Leaders must examine who they are, what they believe, and how these things affect their leadership (Drake & Roe, 1999, p. 486). By examining religion and spirituality in education, we can move discussions of leadership beyond those that are one-dimensional and unconstructive. Rather than reduce discussion of education to limited ideas, is there a way to explore these differing viewpoints that is open and constructive? Can discussions in this manner offer us any insights into schooling and faith beyond the habitual ways in which we conduct them?

Historical and contemporary issues of religion and public schooling can also raise ethical questions facing public school educators through the lens of personal faith. How can public school educators negotiate their personal faith in the context of public education in a way that is ethical? Can an exploration of the personal faith of educators offer alternative ways of thinking about faith and education? Can and do these self-identities of Christian educators offer a positive segment in this debate?

Shields (2005) offers that we are facing a crises in educational leadership because of naïve, conservative, androcentric business models that are in place in answer to an increasingly complex society. These crises cause a reconceputalization of the principalship, requiring that we rethink how principals are evaluated. Can these calls for increased social justice, equity, and care exist with the unchanged and uniform methods of evaluation? Research in this area will be needed. Examining issues of religion and spirituality may help:

> Many researchers exhibit only minimal interest in the women's theology and theological significance. They read early Black spiritual autobiographers primarily to argue that these early writers' rhetorical strategies problematized hegemonic definitions of who they were and proscriptions of what they could and should do. This is valuable scholarship. But by ignoring or depreciating the *theology* of these women's spiritual autobiographies, contemporary scholars perpetuate the academy's proclivity toward keeping the personal and the private outside its walls, as if it were possible to sever

the personal from the professional.... I seek to add, and to urge more scholars to add, an appreciation of the theological in their critical frameworks. (Moody, 2003, p. 174)

Womanist ethicist Floyd-Thomas (2006b) espouses the idea of competing ideas "entering one another's worlds." She offers

> a call to discover worlds beyond one's own—to discover that which was once considered unnecessary—going beyond the limits of one's purview by choosing to foreground Black women's worldview.... The concept of world travel obliges us all to set aside our own orientations and inclinations in the hopes of critically engaging another's path to enhance our own perspectives and thereby facilitate radical subjectivity, traditional communalism, and redemptive self-love within the worlds of others as well as our own. (Floyd-Thomas, 2006b, p. 64)

It is my hope that this research has enabled the reader and indeed other researchers "to engage in a dialogical relationship with the text and context of Black women's writings and lives" (Floyd-Thomas, 2006b, p. 62). It is also my hope that the binary that currently exists in education and religio-spirituality can become conversational if not fully accepting. Of this dialogue, the question is not whether one agrees with the stance, but to understand the import of that stance and what can be learned. In this way, critical engagement connects with the womanist tenet of reciprocity and the exchange of ideas.

Quite often in education, "religion is something that educational theorists tend to speak about as outside observers" (Warnick, 2004, p. 345). Because of the deeply personal nature of religio-spirituality, those working within the tradition may be the best to report the tradition (Warnick, 2004). Working within the tradition carries the basic respect for the tradition and a deep knowledge of it. "Those best equipped to interpret a religious tradition and its meanings for life should quite possibly come from that tradition and also provide a base for how the inquiry is done" (Warnick, 2004, p. 347). By using narrative research and a womanist theological frame, the religio-spiritual meanings for the participants, how these meanings inform practice, and how this practice can contribute to educational concerns are able to be unpacked.

Conclusion

Meditations and Musings

It was so important to me to do this research in a way that felt right to me (Lorde, 1984, p. 38) and to complete it in a way that honored the spirituality and culture of Black women. I also wanted to join my love of the literature by and about Black women and the artistic nature of narrative.

The research glitch is never far from exploring and narrating the lives of others. But I suppose I should call this the researcher's glitch. My dissertation chair provided lots of glitches but caused me to think deeply about the work that I was trying to do. The glitch was also caused by the dissonance I experienced while listening to my participants' stories and measuring them against my own. In telling the stories of these principals, I had the unique positionality of being both an insider and an outsider. I found myself extremely connected to this work because I had a relationship with each participant. Yet, I was also connected because of my own knowledge and experience as a Black female religio-spiritual principal. Although I had long abandoned the Baptist congregation of my childhood for a nondenominational one, I still identified with the tenets of my youth and how they shaped what I thought about faith as an adult.

At times I found myself struggling to connect with some of the stories my participants told concerning their lives, their faith, and their principalships. I could relate all too well to racism and sexism in the principalship, but also the particular demands of the job and finding a place for faith at school. In the same way, I found myself critiquing their stories just as heavily against the backdrop of my own life story and the constant clarification and re-defining of what it meant to me to be a Black woman and a Christian. Some of my experiences did not mesh with theirs. Instead of a cathartic and bonding experience that many researchers experience, I ended up feeling in some ways strangely detached. I soon realized that while there is no need for the researchers to stand outside of the hermeneutic circle, being personal and subjective does not include "letting myself be hoodwinked by uncritical everyday practices" (Atkinson, 1990, p. 10). This work caused me to do the inner work as a researcher that I was not ready to do. I was already a professor, but I still wanted to function as a graduate student and basically make it through the "process." I found myself struggling with the deeply interpretive nature of their narratives and the presentations of them.

I remember a TV show that I saw more than ten years ago in which a Black lawyer was asked to describe if he was a Black man or a lawyer. Ever since I saw that episode, I have found myself asking variations of that question with all my many identities: Am I a Black woman or a Christian, am I a Black woman or a principal, am I a Black woman or a researcher, am I a Black woman or an academic? I am all those things, but mostly a Black Christian woman. I place all these things together because my own faith is a personal one and I don't think He makes the demands on each one of these identities, as people think He does. Because of my worldview, I have a harmonious, if messy, embracing of all of them, and they all are constantly dialoguing with one another. In God, I am valued in all ways at all times, even when the world does not value certain parts of me.

I am still not sure of all the roles that religion or spirituality may have to play in education. However, I do know from personal experience that religion and spirituality play a big role in schools. The separation of church and state continues to offer a critical way to examine religion and spirituality in schools, but also to silence certain voices as well. What I believe to be the bigger issue is that the law seems to have little to do with everyday practice in public arenas. What do we do about that and what do we understand about it? I believe there is something about the discussion and critique of the values that can add much to education. This will not be an easy dialogue. The conversation will have to be courageous.

References

Ah Nee-Benham, M. K., & Cooper, J. E. (1998). *Let my spirit soar! Narratives of diverse women in school leadership*. Thousand Oaks, CA: Corwin Press.

Alston, J. A. (2005). Tempered radicals and servant leaders' Black female persevering in the superintendency. *Educational Administration Quarterly, 41*(4), 675–688.

Apple, M. (2001). *Educating the "right" way: Markets, standards, God, and inequality*. New York: Routledge Falmer.

Ashburn, E. A., Mann, M., & Purdue, P. A. (1987, April). *Teacher mentoring: ERIC clearinghouse on teacher education*. Paper presented at the annual meeting of the American Educational Research Association, Washington, DC.

Atkinson, P. (1990). *The ethnographic imagination: Textual constructions of reality*. London: Routledge.

———. (1992). *Understanding ethnographic texts*. Newbury Park, CA: Sage.

Atkinson, R. (1998). The life story interview, *Sage University Paper Series on Qualitative Research Methods, 44*, Thousand Oaks, CA: Sage.

Baker-Fletcher, K. (1996). *A singing something: Womanist reflections on Anna Julia Cooper*. New York: Crossroad.

Bass, B. M. (1981). Women and leadership. In F. Stodgill (Ed.), *Stodgill's handbook of leadership: A survey of theory and research* (Rev. ed., pp. 491–507). New York: Free Press.

Bassard, K. C. (1999). *Spiritual interrogations: Culture, gender, and community in early African American women's writing*. Princeton, NJ: Princeton University Press.

Baumberg, M. (2004). Positioning with Davie Hogan. In C. Daiute & C. Lightfoot (Eds.), *Narrative analysis* (pp. 135–157). Thousand Oaks, CA: Sage.

Beauboeuf, T. (1997). *Politicized mothering among African American women teachers: A qualitative inquiry*. Unpublished doctoral dissertation, Harvard University Graduate School of Education, Cambridge, MA.

Beauboeuf-Lafontant, T. (1999). A movement against and beyond boundaries: "Politically relevant teaching" among African American teachers. *Teachers College Record, 100*(4), 702–723.

———. (2002). Womanist lessons for reinventing teaching. *Journal of Teacher Education, 56*(5), 436–445.

———. (2006). A womanist experience of caring: Understanding the pedagogy of exemplary Black women teachers. In L. Phillips (Ed.), *The womanist reader* (pp. 280–295). New York: Routledge.

Belenky, M. F., Clinchy, B. M., Goldberger, N. R., & Tarule, J. M. (1986). *Women's ways of knowing*. New York: Basic.

Bell, M. (1994). How primordial is narrative? In C. Nash (Ed.), *Narrative in culture* (pp. 172–198). London: Routledge.

Bellah, R. N., Madsen, R., Sullivan, W. M., Swidler, A., & Tipton, S. M. (1985). *Habits of the heart*. New York: Harper & Row.

Benham, M. K. P. (2005). Leading in full vision of the Kiha: A native Hawaiian woman's perspective of leadership and spirituality. In C. C. Shields, M. M. Edwards, & A. Sayani (Eds.), *Inspiring practice: Spirituality and educational leadership* (pp. 117–128). Lancaster, PA: Proactive.

Bennett, L., Jr. (1975). *The shaping of Black America: The struggles and triumphs*. New York: Johnson.

Betsworth, R. G. (1990). *Social ethics: An examination of American moral traditions*. Louisville, KY: Westminster/John Knox Press.

Bettis, P. J., & Adams, N. G. (Eds.). (2005). *Geographies of girlhood: Identities in-between*. Mahwah, NJ: Lawrence Erlbaum.

Black, H. K. (1999). Poverty and prayer: Spiritual narratives of elderly African American women. *Review of Religious Research, 40*(4), 359–374.

Blackmore, J. (1993). In the shadow of men: The historical construction of administration as a masculinist enterprise. In J. Blackmore & J. Kenway (Eds.), *Gender matters in educational administration and policy: A feminist introduction* (pp. 27–48). Bristol, PA: Falmer Press.

———. (1999). *Troubling women: Feminism, leadership, and educational change*. Buckingham, UK: Open University Press.

Blakeney, C. D., & Blakeney, R. F. (2004). Epilogue. In V. Siddle Walker & J. R. Snarey (Eds.), *Race-ing moral formation: African American perspectives on justice and care* (pp. 147–150). New York: Teachers College Press.

Blase, J., & Blase, J. (2000). Effective instructional leadership: Teachers' perspectives on how principals promote teaching and learning in schools. *Journal of Educational Administration, 38*(2), 130–141.

Bloom, C. M., & Erlandson, D. A. (2003). African American women principals in urban schools: Realities, (re)constructions, and resolutions. *Educational Administration Quarterly, 39*(3), 339–369.

Bloom, L. R. (1998). *Under the sign of hope: Feminist methodology and narrative interpretation.* Albany: SUNY Press.

———. (2002). Stories of one's own: Nonunitary subjectivity in narrative representation. In S. B. Merriam (Ed.), *Qualitative research in practice: Examples for discussion and analysis* (pp. 289–309). San Francisco: Jossey-Bass.

Bogdan, R., & Biklen, S. (1992). *Foundations of qualitative research.* Boston: Allyn & Bacon.

Bolman, L. G., & Deal, T. E. (1995). *Leading with soul: An uncommon journey of spirit.* San Francisco: Jossey-Bass.

Book indicates "unchurched" more permissive. (1978, June 16). *The Washington Post,* p. A30.

Books, S. (Ed.). (2003). *Invisible children in the society and its schools* (2nd ed.). Mahwah, NJ: Lawrence Erlbaum.

Borum, V. (2006). Reading and writing womanist poetic prose: African American mothers with deaf daughters. *Qualitative Inquiry,* 12(2), 340–352.

Bowe, B. E. (2003). *Biblical foundations of spirituality: Touching a finger to the flame.* Lanham, MD: Rowman & Littlefield.

Broughton, V. W. (1850). Twenty years' experience of a missionary. In S. Houchins (Ed.), *Spiritual narratives* (pp. 1–140). New York: Oxford University Press.

Brown, R. (1977). *A poetic for sociology.* Cambridge: Cambridge University Press.

Brown, T. L. F. (2000). *God don't like ugly.* Nashville, TN: Abingdon Press.

Brumett, B. (2000). Rhetorical epistemology and rhetorical spirituality. In M. L. Buley-Meissner, M. Thompson, & E. B. Tan (Eds.), *The academy and possibility of belief: Essays on intellectual and spiritual life* (pp. 121–135). Cresskill, NJ: Hampton Press.

Brunner, C. C. (2000). Unsettled moments in settled discourse: Women superintendents' experiences of inequality. *Educational Administration Quarterly,* 36(1), 76–116.

Bullough, R. (1998). Musings on life writing: Biography and case study in teacher education. In C. Kridel (Ed.), *Writing educational biography: Explorations in qualitative research* (pp. 19–32). New York: Garland.

Burck, J. R., & Hunter, R. (1990). Pastoral theology. In *The dictionary of pastoral care and counseling.* Nashville, TN: Abingdon Press.

Burk, M. (2007, March 9). Women's history—still being written. *Ms. Magazine.* Retrieved February 4, 2008, from http://msmagazine.com/radar/2007-03-09-burkwomenshistory.asp

Burroughs, N. H. (1968). *Who started Woman's Day?* Washington, DC: Author.

Caldwell, P. (1983). *The Puritan conversion narrative.* New York: Cambridge University Press.

Cambron-McCabe, N., & McCarthy, N. M. (2005). Educating school leaders for social justice. *Educational Policy,* 19(1), 201–222.

Campbell, R. (1994). The virtues of feminist empiricism. *Hypatia* 9 (1): 90–115.

Campbell, R. F., Cunningham, L. L., Nystrand, R. O., & Usdan, M. D. (1990). *The organization and control of American schools* (6th ed.). New York: Macmillan.

Cannon, K. G. (1988). *Black womanist ethics.* Atlanta, GA: Scholars Press.

———. (1995). *Katie's canon: Womanism and the soul of the Black community.* New York: Continuum Press.

———. (2006). Structured academic amnesia: As if this true womanist story never happened. In S. M. Floyd-Thomas (Ed.), *Deeper shades of purple: Womanism in religion and society* (pp. 19–28). New York: NYU Press.

Cannon, K. G., Johnson, A. P. G., & Sims, A. D. (2005). Womanist works in word. *Journal of Feminist Studies in Religion, 21*(2), 135–146.

Capper, C. A., & Keyes, M. W. (1999, April 17–22). *The role of spirituality in educational leaders leading for justice.* Paper presented at the annual meeting of the American Educational Research Association, Montreal, Canada.

Carby, H. (1998). The multicultural wars. In G. Dent (Ed.), *Black popular culture: A project by Michelle Wallace.* New York: New Press.

Carpenter, D. C. (2000). Black women in religious institutions. In L. G. Murphy (Ed.), *Down by the riverside: Readings in African American religion* (pp. 97–104). New York: NYU Press.

Case, K. (1997). African American othermothering in the urban elementary school. *The Urban Review, 29*(1), 25–39.

Casey, K. (1993). *I answer with my life: Life histories of women teachers working for social change.* New York: Routledge.

Chandler, M. J., Lalonde, C. E., & Teucher, U. (2004). Culture, continuity, and the limits of narrativity: A comparison of the self-narratives of native and non-native youth. In C. Daiute & C. Lightfoot, *Narrative analysis: Studying the development of individuals in society* (pp. 245–266). Thousand Oaks, CA: Sage.

Chase, S. E. (1995). Taking narrative seriously: Consequences for method and theory in interview studies. In R. Josselson & A. Lieblich (Eds.), *Interpreting experience* (pp. 1–26). Thousand Oaks, CA: Sage.

Chireau, Y. (1995). Hidden traditions: Black religion, magic, and alternative spiritual beliefs in womanist perspective. *Journal of the Interdenominational Theological Center,* 65–88.

Clandinin, D. J., & Connelly, F. M. (2000). *Narrative inquiry: Experience and story in qualitative research.* San Francisco: Jossey-Bass.

Cochran-Smith, M. (2003). Blind vision: Unlearning racism in teacher education. In S. Plaut & N. S. Sharkey (Eds.), *Education policy and practice: Bridging the divide* (pp. 95–127). Cambridge, MA: Harvard Educational Review.

Coffey, A., & Atkinson, P. (1996). *Making sense of qualitative data: Complementary research strategies.* Thousand Oaks, CA: Sage.

Coles, R. (1989). *The call of stories: Teaching and the moral imagination.* Boston: Houghton Mifflin.

Collard, J., & Reynolds, C. (2005). *Leadership, gender and culture in education.* New York: Open University Press.

Collins, P. H. (1989). The social construction of Black feminist thought. *Signs, 14,* 771.

———. (1991). *Black feminist thought: Knowledge, consciousness, and the politics of empowerment.* New York: Routledge.

———. (1998). *Fighting words: Black women and the search for justice.* Minneapolis: University of Minnesota Press.

———. (2000). *Black feminist thought: Knowledge, consciousness, and the politics of empowerment* (2nd ed.). New York: Routledge.

Comenius, J. A. (1990). *Panegersia, or universal awakening* (A. M. O. Dobbie, Trans.). Shipston-on-Stour, UK: Peter I. Drinkwater.

Comstock, G., & Mayhall, C. W. (2004). *Religious autobiographies* (2nd ed.). Belmont, CA: Thomson Wadsworth.

Cone, J. (1997). *God of the oppressed.* Maryknoll, NY: Orbis Books.

Conley, D. T., & Goldman, P. (1994). *Facilitative leadership: How leaders lead without dominating.* Eugene, OR: Oregon School Study Council.

Copeland, M. S. (2006). A thinking margin: The womanist movement as critical cognitive praxis. In S. Floyd-Thomas (Ed.), *Deeper shades of purple: Womanism in religion and society* (pp. 226–235). New York: New York University Press, 2006.

Cotterill, P., & Leatherby, G. (1993). Weaving stories: Personal autobiography in feminist research. *Sociology, 27*(1), 67–80.

Court, M. (2005). Negotiating and reconstructing gendered leadership discourses. In J. Collard & C. Reynolds (Eds.), *Leadership, gender and culture in education* (pp. 3–17). New York: Open University Press.

Covey, S. R. (1994). *First things first.* New York: Simon & Schuster.

Crenshaw, K. W. (1991). Mapping the margins: Intersectionality, identity, politics, and violence against women of color. *Stanford Law Review, 43*(6), 1241–1299.

Culp, D. W. (1902). *Twentieth century Negro literature.* Atlanta, GA: J. L. Nichols.

Daiute, C., & Lightfoot, C. (2004). *Narrative analysis.* Thousand Oaks, CA: Sage.

Dantley, M. E. (2003). Critical spirituality: Enhancing transformative leadership through critical theory and African American prophetic spirituality. *International Journal of Leadership in Education, 6*(1), 3–17.

———. (2005). A Christian view of spirituality and educational leadership. In C. M. Shields, M. M. Edwards, & A. Sayani (Eds.), *Inspiring practice: Spirituality and educational leadership* (pp. 129–144). Lancaster, PA: Proactive.

Dantley, M. E., & Tillman, L. C. (2006). Social justice and moral transformative leadership. In C. Marshall & M. Oliva (Eds.), *Leadership for social justice* (pp. 16–30). New York: Pearson.

Daresh, J. C. (2001). *Beginning the principalship: A practical guide for new leaders* (2nd ed.) Thousand Oaks, CA: Corwin Press.

Day, E. (2002, September). Me, my*self and I: Personal professional re-constructions in ethnographic research [59 paragraphs]. *Forum Qualitative Sozialforschung/Forum: Qualitative Social Research, 3*(3). Retrieved April 28, 2007, from http://www.qualitative-research.net/fqs-texte/3-02/3-02day-e.htm

Delgado, R. (1995). *Critical Race Theory: The cutting edge.* Philadelphia, PA: Temple University Press.

Delpit, L. (1995). *Other people's children: Cultural conflict in the classroom.* New York: New Press.

Denard, C. C. (1998). Retrieving and reappropriating the values of Black church tradition. In W. E. Fluker (Ed.), *The stones that builders rejected: The development of ethical leadership from the Black church tradition* (pp. 82–96). Harrisburg, PA: Trinity Press International.

Denzin, N. (1997). *Interpretive ethnography: Ethnographic practices for the 21st century.* Thousand Oaks, CA: Sage.

Denzin, N. K., & Lincoln, Y. S. (1994). Introduction: The discipline and practice of qualitative research. In N. K. Denzin & Y. S. Lincoln (Eds.), *Handbook of Qualitative Research* (pp. 1–17). Thousand Oaks, CA: SAGE Publications.

Dillard, C. B. (2000). The substance of things hoped for, the evidence of things not seen: Examining an endarkened feminist epistemology in educational research and leadership. *Qualitative Studies in Education, 13*(6), 661–681.

Dillard, C., Abdur-Rashid, D., & Tyson, C. (2000). My soul is a witness: Affirming pedagogies of the spirit. *Qualitative Studies in Education, 13*(5), 447–462.

Dodson, J. E., & Gilkes, C. T. (1986). Something within: Social change and collective endurance in the sacred world of Black Christian women. In R. R. Ruether & R. S. Keller (Eds.), *Women & religion in America* (pp. 80–91). San Francisco: Harper & Row.

Douglas, K. B. (2006). Twenty years a womanist: An affirming challenge. In S. M. Floyd-Thomas (Ed.), *Deeper shades of purple: Womanism in religion and society* (pp. 145–157). New York: NYU Press.

Drake, T. L., & Roe, W. H. (1999). *The principalship* (5th ed.). Upper Saddle River, NJ: Merrill.

Du Bois, W. E. B. (1994). *The souls of Black folk* (Unabridged ed.). New York: Dover.

DuCille, A. (1996). *Skin trade.* Cambridge, MA: Harvard University Press.

Eagly, A. H., Karau, S. J., & Johnson, B. T. (1992). Gender and leadership style among principals: A meta-analysis. *Educational Administration Quarterly, 2*(28), 76–102.

Elaw, Z. (1986). Memoirs of the life, religious experience, ministerial travels and labours of Mrs. Zilpha Elaw: An American female of colour. In W. L. Andrews (Ed.), *Sisters of the spirit: Three Black women autobiographies of the nineteenth century* (pp. 45–72). Bloomington: Indiana University Press.

Elizabeth. (1863/1988). Memoir of Old Elizabeth. In H. L. Gates, Jr. (Ed.), *Six women's slave narratives* (pp. 1–40). New York: Oxford University Press.

Elsasser, S. (2005). In the world but not of it: Gendered religious socialization at a Christian school. In P. J. Bettis & N. G. Adams (Eds.), *Geographies of girlhood* (pp. 137–153). Mahwah, NJ: Lawrence Erlbaum.

Ely, M., Vinz, R., Downing, M., & Anzul, M. (1997). *On writing qualitative research: Living by words.* Philadelphia: Falmer Press.

English, F. (2008). An anatomy of professional practice: Reflections on practices, standards, and promising research perspectives on educational leadership. *UCEA Review, 49*(1), 1–2.

Enomoto, E. K., Gardiner, M. E., & Grogan, M. (2000). Notes to Athene. *Urban Education, 35*(5), 567–583.

Epistle. (n.d.) *Wikipedia*. Retrieved May 20, 2007, from http://en.wikipedia.org/ wiki / Epistle

Essed, P. (1991). *Understanding everyday racism: An interdisciplinary theory*. Newbury Park, CA: Sage.

Etter-Lewis, G., & Foster, M. (1996). *Unrelated kin: Race and gender in women's personal narratives*. New York: Routledge.

Eugene, T. M. (2000). Lifting as we climb: Womanist theorizing about religion and the family. In L. G. Murphy (Ed.), *Down by the riverside: Readings in African American religion* (pp. 434–444). New York: NYU Press.

Evans, R. (1996). *The human side of school change: Reform, resistance, and the real-life problems of innovation*. San Francisco: Jossey-Bass.

Ezzy, D. (2002). *Qualitative analysis*. London: Routledge.

Featherston, E. (Ed.). (1994). *Skin deep: Women writing on color, culture, and identity*. Freedom, CA: Crossing Press.

Feldman, S. M. (2000). *Law and religion*. New York: NYU Press.

Floyd-Thomas, S. M. (Ed.). (2006a). *Deeper shades of purple: Womanism in religion and society*. New York: NYU Press.

———. (2006b). *Mining the motherlode: Methods in womanist ethics*. Cleveland, OH: Pilgrim Press.

Fluker, W. E. (1998). *The stones that the builders rejected: The development of ethical leadership from the Black church tradition*. Harrisburg, PA: Trinity Press.

Foster, F. S., & Haywood, C. (1995). Christian recordings: Afro-Protestantism, its press, and the production of African-American literature. *Religion and Literature, 27*, 15–33.

Foster, M. (1993). Othermothers: Exploring the educational philosophy of Black American women teachers. In M. Arnot & K. Weiler (Eds.), *Feminism and social justice in education: International perspectives* (pp. 101–123). Washington, DC: Falmer Press.

Foster, L. (2005). The practice of educational leadership in African American communities of learning: Context, scope and meaning. *Educational Administration Quarterly, 41*(4), 689–700.

Foster, W. (1986). *Paradigms and promises: New approaches in educational administration*. Buffalo, NY: Prometheus Books.

Frederick, M. F. (2003). *Between Sundays: Black women and everyday struggles of faith*. Berkeley: University of California Press.

Freire, P. (1996). *Pedagogy of the oppressed* (Rev. ed.). New York: Continuum.

Frey, S. (1993). Shaking the dry bones: The dialectic of conversion. In T. Owenby (Ed.), *Black and white cultural interaction in the antebellum South* (pp. 23–44). Jackson: University of Mississippi Press.

Fullan, M. (2002). Moral purpose writ large. *The School Administrator, 59*(8), 14–16.

Fusarelli, L. D. (2003). *The political dynamics of school choice: Negotiating contested terrain*. New York: Palgrave Macmillan.

Gates, H. L., Jr. (1991). Introduction: On bearing witness. In H. L. Gates, Jr. (Ed.), *Bearing witness: Selections from African-American autobiography in the twentieth century*. New York: Pantheon.

Gaustad, E. S. (Ed.). (1968). *Religious issues in American history*. New York: Harper & Row.

Geertz, C. (1973). *The interpretation of cultures: Selected essays by Clifford Geertz*. New York: Basic Books.

Gergen, M. (2004). A narratologist's tale. In C. Daiute & C. Lightfoot (Eds.), *Narrative analysis* (pp. 267–285). Thousand Oaks, CA: Sage.

Gibbs, P. (2007). Narrative and context in a practical theology for Papua New Guinea. *Australian Journal of Theology, 9*, 1–24.

Giles, M. S., Nance, O., & Witherspoon, N. (2008). Encountering faith in the secular classroom: An African American view. In M. R. Diamond (Ed.), *Encountering faith in the classroom: Turning difficult discussions into constructive engagement* (pp. 90–101). Sterling, VA: Stylus.

Gilgun, J. F. (2004). Fictionalizing life stories: Yukee the wine thief. *Qualitative Inquiry, 10*(5), 691–705.

Gilkes, C. T. (1987). Some mother's son and some father's daughter: Gender and biblical language in Afro-Christian worship tradition. In C. W. Atkinson, C. H. Buchanan, & M. R. Miles (Eds.), *Shaping new visions: Gender and values in American culture* (pp. 365–388). Ann Arbor, MI: UMI Research Press.

———. (1989). Roundtable discussion: Christian ethics and theology in womanist perspective. *Journal of Feminist Studies in Religion, 5*, 108–109.

———. (1993). The loves and troubles of African-American women's bodies. In E. M. Townes (Ed.), *Troubling in my soul: Womanist perspectives on evil and suffering* (pp. 239–240). Maryknoll, NY: Orbis Books.

———. (2001). *If it wasn't for the women*. Maryknoll, NY: Orbis Books.

Gilligan, C. (1982). *In a different voice: Psychological theory and women's development*. Cambridge, MA: Harvard University Press.

Giroux, H. (1991). *Border crossings*. London: Routledge & Kegan Paul.

Glasman, N. S. (1984). Student achievement and the school principal. *Educational Evaluation and Policy Analysis, 6*(3), 283–296.

Glazer, S. (Ed.). (1999). *The heart of learning: Spirituality in education*. New York: Jeremy P. Tarcher/Putnam.

Gilmour, P. (n.d.). *Pre-historic, historic, and post-historic fabulation narratives in religious/spiritual traditions and their implications for religious education*. Unpublished manuscript.

Gold, N., & Bogo, M. (1992). Social work research in a multicultural society: Challenges and approaches. *Journal of Multicultural Social Work, 2*(4), 7–22.

Goodley, D., Lawthom, R., Clough, P., & Moore, M. (Eds.). (2004). *Researching life stories*. New York: Routledge Falmer.

Goodson, I., & Sikes, P. (2001) *Life history in educational settings: Learning from lives*. Buckingham, UK: Open University Press.

Gottlieb, R. S. (2003). *A spirituality of resistance: Finding a peaceful heart and protecting the Earth*. Lanham, MD: Rowman & Littlefield.

Grant, J. (1989). *White women's Christ, Black women's Jesus: Feminist Christology and womanist response*. Atlanta, GA: Scholars Press.

Greenfield, W. D. (1991, April). *The micropolitics of leadership in an urban elementary school*. Paper presented at the annual meeting of the American Educational Research Association, Chicago, IL.

Greenleaf, R. K. (1995). Life choices and markers. In L. Spears (Ed.), *Reflections on leadership: How Greenleaf's theory of servant leadership influenced today's top management thinkers* (pp. 17–21). New York: John Wiley & Sons.

Griffiths, M. (1998). *Educational research for social justice: Getting off the fence*. Philadelphia: Open University Press.

Grogan, M., & Crow, G. (2004). Mentoring in the context of educational leadership preparation and development—old wine in new bottles? Introduction to special issue. *Educational Administration Quarterly, 40*(4), 463–467.

Guy-Sheftall, B. (Ed.). (1995). *Words of fire: An anthology of African-American feminist thought*. New York: New Press.

Hallinger, P., Bickman, L., & Davis, K. (1990). *What makes a difference: School context, principal leadership, and student achievement* (Occasional Paper No. 3). Cambridge, MA: National Center for Educational Leadership, Harvard Graduate School of Education.

Hambrick, A. (1997). You haven't seen anything until you make a Black woman mad. In K. M. Vaz (Ed.), *Oral narrative research with Black women*. Thousand Oaks, CA: Sage.

Hardesty, N. (1984). *Women called to witness: Evangelical feminism in the 19th century*. Nashville, TN: Abington Press.

Harley, S. (1982). Beyond the classroom: The organizational lives of Black female educators in the District of Columbia, 1890–1930. *Journal of Negro Education, 51*, 254–265.

Harmon, W. (2000). *A handbook to literature* (8th ed.). Upper Saddle River, NJ: Prentice Hall.

Harris, M. L. (2006). Womanist humanism. In S. M. Floyd-Thomas (Ed.), *Deeper shades of purple: Womanism in religion and society* (pp. 54–76). New York: NYU Press.

Hatch, J. A., & Wisniewski, R. (1995). *Life history and narrative*. London: Falmer Press.

Hauerwas, S., & Jones, L. G. (Eds.). (1989). *Why narrative? Readings in narrative theology*. Grand Rapids, MI: Eerdmans.

Hayes, D. L. (1997). My hope is in the Lord: Transformation and salvation in the African American community. In E. M. Townes (Ed.), *Embracing the spirit: Womanist perspectives on hope, salvation, and transformation* (pp. 9–28). Maryknoll, NY: Orbis Books.

———. (2006). Standing in the shoes my mother made. In S. M. Floyd-Thomas (Ed.), *Deeper shades of purple: Womanism in religion and society* (pp. 54–76). New York: NYU Press.

Haynes, E. A., & Licata, J. W. (1995). Creative insubordination of school principals and the legitimacy of the justifiable. *Journal of Educational Administration, 33*(4), pp. 21–35.

Healey, J., & Sybertz, D. (1996). *Towards an African narrative theology.* Maryknoll, NY: Orbis Books.

Held, V. (1993). *Feminist morality: Transforming culture, society, and politics.* Chicago: University of Chicago Press.

Hendry, P. H. (2007). The future of narrative. *Qualitative Inquiry, 12*(4), 487–499.

Hersey, P., & Blanchard, K. H. (2007). *Management of organizational behavior* (9th ed.). Upper Saddle River, NJ: Prentice Hall.

Higginbotham, E. B. (1993). *Righteous discontent: The women's movement in the Black Baptist Church, 1880–1920.* Cambridge, MA: Harvard University Press.

———. (2003). The Black church: A gender perspective. In C. West & E. Glaude (Eds.), *African American religious thought: An anthology.* Louisville, KY: Westminster/John Knox Press.

Hill, R. (2003). *The strength of Black families.* New York: University Press of America.

Hine, D. C. (1994). *Hine sight: Black women and the re-construction of American history.* New York: Carlson.

Holloway, K. F. C. (1997). Cultural narratives passed on: African American mourning stories. *College English, 59*(1), 32–40.

Hong, Y. (2000). Revisiting church growth in Korean Protestantism: A theological perspective. *International Review of Missions, 89*(353), 190.

hooks, b. (1999). *Yearning: Race, gender, and cultural politics.* Cambridge, MA: South End Press.

———. (2000). *All about love.* New York: William Morrow.

———. (2005). *Sisters of the yam: Black women and self-recovery.* Cambridge, MA: South End Press.

hooks, b., & West, C. (1991). *Breaking bread: Insurgent Black intellectual life.* Cambridge, MA: South End Press.

Hoopes, J. (1979). *Oral history.* Chapel Hill: University of North Carolina Press.

Hopkins, D. N. (2005). *Being human: Race, culture and religion.* Minneapolis, MN: Fortress.

Houchins, S. (1988). *Spiritual narratives.* New York: Oxford University Press.

Houston, P. D. (2002). Why spirituality, and why now? *The School Administrator.* Retrieved June 15, 2007, from http://www.aasa.org/publications/saarticle detail.cfm?ItemNumber=1922&ItemNumber=950&tnItemNumber=1955database

Hoyle, J. R. (2002). The highest form of leadership. *The School Administrator.* Retrieved June 15, 2007, from http://www.aasa.org/publications/saarticle detail.cfm?ItemNumber=1917&snItemNumber=950&tnItemNumber=1955database

Hudak, G. M. (2005). School leadership and spirituality: A critical dialogue [Special issue]. *Journal of School Leadership, 15*(6).

Hughes, L. W. (1999). *The principal as leader* (2nd ed.). Upper Saddle River, NJ: Merrill.

———. (Ed.). (2005). *Current issues in school leadership*. Mahwah, NJ: Lawrence Erlbaum.

Hull, J. M. (1996). The ambiguity of spiritual values. In J. M. Halstead & M. J. Taylor (Eds.), *Values in education and education in values* (pp. 33–44). London: Falmer Press.

Humez, J. M. (1984). My spirit eye: Some functions of visionary and spiritual experiences in the lives of five black women preachers, 1810–1880. In B. J. Harris & J. K. McNamara (Eds.), *Women and the structure of society: Selected research from the Fifth Berkshire Conference of the History of Women* (pp. 129–146). Durham, NC: Duke University Press.

Hurston, Z. N. (1990). *Their eyes were watching God*. New York: Harper Perennial.

Irvine, J. J. (1999). The education of children whose nightmares come both day and night. *Journal of Negro Education, 68*, 224–253.

Isasi-Diaz, A. M. (1993). *En la lucha—In the struggle: A Hispanic women's liberation theology*. Minneapolis, MN: Fortress Press.

Jacobs, H. (Ed.). (1861/1987). *Incidents in the life of a slave girl, written by herself* (J. F. Yellin, Ed.). Cambridge, MA: Harvard University Press.

Jacobson, S. (2008). An E. C. minute. *UCEA Review, 49*(1), 4–5.

James, W. (1902/1982). *The varieties of religious experience*. New York: Penguin.

Jim Crow and the fight for civil rights. (2007). City University of New York, La Guardia Community College, and the New York Times Knowledge Network. Retrieved February 17, 2008, from http://www1.cuny.edu/portalur/content/voting_curriculum/jimcrow_civil_rights.html

Johansson, O. (2005). Gender and school leadership in Sweden. In J. Collard & C. Reynolds (Eds.), *Leadership, gender & culture in education* (pp. 38–49). New York: Open University Press.

Johnson, K. A. (2000). *Uplifting the women and the race: The educational philosophies and social activism of Anna Julia Cooper and Nannie Helen Burroughs*. New York: Garland.

Johnson, P. (2006, June 11). Churched [Comment 3]. *A Way with Words*. Retrieved February 19, 2008, from http://www.doubletongued.org/index.php/dictionary/churched/

Johnson-Bailey, J. (2002). Dancing between the swords: My foray into constructing narratives. In S. Merriam (Ed.), *Qualitative research in practice: Examples for discussion and analysis* (pp. 323–326). San Francisco: Jossey-Bass.

Jones, L. B. (1995). *Jesus CEO: Using ancient wisdom for visionary leadership*. New York: Hyperion.

Jones, S. N. (2003). *The praxis of black female educational leadership from a systems thinking perspective*. Unpublished doctoral dissertation, Bowling Green State University, Bowling Green, KY.

Judge, T. A., & Piccolo, R. F. (2004). Transformational and transactional leadership: A meta-analytic test of their relative ability. *Journal of Applied Psychology, 1*(2), 755–768.

Kerby, A. P. (1991). *Narrative and the self*. Bloomington: Indiana University Press.

Kessler, R. (2002). Nurturing deep connections. *The School Administrator*. Retrieved June 15, 2007, from http://www.aasa.org/publications/saarticledetail.cfm?ItemNumber=1922&ItemNumber=950&tnItemNumber=1955database

Keyes, M. W., Hanley-Maxwell, C., & Capper, C. A. (1995). "Spirituality? It's the core of my leadership." *Educational Administration Quarterly, 35*(2), 203–237.

Kezar, A. (2000). Pluralistic leadership. *Journal of Higher Education, 71*(6), 722–743.

Khanna, H., & Srinivas, E. S. (2000, December 15–16). *Spirituality and leadership development*. Paper presented at the annual meeting of the Management Development Institute, Gurgaon, India.

Krug, S. E., Scott, C., & Ahadi, S. (1990). *An experience sampling approach to the study of principal instructional leadership I: Results from the Principal Activity Sampling Form*. Urbana, IL: The National Center for School Leadership, University of Illinois at Urbana-Champaign.

Labov, W. (1982). Objectivity and commitment in linguistic science: The case of the Black English trial in Ann Arbor. *Language in Society 11*, 165–201.

Ladson-Billings, G. (2005, November 4). *What if we leave all children behind? The challenge of teaching in the new millennium*. Keynote address presented at the Teachers of Color Summit, Boulder, CO.

Lecompte, M. D. (1993). A framework for hearing silence: What does telling stories mean when we are supposed to be doing science? In D. McLaughlin & W. G. Tierney (Eds.), *Naming silenced lives: Personal narratives and the process of educational change* (pp. 9–27). New York: Routledge.

Lee, C. D., Rosenfeld, S., Mendenhall, R., Rivers, A., & Tynes, B. (2004). Cultural modeling as a frame for narrative analysis. In C. Daiute & C. Lightfoot (Eds.), *Narrative analysis* (pp. 39–62). Thousand Oaks, CA: Sage.

Lee, J. (1836). *The life and religious experiences of Jarena Lee*. Philadelphia: Author.

Lee, R. M., & Renzetti, C. M. (1993). The problems of researching sensitive topics: An overview and introduction. In. C. Renzetti & R. Lee (Eds.), *Researching sensitive topics* (pp. 3–13). Newbury Park, CA: Sage.

Lei, E. V., & Kyburz, B. L. (Eds.). (2005). *Negotiating religious faith in the composition classroom*. Portsmouth, NH: Heinemann.

Leithwood, K. A. (1992). The move towards transformational leadership. *Educational Leadership, 49*(5), 8–12.

Lerner, M. (2000). *Spirit matters*. Charlottesville, VA: Hampton Roads.

Lewin, K., Lippitt, R., & White, R. K. (1939). Patterns of aggressive behavior in experimentally created social climates. *Journal of Social Psychology, 10*, 271–301.

Lichtman, M. (2006). *Qualitative research in education: A user's guide*. Thousand Oaks, CA: Sage.

Lincoln, C. E. (1999). *Race, religion, and the continuing American dilemma*. New York: Hill & Wang.

Lincoln, C. E., & Mamiya, L. H. (1990). *The Black church in the African American experience*. Durham, NC: Duke University Press.

Lincoln, Y., & Guba, E. (1985). *Naturalistic inquiry*. New York: Sage.

Loder, T. L. (2005). African American women principals' reflections on social change, community, othermothering, and Chicago public school reform. *Urban Education, 40*(3), 298–320.

Lomotey, K. (1989). *African-American principals: School leadership and success; Contributions in Afro-American and African studies.* New York: Greenwood.

Long, J. C. (2005). Encouraging spirituality: Constraints and opportunities. In C. M. Shields, M. M. Edwards, & A. Sayani (Eds.), *Spirituality and educational leadership* (pp. 17–50). Lancaster, PA: Proactive.

Lorde, A. (1984). *Sister outsider: Essays and speeches.* Trumansburg, NY: Crossing Press.

Lynn, M. (2001). *Portraits in Black: Storying the lives and pedagogies of Black men educators.* Unpublished doctoral dissertation, University of California, Los Angeles.

Macintyre, A. (1984). *After virtue: A study in moral theory.* Notre Dame, IN: University of Notre Dame Press.

Marshall, J. (1996). *Women managers moving on: Exploring career and life choices.* London: Routledge.

Martin, C. J. (1998). Normative biblical motifs in African-American women leaders' moral discourse: Maria Stewart's autobiography as a resource for nurturing leadership from the Black church tradition. In W. E. Fluker (Ed.), *The stone that the builders rejected: The development of ethical leadership from the Black church tradition* (pp. 47–72). Harrisburg, PA: Trinity Press International.

Marx, J. H., & Seldin, J. E. (1973). Crossroads of crisis: Organizational and ideological models for contemporary and quasi-therapeutic communes. *Journal of Health and Social Behavior, 14*(2), 183–191.

Mattis, J. S. (2002). Religion and spirituality in the meaning-making and coping experiences of African American women: A qualitative analysis. *Psychology of Women Quarterly, 25,* 309–321.

Mbilinyi, M. 1989. 'I'd have been a man': Politics and the labor process in producing personal narratives. In Personal Narratives Group (Eds.), Interpreting Women's Lives (pp. 204–227). Bloomington: Indiana University Press.

McCluskey, A. T. (1993). The historical context of the single-sex schooling debate among African Americans. *Western Journal of Black Studies, 17*(4), 194.

McCracken, G. (1988). *The long interview.* Newbury Park, CA: Sage.

McKay, N. (1989). Nineteenth-century Black women's spiritual autobiographies: Religious faith and self-empowerment. In The Personal Narratives Group (Ed.), *Interpreting women's lives: Feminist theory and personal narratives* (pp. 139–154). Bloomington: Indiana University Press.

McKay, N. Y. (1995). The narrative self: Race, politics, and culture in Black American women's autobiography. In D. C. Stanton & A. J. Stewart (Eds.), *Feminisms in the academy* (pp. 74–100). Ann Arbor: University of Michigan Press.

McLaughlin, D. (1993). Coda: Toward the pathway of a true human being. In D. McLaughlin & W. G. Tierney (Eds.), *Naming silenced lives: Personal narratives and the process of change* (pp. 237–240). New York: Routledge.

McLaughlin, D., & Tierney, W. G. (1993). *Naming silenced lives: Personal narratives and the process of change.* New York: Routledge.

Mendez-Morse, S. (2004). Constructing mentors: Latina educational leaders' role models and mentors. *Educational Administration Quarterly, 40*(4), 561–590.

Merchant, B. M., & Shoho, A. R. (2006). Bridge people: Civic and educational leaders for social justice. In C. Marshall & M. Oliva (Eds.), *Leadership for social justice: Making revolutions in education* (pp. 85–108). New York: Pearson.

Merriam, S. B. (2002). *Qualitative research in practice: Examples for discussion and analysis.* San Francisco: Jossey-Bass.

Meux, C. S. (2002). *African American leadership in the context of its social and cultural background: A multiple case study.* Unpublished doctoral dissertation, Fielding Graduate Institute, Santa Barbara, CA.

Meyerson, D., & Scully, M. (1995). Tempered radicalism and the politics of ambivalence and change.' *Organization Science 6*(6): 585–600).

Michaels, S. (1981). "Sharing time": Children's narrative styles and differential access to literacy. *Language in Society, 10,* 423–442.

Middleton, S. (1993). *Educating feminists: Life histories and pedagogy.* New York: Teachers College Press.

Mink, L. O. (1970). History and fiction as modes of comprehension. *New Literary History, 1,* 541–558.

Mischler, E. G. (1995). Models of narrative analysis. *Journal of Narrative and Life History, 5,* 87–123.

Mitchell, C., & Weber, S. (1999). *Reinventing ourselves as teachers: Beyond nostalgia.* London: Falmer Press.

Mitchell, G. J., & Cody, W. K. (1993). The role of theory in qualitative research. *Nursing Science Quarterly, 6*(4), 170–178.

Mitchell, H. H., & Lewter, N. C. (1986). *Soul theology: The heart of American Black culture.* San Francisco: Harper & Row.

Mitchell, L., & Romans, S. (2003). Spiritual beliefs in bipolar affective disorder: Their relevance for illness management. *Journal of Affective Disorders, 75*(3), 247–257.

Mitchem, S. Y. (2002). *Womanist theology.* Maryknoll, NY: Orbis Books.

Mitroff, I., & Denton, E. (1999). *A spiritual audit of corporate America: A hard look at spirituality, religion, and values in the workplace.* San Francisco: Jossey-Bass/Pfeiffer.

Mohamed, A., Hassan, A., & Wisnieski, J. (2001). Spirituality in the workplace: A literature review. *Global Competiveness, 9*(1), 644–652.

Moody, J. (1997). Professions of faith: A teacher reflects on women, race, church, and spirit. In K. M. Vaz (Ed.), *Oral narrative research with Black women* (pp. 24–37). Thousand Oaks, CA: Sage.

———. (2003). *Sentimental confessions: Spiritual narratives of nineteenth-century African American women.* Athens: University of Georgia Press.

Morris, T. V. (Ed.). (1994). *God and the philosophers: The reconciliation of faith and reason.* New York: Oxford University Press.

Morton, N. (1985). *The journey is home.* Boston: Beacon Press.

Mott-Thornton, K. (1996). *Common faith: Education, spirituality and the state.* Aldershot: Ashgate.

Mullane, D. (Ed.). (1993). *Crossing the danger water: Four hundred years of African American writing.* New York: Anchor Books.

Munro, P. (1991). *A life of work: Stories women teachers tell.* Unpublished doctoral dissertation, University of Oregon, Eugene.

———. (1998). *Subject to fiction: Women teachers' life history narratives and the cultural politics of resistance.* Philadelphia: Open University Press.

Murphy, E. (1996). *Handbook for spiritual warfare* (Rev. ed.). Nashville, TN: Thomas Nelson.

Murphy, L. G. (2000). *Down by the riverside: Readings in African American religion.* New York: NYU Press.

Murtadha-Watts, K. (1999). Spirited sisters: Spirituality and the activism of African American women in educational leadership. In L. T. Fenwick & P. Jenlink (Eds), *School leadership: Expanding the horizons of the mind and spirit* (pp. 155–167). Lancaster: Technomic.

Murtadha, K., & Watts, D. M. (2005). Linking the struggle for education and social justice: Historical perspectives of African American leadership in schools. *Educational Administration Quarterly, 41*(4), 591–608.

Napier, W. (Ed.). (2000). *African American literary theory: A reader.* New York: NYU Press.

Nash, R. J. (1999). *Faith, hype, and clarity: Teaching about religion in America's schools and colleges.* New York: Teachers College Press.

Nelson, K. (2004). Construction of the cultural self in early narratives. In C. Daiute & C. Lightfoot, *Narrative analysis* (pp. 87–109). Thousand Oaks, CA: Sage.

Nelson-Brown, J. E. (2006). *The keys of the kingdom: How teacher beliefs about religion impact their experience of teaching.* Unpublished doctoral dissertation, University of Washington, Seattle.

Neuhaus, R. J. (2000). A new order of religious freedom. In S. Feldman (Ed.), *Law and religion: A critical anthology* (pp. 89–95). New York: NYU Press.

Noddings, N. (1984). *Caring: A feminine approach to the ethics and moral education.* Berkeley: University of California Press.

Noel, J. A. (n.d.). *Phenomenological hermeneutics, Black theology and the study of Black religion: A primer.* Unpublished manuscript.

Oliviera, M. (2004). The function of self-aggrandizement in storytelling. *Narrative Inquiry, 9,* 25–48.

Olney, J. (1985). "I was born": Slave narratives, their status as autobiography and as literature. In C. T. Davis & H. L. Gates, Jr. (Eds.), *The slave's narrative* (pp. 152–153). New York: Oxford University Press.

Ong, W. (1982). *Orality and literacy: The technologizing of the word.* London: Methuen.

Ontology. (2007, June 20). *Wikipedia.* Retrieved June 26, 2007, from http://en.wikipedia.org/w/index.php?title=Ontology&oldid=139408242

Parachurch. (2007, November 14). *Wikipedia.* Retrieved February 18, 2008, from http://en.wikipedia.org/wiki/Parachurch

Paris, P. (1985). *The social teaching of the Black churches*. Philadelphia: Fortress Press.
Patton, M. Q. (2002). *Qualitative evaluation and research methods*. London: Sage.
Perkins, L. M. (1989). The history of Blacks in teaching. In D. Warren (Ed.), *American teachers: Histories of a profession at work* (pp. 344–369). New York: Macmillan.
Peterson, E. (1992). *African American women: A study of will and success*. Jefferson, NC: McFarland.
Peterson, E. A. (1997). African American women and the emergence of self-will. In K. M. Vaz (Ed.), *Oral narrative research with Black women* (pp. 156–174). Thousand Oaks, CA: Sage.
Phillips, L. (2006). *The womanist reader*. New York: Routledge.
Pierce, Y. N. (1999). *On the road to Damascus: The African American conversion experience*. Unpublished doctoral dissertation, Cornell University, Ithaca, NY.
Pierce-Baker, C. (1998). *Surviving the silence: Black women's stories of rape*. New York: Norton.
Pinar, W., Reynolds, W., Slattery, P., & Taubman, P. (1995). Understanding curriculum: An introduction. New York: Peter Lang.
Plaskow, J. (1980). Blaming Jews for inventing patriarchy. *Lilith, 7,* 11–12.
Polkinghorne, C. (1988). *Narrative knowing and the human sciences*. Albany, NY: SUNY Press.
Pollard, D. S. (1997). Race, gender, and educational leadership: Perspectives from African American principals. *Educational Policy, 11*(3), 353–374.
Postman, N. (1996). *The end of education: Redefining the value of school*. New York: Vintage.
Purpel, D. E., & McLaurin, W. M. (2004). *Reflections on the moral & spiritual crisis in education*. New York: Peter Lang.
Raboteau, A. J. (2000). In search of the promised land. In L. G. Murphy (Ed.), *Down by the riverside: Readings in African American religion* (pp. 289–292). New York: NYU Press.
Ratner, C. (2002, September). Subjectivity and objectivity in qualitative methodology [29 paragraphs]. *Forum Qualitative Sozialforschung/Forum: Qualitative Social Research, 3*(3). Retrieved April 28, 2007, from http://www.qualitative-research.net/fqs-texte/3-02/3-02ratner-e.htm
Reid-Merritt, P. (1996). *Sister power: How phenomenal Black women are rising to the top*. New York: John Wiley & Sons.
Richie, B. E. (1996). *Compelled to crime: The gender entrapment of battered Black women*. New York: Routledge.
Ricoeur, P. (1976). *Interpretation theory: Discourse and the surplus of meaning*. Fort Worth, TX: Texas Christian University Press.
———. (1980). Narrative time. *Critical inquiry, 7*(1), 160–180.
———. (1995). *Figuring the sacred* (M. I. Wallace, Ed., & D. Pellauer, Trans.). Minneapolis, MN: Fortress Press.
Riehl, C. (2007). Some observations on useful approaches to research on educational leadership. *UCEA Review, 46*(3), 9–12.
Riessman, C. K. (1993). *Narrative analysis*. Newbury Park, CA: Sage.

Riessman, C. K., & Quinney, L. (2005). Narrative in social work: A critical review. *Qualitative Social Work, 4*(4), 383–404.

Riggs, M. Y. (1994). *Awake, rise, and act: A womanist call for Black liberation.* Cleveland, OH: Pilgrim.

———. (1997). *Can I get a witness? Prophetic religious voices of African American women: An anthology.* Maryknoll, NY: Orbis Books.

———. (1998). Living into the bonds of justice. In W. E. Fluker (Ed.), *The stones that the builders rejected: The development of ethical leadership from the Black church tradition* (pp. 33–46). Harrisburg, PA: Trinity Press International.

Rizvi, F. (1998). Some thoughts on contemporary theories of social justice. In B. Atwel, S. Kemmis, & P. Weeks (Eds.), *Partnerships for social justice in education* (pp. 47–56). New York: Routledge.

Rogan, A. I., & De Kock, D. M. (2005). Chronicles from the classroom: Making sense of the methodology of methods of narrative analysis. *Qualitative Inquiry, 11*(4), 628–649.

Rogers, J. L., & Dantley, M. E. (2001). Invoking the spiritual in campus life and leadership. *Journal of College Student Development, 42*(6), 589–603.

Romo, J., & Roseman, M. (2005). Educational warriors for social justice. In L. W. Hughes (Ed.), *Current issues in school leadership* (pp. 37–57). Mahwah, NJ: Lawrence Erlbaum.

Roof, W. C. (1993). Religion and narrative. *Review of Religious Research, 34*(4), 1–13.

Rosiek, J., & Atkinson, B. (2007). The inevitability and importance of genre in narrative research. *Qualitative Inquiry, 13*(2).

Ross, R. E. (2002). *Witnessing and testifying: Black women, religion, and civil rights.* Minneapolis, MN: Fortress.

———. (2006). Lessons and treasures in our mothers' witness: Why I write about Black women's activism. In S. M. Floyd-Thomas (Ed.), *Deeper shades of purple: Womanism in religion and society* (pp. 115–127). New York: NYU Press.

Rost, J. C. (1991). *Leadership for the twenty-first century.* New York: Praeger.

Rousmaniere, K. (2008). School principals in America: A review of three biographical studies. *Journal of Educational Administration and History, 40* (1), 75–80.

Sakar, T. (2001). *Hindu wife, Hindu nation: Community, religion, and cultural nationalism.* London: Hurst.

Sanchez-Eppler, K. (1992). Bodily bonds: The intersecting rhetorics of feminism and abolition. In S. Samuels (Ed.), *The culture of sentiment: Race, gender, and sentimentality in nineteenth-century America* (pp. 92–114). New York: Oxford University Press.

Sanders, C. J. (1989). Christian ethics and theology in womanist perspective. *Journal of Feminist Studies in Religion 5,* 83–91. Sanders, C. J.., Cannon, K. G., Townes, E. M., Copeland, M. S., hooks, b., & Gilkes, C. T. (1989). Roundtable discussion: Christian ethics and theology in womanist perspective. *Journal of Feminist Studies in Religion, 5,* 87–95.

Sanders-Lawson, E. R. (2001). *Black women school superintendents: Leading for social justice.* Unpublished doctoral dissertation, Michigan State University, East Lansing.

Sanders-Lawson, R., Smith-Campbell, S., & Benham, M. K. P. (2006). Wholistic visioning for social justice: Black women theorizing practice. In C. Marshall & M. Oliva (Eds.), *Leadership for social justice: Making revolutions in education* (pp. 31–63). New York: Pearson.

Sawyer, M. R. (2000). The Black church and Black politics. In L. G. Murphy (Ed.), *Down by the riverside: Readings in African American religion* (pp. 293–302). New York: NYU Press.

Sayani, A. (2005). Allah-consciousness: A meta-meaning system to understand Muslim spirituality in an educational context. In C. M. Shields, M. M. Edwards, & A. Sayani (Eds.), *Inspiring practices: Spirituality and educational leadership* (pp. 101–117). Lancaster, PA: Proactive.

Scott, J. W. (1986). Gender: A useful category of historical analysis. *The American Historical Review, 91* (5), 1053–1075.

Sered, S. S. (1994). Ideology, autonomy, and sisterhood: An analysis of the secular consequences of women's religions. *Gender and Society, 8*(4), 486–506.

Sergiovanni, T. J. (1992). *Moral leadership: Getting to the heart of school leadership.* San Francisco: Jossey-Bass.

———. (1994). Organizations or community? Changing the metaphor changes the theory. *Educational Administration Quarterly, 30*(2), 214–226.

Settles, S. (2006). The sweet fire of honey: Womanist visions of Osun, a methodology of emancipation. In S. M. Floyd-Thomas (Ed.), *Deeper shades of purple: Womanism in religion and society* (pp. 191–207). New York: NYU Press.

Shakeshaft, C. (1987, April). *Organizational theory and women: Where are we?* Paper presented at the annual meeting of the American Educational Research Association, Washington, DC.

———. (1999). The struggle to create a more gender-inclusive profession. In J. Murray & K. Seashore Louis (Eds.), *The handbook of research on educational administration* (pp. 99–118). San Francisco: Jossey-Bass.

Shaneo. (2003, October 7). Schooled [Definition 2]. *Urban dictionary.* Retrieved October 7, 2003, from http://www.urbandictionary.com/define.php?term=schooled

Shange, N. (1977). *For colored girls who have considered suicide when the rainbow is enough.* New York: Macmillan.

Shapiro, J. P., & Gross, S. J. (2008). *Ethical educational leadership in turbulent times: (Re)solving moral dilemmas.* Mahwah, NJ: Lawrence Erlbaum.

Shapiro, J. P., & Stefkovich, J. A. (2005). *Ethical leadership and decision making in education: Applying theoretical perspectives to complex dilemmas* (2nd ed.). Mahwah, NJ: Lawrence Erlbaum.

Sheared, V. (2006). Giving voice: An inclusive model of instruction—a womanist perspective. In L. Phillips (Ed.), *The womanist reader* (pp. 269–279). New York: Routledge.

Shields, C. (2005). Liberating discourses: Spirituality and educational leadership. *Journal of School Leadership, 15*(6), 608–623.

Shorter, E. (1982). *The history of women's bodies.* New York: Penguin.

Siddle Walker, V. (1996). *Their highest potential: An African American school community in the segregated south.* Chapel Hill: University of North Carolina Press.

Siddle Walker, V., & Snarey, J. R. (Eds.). (2004). *Race-ing moral formation: African American perspectives on care and justice.* New York: Teachers College Press.

Simonsen, T. (1986). *You may plow here: The narrative of Sara Brooks.* New York: Touchstone.

Slife, B. D., & Richards, P. S. (2001). How separable are spirituality and theology in psychotherapy? *Counseling and Values, 45*, 190–206.

Smith, A. (1982). *The relational self: Ethics & therapy from a Black church perspective.* Nashville, TN: Abingdon Press.

Smith, C. (1991). *The emergence of liberation theology: Radical religion and social movement theory.* Chicago: Chicago University Press.

Smith, L. T. (1999). *Decolonizing methodologies: Research and indigenous peoples.* London: Zed Books.

Smith, S. (2001). *Getting over equality: A critical diagnosis of religious freedom in America.* New York: NYU Press.

Smith, S. C., & Piele, P. K. (1996). *School leadership* (3rd ed.). Eugene: University of Oregon Press.

Smith, W. C. (1985). *The church in the life of the Black family.* Valley Forge, PA: Judson Press.

Smitherman, G. (2000). *Talk that talk: Language, culture, and education in African America.* New York: Routledge.

Snarey, J. R., & Siddle Walker, V. (2004). Primary values and developing virtues of African American ethics. In V. Siddle Walker & J. R. Snarey (Eds.), *Race-ing moral formation: African American perspectives on care and justice* (pp. 130–146). New York: Teachers College Press.

Soder, R. (2002). A way to engage not escape. *The School Administrator.* Retrieved June 15, 2007, from http://www.aasa.org/publications/saarticledetail.cfm?ItemNumber=1919&snItemNumber=950&tnItemNumber=1955 database

Solomon, J., & Hunter, J. (2002). A psychological view of spirituality and leadership. *The School Administrator.* Retrieved June 15, 2007, from http://www.aasa.org/publications/saarticledetail.cfm?ItemNumber=1922&snItemNumber=950&tnItemNumber=1955 database

Spencer, B. (2006). *The body as fiction/fiction as a way of thinking.* Unpublished doctoral dissertation, University of Ballarat, Victoria, Australia.

Stack, C. (1974). *All our kin: Strategies for survival in a black community.* New York: Harper and Row.

Stanley, C. A. (2007). When counter narratives meet master narratives in the journal editorial-review process. *Educational Researcher, 36*(1), 14–24.

Stanley, L. (1993). On auto/biography in sociology. *Sociology, 27*(1), 44–53.

Stanley, S., & Billig, M. (2004). Dilemmas of storytelling and identity. In C. Daiute & C. Lightfoot (Eds.), *Narrative analysis* (pp. 159–176). Thousand Oaks, CA: Sage.

Starratt, R. J. (1995). *Leaders with vision: The quest for school renewal.* Thousand Oaks, CA: Corwin Press.

———. (1996). *Transforming educational leadership: Meaning, community and excellence.* New York: McGraw-Hill.

———. (1999, June 17–25). *Historical frameworks for understanding spirituality: Implications for contemporary education.* Paper presented at the annual meeting of the American Educational Research Association, Montreal, Canada.

———. (2005a). Prologue. In C. M. Shields, M. M. Edwards, & A. Sayani (Eds.), *Inspiring practice: Spirituality and educational leadership* (pp. xi–xiii). Lancaster, PA: Proactive.

———. (2005b). Responsible leadership. *The Educational Forum, 69*(2), 124–133.

———. (2005c). The spirituality of presence for educational leaders. In C. M. Shields, M. M. Edwards, & A. Sayani (Eds.), *Inspiring practice: Spirituality and educational leadership* (pp. 67–84). Lancaster, PA: Proactive.

Stewart, D. (2005). *Three eyes for journey: African dimensions of the Jamaican religions.* Oxford, UK: Oxford University Press.

Stewart, M. W. (1835/1988). Productions of Mrs. Maria W. Stewart. In S. Houchins (Ed.), *Spiritual narratives* (pp. 1–80). New York: Oxford University Press.

Stringer, E. T. (1999). *Action research* (2nd ed.). Thousand Oaks, CA: Sage.

Sudarkasa, N. (1997). African American families and family values. In H. P. McAdoo (Ed.), *Black families* (3rd ed.). Thousand Oaks, CA: Sage.

Sutherland, J., Poloma, M. M., & Pendleton, B. F. (2004). Religion, spirituality, and alternative health practices: The baby boomer and cold war cohorts. *Journal of Religion and Health, 42*(4), 315–338.

Tate, C. (1992). *Domestic allegories of political desire: The Black heroine's text at the turn of the century.* New York: Oxford University Press.

Taylor, T. L. (2002). Womanhood glorified: Nannie Helen Burroughs and the National Training School for Women and Girls, Inc., 1909–1961. *Journal of African American History, 13*, 390–401.

Terry, R. W. (1993). *Authentic leadership: Courage in action.* San Francisco: Jossey-Bass.

Thompson, A. (1998). Not the color purple: Black feminist lessons for educational caring. *Harvard Educational Review, 66*, 522–554.

Thompson, C. M. (2000). *The congruent life: Following the inward path to fulfilling work and inspired leadership.* San Francisco: Jossey-Bass.

Tierney, W. G. (1993). Self and identity in a postmodern world: A life story. In D. McLaughlin & W. G. Tierney (Eds.), *Naming silenced lives: Personal narratives and the process of educational change* (pp. 119–134). New York: Routledge.

Tillman, L. (2002). The impact of diversity in educational administration. In G. Perreault & E. Lunenburg (Eds.), *The changing world of school administration* (pp. 144–156). Lanham, MD: Scarecrow Press.

Tillman, L. C. (2003). From rhetoric or reality? Educational administration and the lack of racial and ethnic diversity in the profession. *University Council of Educational Administration Review, 45*(3), 1–4.

Tisdell, E. (2003). *Exploring spirituality and culture in adult and higher education.* San Francisco: Jossey-Bass.

Townes, E. M. (Ed.). (1993a). *Troubling in my soul: Womanist perspectives on evil and suffering.* Maryknoll, NY: Orbis Books.

———. (1993b). *Womanist justice, womanist hope.* Atlanta, GA: Scholars Press.

———. (1995). *In a blaze of glory: Womanist spirituality as social witness.* Nashville, TN: Abingdon Press.

Travick-Jackson, C. J. (2003). *Christianity in the lives of highly educated African American women: Womanist narratives.* Unpublished doctoral dissertation, University of New Mexico, Albuquerque.

Truth, S. (1851/1993). Address to the Ohio Women's Convention. In D. Mullane (Ed.), *Crossing the water: Three hundred years of African American writing* (p. 186). New York: Anchor Books.

Tseng, W. S., & Hsu, J. (1991). *Culture and family: Problems and therapy.* Binghamton, NY: Haworth Press.

Vaz, K. (1995). *The woman with the artistic brush: A life history of Nike Davis.* Armonk, NY: M. E. Sharpe.

Vaz, K. M. (Ed.). (1997). *Oral narrative research with Black women.* Thousand Oaks, CA: Sage.

Walker, A. (1983). *In search of our mothers' gardens.* San Diego: Harcourt Brace Jovanovich.

Wallace, M. (1978). *Black macho and the myth of the superwoman.* New York: Dial Press.

Warnick, B. R. (2004). Bringing religious traditions into educational theory: Making an example of Joseph Smith, Jr. *Educational Theory, 54*(4), 345–364.

Webb, L. S. (2000). *The power of faith: Spirituality as a success factor for African American women administrators on predominately white campuses.* Unpublished doctoral dissertation, University of San Francisco, California.

Weems, R. (1993). *Just a sister away: A womanist vision of women's relationships in the Bible.* San Diego, CA: LuraMedia Press.

Weiler, K. (1988). *Women teaching for change: Gender, class and power.* New York: Bergin & Garvey.

Wells, I. B. (1892). The requisites of true leadership. *Journal of the Proceedings of the American Association of Educators of Colored Youth: The Session of 1891, Held in Nashville, Tennessee, December 29th to 31st, 1891,* 73–79.

West, C. (2008, February). *State of the Black Union Address.* Panel presentation at the State of the Black Union symposium, New Orleans, LA.

West, C., & Glaude, E. S. (Eds.). (2003). *African American religious thought.* Louisville, KY: John Knox Press.

West, T. C. (1999). *Wounds of the spirit: Black women, violence, and resistance ethics.* New York: NYU Press.

White, E. F. (2001). *Dark continent of our bodies: Black feminism and the politics of respectability.* Philadelphia: Temple University Press.

White, J. L., & Parham, T. A. (1990). *The psychology of Blacks: An African American perspective* (2nd ed.). Englewood Cliffs, NJ: Prentice Hall.

White, M. I. (2007). *Leadership, educational leadership, technologies of leadership and feeling valued: A review of the literatures.* Paper presented at the meeting of the Center for Excellence in Leadership, Lancaster University, Lancaster, UK.

White, R. T. (1997). Talking about sex and HIV. In K. M. Vaz (Ed.), *Oral narrative research with Black women* (pp. 99–118). Thousand Oaks, CA: Sage.

Wiggins, D. C. (2004). *Righteous content: Black women speak of church and faith.* New York: NYU Press.

Williams, D., & Williams-Morris, R. (2002). Racism and mental health: The African American experience. *Ethnicity & Health, 5*(3–4), 243–268.

Williams, D. S. (1993). *Sisters in the wilderness: The challenge of womanist God-talk.* Maryknoll, NY: Orbis Books.

———. (1986). Afrocentrism and male-female relationships in church and society. In C. Sanders (Ed.), *Living the intersection: Womanism and Afrocentrism in theology* (pp. 43–56). Minneapolis, MN: Fortress Press.

Williams, S. A. (2000). Some implications of womanist theory. In W. Napier (Ed.), *African American literary theory: A reader* (pp. 218–223). New York: NYU Press.

Wilmore, G. S. (1996). *Black religion, Black radicalism: An interpretation of the religious history of the Afro-American people* (2nd ed.). Maryknoll, NY: Orbis.

Wolff, R. F. (2002). A phenomenological study of in-church and televised worship. In S. B. Merriam (Ed.), *Qualitative research in practice* (pp. 96–119). San Francisco: Jossey-Bass.

Wolterstorff, N. (2006). Teaching justly for justice. *Journal of Education and Christian Belief, 10*(2), 13–15.

Woodward, M. (1997). No greater legacy. In M. Y. Riggs (Ed.), *Can I get a witness? Prophetic religious voice of African American women: An anthology.* Maryknoll, NY: Orbis Books.

Yancey, P. (1999). *The Bible Jesus read.* Grand Rapids, MI: Zondervan.

Yoder, N. A. (1998). *Inspired leadership: Exploring the spiritual dimension of educational leadership.* Unpublished doctoral dissertation, University of Wisconsin, Madison.

Young, M. D. (2008). From the director: Newly revised ISSLC standards are now available. *UCEA Review, 49*(1), 6–7.

Index

Abolition, 25, 45

Abuse, 82, 87, 92, 115–118, 121, 123, 126

Adequate Yearly Progress (AYP), 112, 180, 206

Advocacy, 20, 176, 189, 196

African American, 5, 7–8, 11–12, 16, 18, 22–24, 26–27, 31, 40–41, 47, 49–51, 57, 62–63, 67, 69, 73, 75–76, 105, 107–108, 121, 123–127, 137–138, 141, 143, 145, 156, 165–166, 176, 183, 188–190, 196, 201–202, 213–217, 224, 226, 228–229

Alice Walker, 6, 18, 20, 25, 45, 75

Appropriation, 5, 18, 21, 48–49, 60, 62, 107

At-risk, 136, 177, 182, 207

Audre Lorde, 75

Autobiography, 4, 41, 43, 45, 48, 66, 75

Baptist, 10, 30, 45, 72, 86–87, 101–102, 110, 141, 150, 157–163, 213, 229, 233

Baptist convention, 12–13, 28–29, 65, 100, 124

Bible, 16, 23–25, 46, 68–70, 74, 79, 82–83, 91, 96, 103, 131, 134–135, 137, 141, 143, 148–150, 152–153, 155, 158–160, 162–163, 177, 187–191, 201

Biblical, 4, 8, 16, 17, 23, 41, 45, 66, 103, 124, 138
Black Church, 12–13, 17, 25, 27–29, 40, 62, 99–101, 106, 108, 166–167
Brown v. Board of Education, 101
Care, 7, 17, 19, 33, 46, 64, 70–71, 89, 93, 96, 115, 117, 120, 122, 124–125, 132, 140, 143–145, 147, 149, 151, 153, 158, 164, 168, 172–174, 176–178, 182, 184–185, 193, 202, 206, 217–219, 225, 227, 230
Charismatic, 102
Children of God, 47, 103, 150–152
Christian, 7–10, 16, 22–24, 26–27, 39, 46–47, 49–50, 52, 55, 61, 63–64, 68, 72, 76, 83–84, 90, 92, 95, 101–102, 105–106, 111, 118, 120, 122, 125–126, 134–136, 139, 143–144, 146, 148, 153, 156–163, 165–167, 169, 172–175, 179, 184, 186–188, 191, 200, 217, 229–230, 234
Christology, 8, 16
Church, 1, 12–13, 28–30, 34, 40, 46, 61–62, 72, 81–82, 84–90, 92, 96, 99, 100–111, 113, 117–121, 123–126, 128, 132–135, 137, 141, 143–145, 148, 150–152, 155, 157–163, 166–169, 171, 173–174, 183–186, 188, 191, 205–206, 211, 214–215, 219, 234
Civil rights, 28–29, 81, 84–85, 91–92, 101, 104, 143, 165–166, 179
Colorblind, 217
Communalism, 5, 7, 18–19, 42, 48, 51–52, 98, 107, 139, 231
Community, 2, 6–7, 11, 17, 19–20, 22, 27–28, 30, 40, 46, 48, 55, 62–63, 71–72, 81, 90–92, 96, 98–101, 104–105, 107, 109, 116–117, 121, 123–127, 132, 138–141, 143–144, 148, 150, 152, 159–160, 165–166, 168–169, 171–173, 175, 180, 183–185, 187, 189, 193, 195–197, 204, 206, 214, 218–220, 222, 224–226, 229
Conversion, 24, 26, 45–47, 50, 54, 59, 72, 100, 110, 157, 160–164, 213
Counseling, 130, 132–133
Counterdiscourses, 165
Critical engagement, 5, 18, 20, 21, 43, 48, 57–59, 211, 218–219, 231
Culture, 2, 6, 8, 16, 19–20, 22, 24, 28, 30, 38, 41–42, 44, 48–50, 53–

54, 57–59, 62–64, 69, 93, 99, 145, 150, 157, 165–166, 183, 187, 203, 213, 219, 222, 227, 229, 233

Daily Bread, 128, 134, 190

Denominational identity, 101–102, 157, 161

Diversity, 156, 221, 223

Ecumenical, 101

Epistemology, 7, 18, 34–36, 49, 57, 189, 200

Ethic of care, 189, 193

Ethic of critique, 193, 218

Ethic of justice, 193

Ethic of the profession, 193

Ethics, 2, 17, 20, 22, 32, 173, 188, 193–194, 220–221, 223, 226–227

Ethnographic, 52

Exegesis, 13, 155, 199

Faith, 1, 2, 5, 7–10, 12, 16, 17, 23–25, 27, 45–47, 50, 56, 60–61, 67–68, 70, 81–82, 87, 95–97, 99, 101–102, 106, 108–109, 112–113, 117–120, 128, 131, 134, 136, 138, 140, 153, 156–160, 162–165, 167, 172, 178, 183, 187–189, 193, 196, 200, 209, 213–214, 219, 230, 233–234

Family, 7, 23, 42, 72, 81–82, 84–86, 88, 90, 92–93, 97–101, 103–105, 107–109, 114–119, 124–125, 127, 130–132, 134, 137, 139, 143–145, 148, 151, 159–162, 166, 168, 190, 205

Feminism, 6, 20, 22, 63

Feminist, 6–8, 15, 17, 23, 25–26, 49, 52, 73, 117, 216

Gender, 7–9, 15–18, 20, 33, 38, 42, 46, 50, 53, 62, 68, 73, 76, 116, 127, 137–138, 151, 153, 156, 165, 193, 214–217

God, 11, 16, 22, 24–25, 27, 40, 45–47, 50, 63, 70–72, 80, 82–83, 86, 88–89, 94–97, 100–105, 107–111, 113, 118–119, 121, 127, 131–135, 138–139, 142–146, 148–153, 156, 158, 160–161, 163–168, 171–175, 177–178, 183–185, 189–191, 193–195, 198–203, 208, 211–212, 214, 224, 234

Highly Qualified Teachers (HQT), 180

Identity, 2, 22, 27, 46, 48–50, 61, 68–69, 72–73, 76, 99, 101–102, 116, 151, 157–159, 161, 166, 200, 225

Intersectionality, 9, 22, 127, 153

ISLLC, 220

Jeremiad, 12, 80–81
Jesus, 17, 94–96, 137, 151, 153, 158, 163–165, 172–176, 188
Law, 2, 79, 81, 114, 193, 235
Legal, 1, 101, 135, 185–186, 222–223, 226
Liberation, 22, 24, 27, 70
Life history, 8, 11–12, 41, 43–44, 47–48, 50
Literary, 22, 24–26, 42–43, 62–63, 66, 75–76, 217
Love of Spirit, 22, 63, 109, 153
Magnet school, 65, 128, 136, 170
Meditation, 48, 73, 79–80, 109, 126, 140, 152–153, 208, 233, 235
Mentoring, 121–122, 184–185, 206, 228
Method, 5, 13, 41–44, 47, 49–52, 56–57, 59–60, 62, 64, 67, 69, 71, 73, 221–223, 228, 230
Methodology, 11, 13, 41–42, 52, 56–57, 71–73
Mission, 29–30, 33, 45–47, 96, 100, 108, 110, 112–113, 126, 130, 139, 150, 162, 168–169, 171–172, 174, 176–177, 182–183, 186, 193, 199, 203, 208, 216, 219, 226
Missionary, 29–30, 45, 110, 169
Moral, 11, 22, 28, 32, 36, 38–40, 54, 58, 72, 108, 126, 143, 151, 188–189, 193–194, 199, 214, 220, 227
Mourning Story, 127–128
Narrative, 2, 4, 6, 8–13, 15, 17–19, 23–27, 34, 38–62, 64–77, 79–81, 98–104, 107, 109–110, 113, 115, 120–121, 123, 127–128, 134, 138, 141, 153, 155–157, 159, 161, 164–166, 169, 172, 174, 176, 179, 186, 188–190, 194, 197, 200–203, 208–209, 212–213, 215–216, 219, 222–224, 228–229, 231, 233–234
Narrative analysis, 41, 58, 66–67, 71, 153, 155–156
National Baptist Convention, 12–13, 28–29, 65, 100, 124
Nitty-gritty Hermeneutic, 21, 57
No Child Left Behind (NCLB), 180, 182, 207
Ontology, 34–36, 189, 200
Oppression, 5, 7–9, 16–23, 25, 27, 33, 48, 54, 67, 69, 73, 81, 100, 104, 118, 138, 144–145, 150, 152, 165, 177, 196, 224, 226
Oral history, 24, 41
Othermothering, 7, 19, 123–124, 138
Parachurch, 101, 105, 163, 183

Pastoral care, 168, 173, 176, 217–218

Pastoral theology, 173

Pentecostal, 87, 102

Pentecostalism, 102

Phenomenology, 52

Policy, 10, 16, 32, 108, 122, 125, 136, 178–179, 185, 191–192, 196–197, 200–201, 209, 212, 218–220, 222–223, 227, 233–235

Politics, 28, 180, 185

Poverty, 121–122, 137, 142, 146, 150, 172–173, 182, 204, 227

Prayer, 79–80, 83, 85, 89, 94–95, 103–104, 109, 135, 153, 158, 160, 172, 189–190, 197–201

Principal, 2–6, 9–11, 13, 15–16, 23, 31–32, 36–37, 39, 41–42, 44, 50–54, 60–61, 64–66, 68, 70, 73, 77, 79–80, 90, 92–98, 104–105, 107, 111–113, 120–125, 127–129, 135–136, 138–140, 145, 148–153, 155–158, 162, 164–171, 173–191, 194–209, 211–230, 233–234

Protestant, 27, 65, 72, 106, 158

Psalm, 82, 91, 141–142, 148–149, 190

Qualitative, 43, 47–48, 50, 69

Race, 5, 7, 9, 15–17, 20, 23, 33, 42, 44, 46, 50, 53, 62, 67–68, 76, 102, 109, 117–118, 126–127, 137–138, 145, 151, 153, 156, 165–167, 169, 172, 193, 214–217, 225

Racism, 5, 39, 41–77, 108, 118, 145, 148–150, 165–166, 172, 179, 227, 234

Radical subjectivity, 5, 18, 42, 48, 50, 53, 99, 108, 125, 231

Reciprocity, 5, 18, 21, 43, 48, 60, 62, 107, 176, 211, 218, 229, 231

Redemptive self-love, 5, 18–19, 42, 48, 54, 55, 57, 231

Salvation, 23, 138, 158–159, 161

Schomburg Center for Research in Black Culture, 62

School leadership, 33–34, 60, 97

Secular, 2, 11, 22, 28, 31, 105, 183, 185, 201

Sermon, 12, 75, 77, 141, 191, 224

Servant leadership, 36, 138

Situational leadership, 36, 191

Slave, 7, 17, 24–25, 27, 45, 47, 54, 57, 62, 71, 101, 143–144, 146

Social justice, 3, 7–10, 26, 32–33, 35, 40, 42, 46, 60, 63, 80–81, 100, 106, 124, 138, 146, 156–157, 167, 169–170, 172, 176–177, 180, 185–189, 193–195, 201–203, 205, 207–209, 213, 217–

221, 223–228, 230

Sociology, 17

Southern Christian Leadership Conference (SCLC), 84, 101

Spiritual, 1–2, 4–6, 8, 10–13, 16–17, 19, 23–28, 32–40, 42–77, 79–81, 88–89, 94, 96, 99–105, 108–110, 115, 117–121, 123–127, 137–139, 143, 151, 153, 155–157, 159, 162–163, 167, 172–177, 179–181, 183, 187, 189, 192–193, 200–203, 206–209, 211–214, 217–220, 223, 228, 231, 233

Spiritual fruit, 189, 202–203, 207

Spiritual narrative, 4–6, 8, 11–13, 24–27, 39–40, 42–50, 54, 58–60, 62, 65–66, 69–72, 74–77, 79–81, 99, 104, 109–110, 115, 120, 127, 153, 155, 176, 189, 212–213, 223, 228, 233–235

Spiritual warfare, 89, 103–104

Spirituality, 1–5, 7–13, 15–18, 22–23, 25–26, 28, 30–31, 33–40, 44–50, 54–57, 59–64, 66–73, 79–81, 83, 87, 90, 94–102, 106–107, 109, 113, 117, 120–123, 125–127, 133–139, 141, 143–146, 149–150, 152–153, 155–159, 161–168, 171–173, 175–177, 179–180, 182–190, 192–195, 198–202, 208–209, 211–220, 224–231

Student achievement, 121, 145–146, 182, 203, 206, 227, 233–235

Stumbling Blocks, 177, 180, 185

Suffering, 17, 137–138, 140, 144, 165, 177

Superintendent, 31, 74, 93–95, 178, 180, 192, 215

Supreme Court, 1, 101

Televangelists, 102

Tempered radical, 197

Testifying, 11, 71

Testimony, 4, 65, 72, 79, 88, 100, 109–110, 212

Theo-ethics, 194

Theoretical, 10, 15–17, 43–44, 48–49, 51, 59, 190, 202, 216, 222

Theory, 6, 8, 13, 25, 40, 43, 62, 188, 212–213, 225

Therapy, 116–119, 130, 139

Title I, 98, 112, 142, 147

Tradition, 2, 5, 7–8, 10–12, 16, 18–19, 22, 24, 26, 30, 34–38, 40, 42, 48, 51–53, 56–58, 61–63, 67–

69, 72–73, 76, 82, 87, 98, 100–102, 105, 107, 109, 123–125, 148, 158, 160, 173–174, 188, 193, 201, 212–213, 215–218, 221, 223, 227, 229, 231

Traditional Communalism, 5, 18–19, 42, 48, 51–52, 98, 107, 231

UCEA, 221–222

Urban, 3, 26, 31, 39, 217, 219

Urban school, 3, 26, 31, 217

Values, 2, 6–7, 10, 12, 26–27, 32–33, 53, 70, 99, 120, 125, 127, 133, 137, 143, 179, 194, 201, 211, 213, 215–216, 218–219, 221–222, 225–226, 235

Violence, 85, 118, 128–129, 137, 140, 144, 152, 166

Ways of knowing, 7, 34, 61, 201

Wilderness, 137–138, 157, 164–165, 183, 208, 213

Witnessing, 11, 71–72, 159, 192

Womanism, 5–8, 12, 16–20, 22, 40, 49, 63, 104, 140, 176, 202, 213, 227

Womanist, 5–9, 12–13, 15–23, 25–26, 39–43, 45, 48–57, 59–69, 71, 73, 75, 77, 98–99, 106–108, 117–118, 123–127, 137–141, 150, 152–153, 156, 176, 190, 194, 196, 201, 209, 211–213, 217–218, 223–224, 226–228, 231

Womanist theology, 5, 7–9, 12–13, 16–17, 22–23, 40–42, 45, 51, 54, 59, 63–64, 66–67, 69, 71, 73, 77, 98–99, 106, 117–118, 123, 127, 138–139, 150, 156, 176, 190, 194, 201, 209, 211, 213, 217–218, 223–224, 226, 228

Womanist theory, 6

Women's Club Movement, 17, 124, 176

Worldview, 39, 44, 69, 107, 138, 157–158, 161, 167–168, 208, 214, 225, 231, 234

The Author

Noelle Witherspoon Arnold, PhD, is an Associate Professor of Educational Leadership in the Department of Educational Leadership and Policy Analysis at the University of Missouri–Columbia. Prior to that appointment, she taught elementary school, and served as an administrator at the district and state levels. Her research interests include religion and spirituality in education, leadership for social justice and advocacy, leadership socialization, womanist and feminist research methodologies, and the intersection of race and gender in educational leadership. Noelle's most recent articles have appeared in the *International Journal of Leadership in Education, International Journal of Qualitative Studies in Education, The Journal of Educational Administration History, Equity and Excellence in Education, The Journal of Negro Education, Teachers College Record,* and the *Journal of Educational Administration*.

Rochelle Brock &
Richard Greggory Johnson III,
Executive Editors

Black Studies and Critical Thinking is an interdisciplinary series which examines the intellectual traditions of and cultural contributions made by people of African descent throughout the world. Whether it is in literature, art, music, science, or academics, these contributions are vast and far-reaching. As we work to stretch the boundaries of knowledge and understanding of issues critical to the Black experience, this series offers a unique opportunity to study the social, economic, and political forces that have shaped the historic experience of Black America, and that continue to determine our future. Black Studies and Critical Thinking is positioned at the forefront of research on the Black experience, and is the source for dynamic, innovative, and creative exploration of the most vital issues facing African Americans. The series invites contributions from all disciplines but is specially suited for cultural studies, anthropology, history, sociology, literature, art, and music.

Subjects of interest include (but are not limited to):

- Education
- Sociology
- History
- Media/Communication
- Religion/Theology
- Women's Studies
- Policy Studies
- Advertising
- African American Studies
- Political Science
- LGBT Studies

For additional information about this series or for the submission of manuscripts, please contact Dr. Brock (Indiana University Northwest) at brock2@iun.edu or Dr. Johnson (University of San Francisco) at rgjohnsoniii@usfca.edu.

To order other books in this series, please contact our Customer Service Department:

(800) 770-LANG (within the U.S.)
(212) 647-7706 (outside the U.S.)
(212) 647-7707 FAX

Or browse online by series at www.peterlang.com.

www.ingramcontent.com/pod-product-compliance
Ingram Content Group UK Ltd.
Pitfield, Milton Keynes, MK11 3LW, UK
UKHW022238230426
12048UKWH00018BA/1335